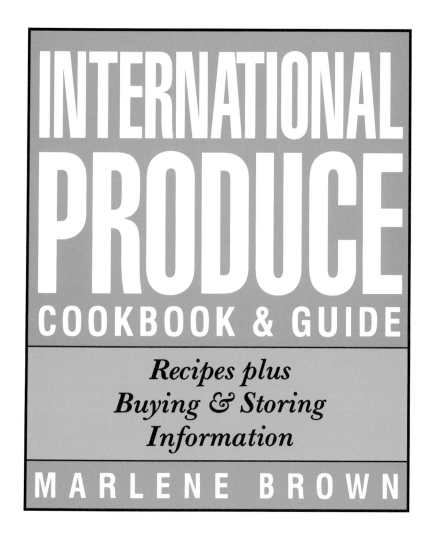

INTERNATIONAL PRODUCE

COOKBOOK & GUIDE

*Recipes plus
Buying & Storing
Information*

MARLENE BROWN

HPBooks
a division of
PRICE STERN SLOAN
Los Angeles

*This book is dedicated to Elaine Woodard, a woman of
vision and a courageous model for us all; and to my
family, who gave me their love and support
throughout this project.*

For their contributions and support, the author wishes to thank Karen and Frieda Caplan, Susan Draudt, Bess Petlak, Ann Henry, Carol Bowman-Williams, Agnes Schepers, Armando Tabora, Lila Dall, Sharon Haven, and Patricia Aaron.

Recipe Tester: Tammi Singer
Market Research: Lorraine Brown

Special thanks to Frieda's Finest/Produce Specialties, Inc., Los Angeles, for supplying much of the exotic produce items used on the cover and inside photographs.

Some accessories for photography were from Freehand, Los Angeles, California; Wilder Place, Los Angeles, California; and The Pavilion at Tanner Market, Pasadena, California.

Photography and food styling by Burke/Triolo Photographic Studio and Peter A. Hōgg Photography.

Published by HPBooks, A division of Price Stern Sloan, Inc.
360 North La Cienega Boulevard, Los Angeles, California 90048

© 1989 Marlene Brown   Printed in U.S.A.

10 9 8 7 6 5 4 3 2 1

Library of Congress Cataloging-in-Publication Data

Brown, Marlene.
    International produce cookbook & guide : recipes plus buying &
storage information / by Marlene Brown.
        p.   cm.
    Includes index.
    ISBN (invalid) 0-89586-792-3
        1. Cookery (Fruit) 2. Cookery (Vegetables) 3. Farm produce.
    I. Title.   II. Title: International produce cookbook and guide.
TX811.B76   1989
    641.65—dc20   89-31214
                                                   CIP

CONTENTS

VEGETABLES

Marlene Brown

With a degree in Consumer Food Science and Business/Marketing from the University of Minnesota, Marlene has been employed as a home economist for the Pillsbury Company and as a food editor for Better Homes & Gardens Magazine. In 1982 she moved to Los Angeles and established her own consulting business, Marlene's Cuisine.

As a consultant to a variety of food industry clients across the U.S., Marlene writes magazine articles and consumer information materials. She also develops recipes, is a food stylist, and acts as a product spokesperson.

One of Marlene's clients is Frieda of California, a Los Angeles-based exotic produce marketer. Developing recipes and consumer information materials for all of the new and unusual produce items has made Marlene an expert on purchasing, preparing and cooking all kinds of fresh fruits and vegetables. She knows that the wide variety of new and unusual items available in markets today can cause confusion for a lot of consumers. In this book, she shares with you her recipes, tips and tricks for enjoying the best of today's fresh produce.

INTRODUCTION

The Supermarket Garden

Chances are, if you shop for food, you've noticed that your supermarket's produce section looks as though it is bursting at the seams. It's true—twenty years ago, an average of 70 different fruits and vegetables were on display; today, larger markets offer as many as 400 items ripe for the picking. Much of this harvest may consist of baffling but beautiful exotica you won't recognize. Just shopping for tomatoes can be filled with new discoveries.

Why? Because regional American specialties such as okra and blueberries, Vidalia onions and Grannysmith apples, can now be bought from Maine to Texas, from Seattle to Chicago. Because lettuce isn't just iceberg anymore—leafy new varieties and hybrids await your salad bowl. Shopping for melon? Take your pick from a dozen flavors. Looking for mushrooms? Try picking just one kind from a succulent array of eight or ten varieties.

Most importantly, progress allows our international neighbors to share their exotic fruits and intriguing vegetables with us. New Zealand, Holland, Fiji, Africa, Thailand, and Brazil, to name a few examples, bring their harvest daily to our doorstep. When our seasonal supplies are on the wane, our neighbors can fill the bill—with strawberries in December, or red bell peppers in May.

There are serious health concerns, too, and a new appreciation of the "apple-a-day" wisdom. Latest research findings indicate that it's possible to decrease the risk of fatal stroke by *40%*—just by eating one serving of fruits and vegetables *per day!* We're just beginning to realize what nutritional powerhouses they are.

This book will show you how to enjoy all of the usual and unusual produce available in abundance now. Beyond the easy recipes specially developed for each fruit and vegetable, you'll find detailed information on how to buy, store, prepare, and cook them, plus helpful hints on incorporating your new finds into your own menus. The time is ripe to seek out new favorites—and rediscover some old ones—in your own supermarket garden.

Shopping Savvy

Beyond supermarkets, you have other options for seeking out the best in fresh produce. Individual produce markets and seasonal farmer's markets (as well as year-round farmer's markets, such as those in Seattle, Indianapolis, and Los Angeles) offer good buys on regional and exotic fruits and vegetables. In summer and fall, you can also take advantage of pick-your-own farms and orchards that allow you to pick the cream of the crop at your leisure, usually for half the price charged in stores.

To find out how to buy the best, check out the "Buying Tips" section provided for each of the fruits and vegetables in this book. And follow these general tips:

Handle all produce with care; don't squeeze the tomatoes so hard they burst! For soft commodities, the best way to judge ripeness is to place the fruit or vegetable between your two palms, then squeeze gently. In general, if it gives to gentle pressure from you, it's ripe.

With vegetables, size is often an indicator of full flavor and/or sweetness. For example, smaller or average-sized turnips or parsnips will be sweeter than very large ones, simply because they are younger. Larger or over-sized vegetables are apt to have pithy centers and either a bland or very bitter taste.

1.Tarragon. 2.Champagne grapes. 3.Kiwano. 4.Yellow crookneck squash. 5.Baby artichoke. 6.Baby carrot. 7.Yellow watermelon. 8.Pomegranate seeds. 9.Freestone peach. 10.Yellow bell pepper. 11.Tomatillo. 12.Red prickly pear. 13.Belgian Endive. 14.Purple wax beans. 15.Italian parsley. 16.Purple salad savoy. 17.Cayenne chile. 18.Papaya. 19.Blackberry. 20.Oyster mushroom. 21.Yellow pear tomato. 22.Yellow tomato. 23.Lady apple. 24.Strawberry. 25. Asparagus.

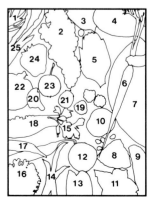

Fruits & Vegetables. See diagram, opposite page.

With fruits, size usually doesn't affect flavor or sweetness. For example, a large strawberry can be every bit as succulent as a petite one.

Buy only what you can use before it spoils. Berries will last just a few days—it's no bargain to buy eight buckets full of them unless you have plans to freeze them, make jam from them, or otherwise use your crop.

For pick-your-own farms, you may want to bring your own buckets or containers to hold the bounty; farmers usually charge extra for them.

You can purchase fruits and vegetables such as tomatoes and pears at different stages of ripeness, depending on how and when you plan to use them. For example, avocados are available *unripe, firm-ripe,* and *ripe.* Ripe ones will be ready to mash for guacamole today or tomorrow; firm-ripe avocados will be perfect for slicing in a salad for the next couple of days. Unripe or very firm ones will ripen for four to six days before they will be ready to eat.

Make a general, not a specific, shopping list for produce, so that you can take advantage of the best buys you find when you get to the market. Let your selection depend on what looks good to you.

Sometimes packaged produce is less expensive than loose; that's because lower quality items are mixed with high quality.

Note that produce departments are usually laid out in much the same way, making shopping more efficient. Lettuces and greens are stocked together, so are potatoes, onions, and squash. Citrus fruits are displayed with apples and year-round fruits, while soft summer fruits like peaches, plums and nectarines are closely grouped. Often exotic items like passion fruit, gingerroot, mangoes, papayas and others will be on a separate display.

Waxed Fruits & Vegetables

In efforts to meet the demand for year-round produce across the country (and the world), certain fruits and vegetables must be protected against dehydration for the long trip to market. Although nature gives fresh produce its own waxy coating, the natural armor is lost during the washing process in the packinghouse. Such commodities as cucumbers, rutabagas, eggplants, yucca root, and apples are often coated with a thin, FDA-approved edible wax that acts to seal in moisture and retard shriveling. Experts tell us that the wax is harmless; in fact, many chocolate candies sport the same waxy coating as a flavor and freshness preservative.

It's important to wash waxed produce thoroughly because dirt and other substances may adhere to the wax. Rinsing these items in very warm water will remove some of the coating. Otherwise, the best way to avoid eating the wax is to remove the peel.

Storing the Bounty

Your refrigerator crisper drawer is probably the best temperature-controlled spot for storing produce that must be chilled. Because refrigerators are filled with dry air, most fruits and vegetables should be tightly wrapped to seal in moisture. Fruits and vegetables that require a cool, dry spot should be kept out of direct light or sunlight for longest shelf life. Don't wash produce before storing it, since you'll be removing any protective coating (natural or otherwise) that will preserve the item during storage. But do sort through such fruits as fresh berries and grapes for moldy or shriveled pieces, and discard the "bad apples." Tear off wilted leaves from the outside of greens. The rest of your bounty will last longer that way.

Very fragile items, such as oriental mushrooms and raspberries, fare best in storage if you layer them on paper towels in a basket or bowl in the fridge (not more than two layers deep). Cover loosely with paper towels. Check the "Storage" section for specific tips on each commodity in this book.

Ripening Produce at Home

There are several easy methods for ripening fresh vegetables and fruits. Never place produce, such as tomatoes, in the sun to speed up the process; a mushy vegetable will result. Stake out a cool, dry spot, out of the light. Place the item(s) next to fruits that give off natural gases, such as bananas, apples, or avocados. Use a fruit ripening bowl, which is a clear plastic bowl with a perforated cover. Filling the bowl with a number of unripe items promotes faster ripening. There's also the brown paper bag technique; closing the bag around unripe foods traps the natural gases given off and creates a good environment for ripening. Remember to check on the progress of ripening fruits and vegetables daily; refrigerate them as soon as they are at their peak.

Washing Your Fresh Favorites

A sturdy colander and a stiff vegetable brush are handy items for washing fresh produce. Scrub roots like potatoes and turnips well with a brush; place fragile items like lettuce leaves and berries in a colander to rinse off dirt and dust. Never allow vegetables or fruits to soak in water; nutrients can leech out into the water and the texture of produce can be adversely affected. Mushrooms act like tiny sponges when soaked. (One exception is spinach; the leaves must be soaked in water to remove dirt. Change the water several times.)

Ice water works to crisp certain vegetables that are eaten raw, such as lettuces, radishes, green onions, celery, and cucumbers. These items all benefit from a short icy bath.

Cooking Produce To Perfection

Now that you've spent some time and energy buying the best, it pays to cook your bounty carefully. For the most part, it's best to err on the side of undercooking, rather than overdoing it (you can always put the pot on a bit longer to soften the crisp edges). Remember that foods always continue to cook after you remove them from the heat.

The age of the vegetable or fruit, stage of ripeness, the variety used, and the season in which you bought it, are all factors that contribute to looks and flavor, and can affect the cooking time considerably. So use the times given in recipes as guidelines, and check frequently for signs of doneness. "Crisp-tender" is a term used often for cooking vegetables; it means to cook until the food is nearly tender, but still has a slight crispness to it. "Tender" means just that: your fork can slip into the soft food easily because all of the fibers have been broken down by cooking.

Note, however, that there is a fine line between tender and mushy—overcooking will cause so much breakdown of the food tissue that the fruit or vegetable no longer retains its shape. Much of the flavor can also be lost. When pre-cooking foods that will later be chilled for use in a salad or a cold entrée, blanch or steam food to doneness desired, then stop the cooking by rinsing the food immediately in cold or iced water.

If cooking vegetables or fruits in liquid, you can use broth, fruit juice, or other appropriately-seasoned liquids instead of water. The broth left from boiling or blanching vegetables is full of flavor; save it to use again in a sauce, soup, or stew.

Use a roomy pot or skillet to cook your produce; this promotes good air circulation and even cooking. Follow these guidelines for the cooking techniques found in this book:

Blanching: Used to partially-cook fruits or vegetables for freezing or chilled salads, or to soften peels for removal. Plunge foods into rapidly boiling water or other liquid briefly according to recipe, then rinse in cold water to stop the cooking.

Boiling: To cook food to desired doneness in liquid heated to 212F (100C), either in a small amount of liquid, or in liquid to cover. The boiled food is drained to stop the cooking.

Braising: Done on top of the range or in the oven. It means to cook in a small amount of liquid, slowly, in a covered pan or skillet until the food is tender.

Broiling: Cooking food under 500F (260C) direct heat in an electric or gas range. Used mainly for tender fruits and vegetables that need to be quickly heated or browned. Food cooked by this method should be carefully watched to avoid drying out or burning.

Deep-Frying: Cooking food while covered in oil that is heated to a very high temperature to create a crisp result. Use a deep-frying thermometer to insure the temperature is high enough; foods will absorb less oil that way. Drain fried foods well on paper towels to serve.

Grilling: Broiling foods on an outdoor unit that provides direct heat, either with a gas element or hot coals. This method is often preceded by blanching or boiling vegetables or fruits briefly to shorten cooking time on the grill.

Micro-cooking: See Microwave Cooking Guidelines, pages 10-11.

Poaching: To cook food that's barely covered in simmering hot liquid, over medium heat.

Sautéing: Cooking foods in a skillet with a small amount of butter or oil over high heat. Butter should not be allowed to brown, nor the oil to smoke before the food is added to the pan, or bitterness may result. Sautéing is done for foods that need some pre-cooking or browning before stewing or long, slow cooking; or to cook vegetables or fruits quickly to desired doneness. Food must be stirred frequently to insure even cooking.

Steaming: This can be done by adding a few tablespoons of liquid to a sautéed mixture to finish the cooking without burning the food before it's tender. The other method of steaming is done by placing the food pieces in a basket set in a covered pan that has a small amount of boiling water in it. The food is cooked by the steam that's created; the water does not come in contact with the food. Occasionally more water must be added during steaming. Steam baskets come in regular and large sizes to fit all types of sauce pans and Dutch ovens.

Stir-Frying: The oriental version of sautéing, done in a large skillet or wok utensil. Usually each ingredient is cooked separately in a small amount of oil (or broth if calories are of concern). The food is stirred constantly over very high heat to distribute the heat evenly and cook the food quickly.

Microwave Cooking Guidelines

Microwaves do marvelous things for both fruits and vegetables. Like blanching and steaming, microwave cooking preserves the colors, flavors, nutrients, and textures beautifully—and it's a fast way to bring your fresh finds to your table.

Once you've mastered the basic techniques of cooking with microwaves, you'll find it a great way to serve cooked fruits and vegetables at their best.

Microwave timings given in this book come from testing in a 700-watt microwave oven. Timings may vary depending on the wattage of your oven, the ripeness of the food, and the way the food is prepared. Check food at the minimum time, and frequently thereafter.

• Be sure foods are cut uniformly, or cook same-size items together for best results.

• Pierce whole vegetables with the peels left on, to prevent them from bursting during the cooking process.

• Standing time is important, because foods continue to cook after you remove them from the oven. Allow food to stand, covered, for the amount of time specified.

• Timings depend on the number of foods you are cooking at the same time. Four apples will take longer to cook than one (about four times longer). Take this into account when checking on timings.

• Stir foods once or twice during cooking. Foods will cook more evenly throughout.

• To cover foods loosely means to leave one corner of your dish or container uncovered, to allow for escape of steam. Otherwise, your container cover may burst from steam pressure, causing spatters.

• Take advantage of special microwave cookware and products that will make the job easier: specially designed steamers, stirring spoons that stay cool, self-sealing cooking bags, and certain brands of plastic wrap and paper towels designed specifically for microwave use.

Preserving Precious Nutrients

Whether you enjoy fruits or vegetables raw or cooked, there are things you can do to insure you're getting the most from them. Cooking vegetables carefully to just-right doneness goes a long way toward keeping vitamins and minerals locked inside. Don't use more liquid than is actually required; save the cooking liquids to use again as they contain dissolved nutrients.

In general, the peelings contain concentrated amounts of nutrients; leave them on whenever possible for cooking or eating. Trim outer leaves and skin carefully; many fruits and vegetables have more nutrients just below the skin than at the center. Don't soak fruits and vegetables unless necessary.

Finally, enjoy your produce at the peak of ripeness; overripe foods usually have decreased vitamin and mineral content.

Freezing Fresh Produce

So you've been to the berry farm and you'd like to preserve the pickings for a winter treat. It's simple to do, if you keep a few points in mind.

Start with perfectly ripe fruits or vegetables that have not passed their prime. For vegetables, precooking, such as blanching or brief steaming, helps to preserve the color and texture. Rinse the food immediately after cooking with cold water and pack food into containers when completely cooled. Do not freeze such vegetables as lettuces or other greens, potatoes, tomatoes, cucumbers, Chinese vegetables, eggplant, sprouts or artichokes.

To freeze fruits, it isn't necessary to sweeten them first. Such fruits as berries, cherries and persimmons can be laid out in a single layer on a tray in the freezer until solid. Then turn them into plastic freezer bags or containers and seal airtight. Or you can stew or puree the fruits to freeze for future use. Check each chapter for information on whether freezing is feasible for your favorites.

Label all containers clearly with contents and date. Freeze containers or bags in a single layer until frozen solid, so they'll reach proper temperature quickly. Then you can stack them. Maximum storage life for vegetables is about eight months, for fruit, one year.

Cutting Techniques

Sharp knives plus a good solid cutting board near

the sink are the key ingredients you'll need to make quick work of chopping fresh produce. Practice will teach you how to quickly julienne, mince, and dice. The best thing to remember is to cut uniformly in same-size pieces; you'll find all produce cooks more evenly that way. The only difference between mincing, dicing, and chopping is the size of the pieces; the technique is the same. For extra convenience, enlist the help of a food processor, mini-processor, chopper, or blender where appropriate. Follow these guidelines for the cutting and slicing terms used in the recipes throughout this book.

Chop: To cut up food coarsely, to about the size of large peas. To chop, slice food, such as an onion, vertically in one direction, then slice across the cuts horizontally.

Bias-slice: Used for slicing long vegetables such as green beans or for stir-fried items such as carrots or green onions. Slice into pieces to the thickness specified in recipe with knife held at a 45-degree angle.

Cube: Cut food approximately 1/2 inch on a side. Use the chopping technique.

Dice: To chop food into cubes about 1/4 inch on each side. Use the chopping technique.

Grate: Reduce to fine, granular pieces using the smallest holes on a grater or shredder.

Julienne-cut: These are matchstick-sized pieces, no more than 1- to 1-1/2 inches long and 1/8 inch wide. Cut thin slices from the item and stack them flat; then cut lengthwise into slices 1/8 inch thick.

Mince: To chop into very fine pieces, so small that they appear as flecks in the recipe, such as garlic or parsley.

Purée: To reduce a fruit or vegetable to a pulp by mashing or pulverizing. A blender or food processor are musts for this. For coarse-textured vegetables, it may be necessary to push the pulp through a sieve or strainer for a smoother texture.

Roll-cut: Used for cylinder-shaped vegetables, such as carrots or zucchini, to increase the amount of surface area exposed to the heat for faster cooking. For example, cut one end of a carrot at a 45-degree angle; roll the carrot forward 1/4 turn and slice again at the same angle, 1/4 to 1 inch from the first cut, depending on your recipe. Continue along the length of the vegetable.

Slice: To make uniform diagonal or vertical cuts; width of cuts depends on the recipe.

Snip: In the case of fresh herbs or vegetable tops, it means to cut into small pieces with kitchen shears. This is an efficient way to mince a few sprigs of fresh parsley, for example.

Shred: Using a shredder or large chef's knife, slice food into paper-thin strips. On a shredder there are usually fine and large holes for desired shred. To shred a many-layered vegetable such as cabbage, slice head in half; place cut side down on board. Cut crosswise into 1/8-to 1/4-inch-thick slices.

USING FRESH FRUITS & VEGETABLES IN MENUS

Everyone knows that fresh produce counts for a lot in terms of taste and value, but it's a challenge sometimes to use those fresh finds wisely. That's where this book comes in. You will find recipes for every course of the meal and every season of the year. For more ideas on making the most of your produce, check the "Basic Preparation" and "Serving Ideas" sections for each fruit and vegetable in this book.

Also, each recipe has a note on preparation time, which is the average amount of time it will take you to prepare the recipe (cooking, baking, or standing time not included).

Take advantage of these sample menus, taken from recipes in this book. Of course, the possible combinations are limitless. After you've tried some of these ideas, you'll be cultivating favorite meals of your own.

Breakfasts & Brunches

Laura's Apple Pancakes, page 17
Bacon or Sausage Links
Hot Citrus Compote, page 34

Southern-Style Frittata, page 125
Fruit-Stuffed Avocados, page 23
Sante Fe Cornbread, page 97
Tropical Prickly Pear Mousse, page 72

Mini Potato Hors d'oeuvres, page 138
Queen Anne Sunday Omelet, page 31
Mushrooms & Shallots Zinfandel, page 122
Toasted Bagels
Fig-Walnut Crumble, page 41

Light & Easy Lunches

Berry Seafood Salad, page 28
French Bread
Chocolate Parsnip Cake, page 132

Roasted Bell Pepper Soup, page 90
Roast Beef & Turkey Sandwiches
Grapefruit Ice Cream, page 35, and Cookies

Bow-Tie Chicken & Fruit Salad, page 44
Twisted Herb Bread, page 110
Ice Cream Sandwiches

Family Suppers

Lamb Chops With Tamarillo Relish, page 77
Baked Leeks With Shallots & Almonds, page 117
Old-Fashioned Date Rice Pudding, page 39

Pasta With Asparagus & Ham, page 83
Pear-Struesel Muffins, page 65
Passion Fruit-Strawberry Mousse, page 61

Tomato, Greens & Cheese Pizza, page 108
Summer Fruit Slaw, page 57
Chocolate-Dipped Bananas, page 26

Turkey & Eggplant Provençale, page 100
Romaine Lettuce Salad
Fresh Apricot Crisp, page 19

Broiled Veal Chops
Sunchokes with Yams, page 150
Steamed Zucchini & Yellow Crookneck Squash
German Apple Kuchen, page 18

Tortellini-Sausage Soup, page 108
Hot Biscuits
Kiwano Fruit Sundaes, page 46

Apple-Bratwurst Skillet, page 17
Buttered Noodles
Tossed Green Salad
Apricot Butter Cookies, page 20

Entertaining Menus

Deep-Fried Jicama Sticks, page 114
Garlic-Studded Pork Roast, page 104
Sautéed Baby Carrots
Stir-Fried Sorrel with Mushrooms, page 120
Banana Beignets, page 26

Nectarine Daiquiris, page 57
Shrimp-Stuffed Artichokes, page 81
Leek Skillet Bread, page 116
Mango-Topped Gingerbread, page 51

Western-Style Spring Rolls, page 131
Turkey Kabobs with Plum Sauce, page 69
Chinese Fried Rice, page 131
Spirited Mangoes, page 52, and Fortune Cookies

Apricot Margaritas, page 20
Appetizer Tostadas with Guacamole, page 22
Fajitas, page 89
Homemade Salsa, page 97
Kiwi Fruit Meringues, page 48

Herb-Stuffed Roast Lamb, page 110
Fruited Saffron Rice, page 58
Asparagus Bundles with Lemon Butter, page 82
Cherimoya-Pineapple Sorbet, page 30

Barbecued Red Snapper
Grilled Melon with Herbs, page 54
Two-Cheese Cabbage Slaw, page 92
Shimmering Grape Tart, page 43

Coconut-Almond Crusted Fish, page 37
Steamed Baby Carrots & Potatoes
Avocado & Tomato Salad Viniagrette, page 22
Black Forest Decadence, page 32

Roast Chicken with
Apricot-Pecan Stuffing, page 20
Herb-Roasted Sweet Onions, page 127
Fennel & Carrot Salad, page 101
Twenty-Minute Coconut Custard Pie, page 37

Artichokes With Curry-Mustard
Mayonnaise, page 81
Poached Fish in Orange Sauce, page 34
Wild Rice Shiitake, page 122
Berry Tart a la Creme, page 28

Turkey Roll or Roast Beef
Finnish Potato Rosti, page 140
Roasted Bell Pepper Salad, page 90
Persimmon Clafouti, page 67

Cheese-Stuffed Belgian Endive, page 120
Grilled Flank Steak with Mangoes, page 52
Baby Potatoes Polonaise, page 140
Chilled Fresh Grapes

Appetizer Buffet I

French Afternoon Platter, page 40
Baby Vegetables with Spinach Dip, page 85
Cocktail Avocados
Curried Eggplant Spread, page 100
French Bread or Crackers

Appetizer Buffet II

Cheese-Stuffed Artichoke Bottoms, page 81
Asparagus Pâté Rafts, page 83
Roasted Garlic, page 103
Mini Potato Hors d'oeuvres, page 138
Proscuitto & Melon Appetizer Balls, page 56

EASY FRUIT & VEGETABLE GARNISHES

Your finished dishes, whether soup, salad, main course, or dessert, will have a lot of appeal with a simple garnish. It's not necessary to carry a cooking school diploma to make these garnishes; just follow these simple suggestions:

Fruit Garnishes:

Citrus Curls: Make curls from the skin of citrus fruits with a zester, paring knife, or peeler; place strips of the rind in ice water so they'll curl in no time.

Citrus Twists: Use slices of the fruit, slit to the center to twist for a salad or roast garnish.

Kumquat Flowers: Make an "X" cut in the top of a kumquat; turn fruit slightly and make another "X", then turn and make another. Place in ice water to make the flower open.

Mango Flowers: See tip on page 51.

Apple Birds: Core an apple; cut in quarters. Lay one quarter, skin side up, on a flat surface; make a "V" cut to cut out a deep wedge. Cut another wedge out of the wedge you just made; repeat with the second wedge to make a third wedge. Reassemble wedges, one on top of the other, spreading them apart just a bit so the inside of the apple shows.

Berry Fans: From stem to tip of a large strawberry, make vertical cuts very close to each other, cutting through the fruit, but not the stem (it holds the "fan" together). Spread the fruit slices like a fan. You can do the same with kumquats.

Drink Garnishes: Use thin slices of kiwi fruit, star fruit, Kiwano, loquats, peaches, plums, nectarines, citrus fruits and babaco with a small slit cut to the center, to slip over the rim of a glass.

Garnishes From Vegetables:

Platter Liners: Use cooked leaves of artichokes, salad savoy, red leaf lettuce, radiccio, Belgian Endive or alfalfa sprouts as attractive underliners for salads, side dishes and roasts or seafood.

Chili Flowers: Use a red or green jalapeño, serrano or a yellow chili. With a sharp paring knife, make two cross cuts from tip to stem of chili, cutting to, but not through, the stem. Turn chili 1/4 inch; continue making cross cuts from tip to stem. Place in ice water until flower opens.

Radish Roses: "V" cutters, or knives with a "V"-shaped tip, are great for making radish roses without carving skills. Trim stems off radishes, then make rows of "V"-cuts all around radishes. Place in ice water to open.

Green Onion Ties: Cut long 1/8-inch-wide strips of green onions (tops only); plunge in boiling water and immediately transfer to ice water. Use these flexible green onion "ties" to tie bunches of herbs, a pair of baby vegetables, 2 stalks of asparagus, or a few slender beans together to garnish a meat platter or vegetable tray.

Fluted Mushrooms: Use a citrus peel stripper or the tip of a paring knife to make diagonal "V" cuts into tops of mushrooms, working from the center to the edge of caps. Cook or use raw as a garnish.

Green Onion Fronds: Trim green onions; slice off all but 1 inch of green tops. Lay green onion on its side. With a paring knife, make cuts from center through ends of onions, turning onion as you cut until the edges are frilled (leave the centers of onions intact to hold fronds together). Place in ice water to open.

Tomato Roses: Using a small tomato or a plum or Roma tomato, turn stem end down in your palm. Working with a small paring knife, as if you are peeling the tomato, start from the bottom and peel a continuous strip from entire surface of tomato to stem, taking some of the flesh with it. Take the beginning end of the long coil you've made and reassemble the coil, twisting it back into a rounded shape, tucking each layer of the coil inside the previous layer. The resulting shape will resemble a rose. Tuck a sprig of parsley in the center.

Fruits. See diagram, page 156.

APPLES

Apples are by far the most popular fruit in America. Grown since ancient times, experts can only estimate the number of varieties that have existed—anywhere from 5,000 to 20,000. Early American colonists are responsible for harvesting and developing quite a few different types of apples; one of them was the legendary Johnny Appleseed.

So many apple varieties exist mainly because of a botanical quirk: apple seeds from one tree do not necessarily reproduce exactly the same way again. If you planted the seeds from the apple you're eating, you would wind up with several different apple trees that wouldn't resemble each other at all! Today's most desirable apple varieties are reproduced by budding and grafting.

Between supermarkets, farmer's markets and roadside stands, about two dozen types of apples are sold. Apples are in their prime from late August through October, but storage makes a year-round supply possible. (For Asian Pears or apple pears, see Pears, page 64.)

Buying Tips: Look for apples that are free of bruises and firm to the touch. Larger apples should be very firm, since they mature faster than small apples and become mushy sooner. Color should be good for the variety and free of "russeting," which is a brown scab-like condition near the stem end.

Storage: Keep apples in a plastic bag in the refrigerator, away from strong-smelling foods. Apples stored at room temperature will soften about 10 times faster than if refrigerated.

Basic Preparation: Peel apples, if desired, remove cores and slice or cut into wedges. Use an apple corer, if desired, or an apple cutter to separate fruit into neat wedges. When cut, apple's inner color turns brown quickly, so dip slices or wedges in lemon juice and water to preserve the color.

Serving Ideas: Apples can be baked, poached, sautéed, fried in batter and used in every course of the meal from appetizer to dessert. Dice them to add to rice pilaf, shred for a meatloaf or stir-fry with onions for an unusual side dish. Or use them in delectable desserts like a flaky pie or tart, dipped in melted chocolate, wrapped in filo dough, chopped into muffins or made into applesauce.

Yield: 1 lb. apples = 3 medium or 4 small apples or about 3 cups sliced or diced.
2 lb. apples = enough for a 9-inch pie.

Nutrition Facts: 1 medium-sized apple yields about 90 calories. Apples are generous in dietary fiber; the apple-a-day proverb applies. They're rich in vitamins A, B, and C, and in minerals such as iron and potassium.

Unusual Apple Varieties:

Braeburn: A New Zealand variety, slightly tart apple with a crisp texture. Excellent for pies, sauces, baking.

Cortland: Richly red-colored with very white meat. Very juicy sweet flavor that intensifies with baking or cooking.

Crab: Enjoying a comeback, crab apples are diminutive, tart red apples that fare best cooked or baked. A good garnishing apple for meat platters at the holidays.

Empire: Large brilliant apple that's sweet, almost spicy in flavor. Juicy, good eating apple, even better for baking.

Gala: Another New Zealand apple. Mildly sweet, with a softer texture than Braeburns. Recommended for pies and salads.

Grannysmith: These pale green apples with the red blush are very crisp and juicy, a superb eating apple. With a pleasantly tart flavor, they also make fabulous pies, brown Bettys and sauces.

Jonagold: A cross between Jonathan and Golden Delicious, this apple is large with red streaks on a yellow skin. Inside, it's creamy-white, firm, juicy and sweet. For eating or cooking.

Lady: As tiny as crab apples, these bright yellow apples have a red blush and are pretty garnishes for late fall holiday meals. They have a sophisticated sweet-tart taste. Do not peel; the outer skin holds much of the flavor.

Newtown Pippin: With yellowish-green skin, this apple has a slightly tart flavor and a firm texture. It's a good keeper, ideal for baked desserts, salads and snacks.

Northern Spy: An all-purpose pale green or yellow apple striped with red. Exceptionally juicy, sweet-tart flavor. Available in the Midwest and Northeast.

Stayman: A descendant of the Winesap apple; red with green streaks. Large, crisp and juicy; good for eating or cooking.

Apple-Bratwurst Skillet

Serve this easy main dish for a quick family supper.

1 tablespoon vegetable oil
1 cup thinly sliced red onion
2 medium apples, cored, thinly
   sliced (2 cups)
3 tablespoons packed brown sugar
1/2 cup dry red wine
1/2 cup water
1 bay leaf
1 lb. bratwurst, cut into 1-inch
   diagonal slices
1-1/2 cups sauerkraut,
   well-drained
1/4 teaspoon pepper
1/8 teaspoon caraway seed
Hot cooked spaetzle or noodles

Heat oil in a large skillet. Sauté onion and apples in oil with brown sugar about 5 minutes or until nearly tender. Add wine, water and bay leaf; bring mixture to boiling. Add bratwurst and sauerkraut; stir in pepper and caraway seed. Reduce heat; simmer 5 minutes or until bratwurst is heated through. Arrange spaetzle or noodles on a serving platter. Transfer bratwurst mixture to platter with a slotted spoon. Makes 4 servings.

Preparation time: 20 minutes

Laura's Apple Pancakes

These German-style pancakes are traditionally served with butter and a sprinkling of sugar.

1 cup all-purpose flour
1/2 teaspoon baking soda
3 tablespoons packed brown sugar
1/2 teaspoon salt
1/8 teaspoon ground nutmeg
1-1/4 cups buttermilk
2 tablespoons vegetable oil
2 eggs, separated
1 teaspoon vanilla extract
1-1/2 cups very thinly sliced
   apples

In a medium bowl, stir together flour, baking soda, brown sugar, salt and nutmeg. In a large bowl, beat milk, oil, egg yolks and vanilla together until blended. Add dry ingredients all at once to milk mixture, stirring just to moisten (batter will be lumpy). Stir in apples. Beat egg whites until stiff. Fold into batter just until blended; do not stir. Lightly grease a large skillet or griddle over medium heat. For each pancake, pour about 1/4 cup batter into pan. Cook until bubbles appear over top surface of pancakes. Turn and brown second side. Keep finished pancakes warm on an ovenproof plate in a 250F (120C) oven while preparing remaining pancakes. Makes about 16 pancakes.

Preparation time: 15 minutes

Apple 'n Cheese Hors d'oeuvres

Your favorite apple, from the tart Grannysmith to a petite Lady apple, will complement this flavorful spread. (photo on page 23.)

2 (3-oz.) pkgs. cream cheese, room
   temperature
1/2 cup crumbled blue cheese
   (2 oz.)
1/2 cup shredded Cheddar cheese
   (2 oz.)
2 tablespoons milk
1/4 teaspoon Worcestershire sauce
1/4 teaspoon hot-pepper sauce
2 tablespoons finely chopped
   fresh parsley or watercress
About 30 apple slices
About 30 (2- x 1-inch) crackers or
   party-sliced dark bread

In a blender container or food processor fitted with a metal blade, process cheeses, milk, Worcestershire and hot-pepper sauce until smooth, stopping machine several times to scrape down sides of container. Use enough milk to make a spreading consistency. Spoon mixture into a crock or bowl. Sprinkle with parsley. If preparing ahead, cover and chill in refrigerator for up to 1 week. Spread a generous teaspoonful of cheese mixture over each apple slice; place each apple slice on a cracker or bread piece. Makes about 30 appetizers, 1-1/3 cups spread.

Preparation time: 15 minutes

Tip:
Recipe can be doubled or tripled.

German Apple Kuchen

This sweet-apple yeast coffeecake requires only ten minutes to rise, then mix and bake.

1 (.25-oz.) package active dry
   yeast (1 tablespoon)
3 tablespoons warm water
   (110F/45C)
1 teaspoon sugar
1-3/4 cups all-purpose flour
1 tablespoon baking powder
1/4 teaspoon salt
1/2 cup sugar
3/4 cup butter or margarine,
   softened
1 egg
1/2 cup milk
1 teaspoon vanilla extract
3 medium apples, cored, thinly
   sliced (3 cups)
3 tablespoons sugar
1 teaspoon ground cinnamon
1 teaspoon grated lemon peel

Preheat oven to 350F (175C). Lightly grease a 12" x 8" baking dish. In a small bowl, dissolve yeast in warm water; stir in 1 teaspoon sugar. Let mixture stand 10 minutes or until yeast starts to bubble. In a medium bowl, combine flour, baking powder and salt. Set aside. In another medium bowl, cream together 1/2 cup sugar, 1/2 cup butter or margarine and egg on medium speed of electric mixer until fluffy. Beat in milk and vanilla; beat in yeast mixture just till blended. Stir flour mixture into milk mixture just until moistened; spread evenly in bottom of baking dish. Arrange apple slices, overlapping slightly, in neat rows over batter. Dot with remaining 1/4 cup butter or margarine. Stir together 3 tablespoons sugar, cinnamon and lemon peel; sprinkle over apples. Bake 30 to 40 minutes or un-

til a wooden pick inserted in center comes out clean. Cut into squares and serve warm. Makes 9 servings.

Variation:
Any-Fruit Kuchen: Substitute 3 cups peeled, pitted, sliced peaches, nectarines, apricots, pears or plums for sliced apples.

Preparation time: 20 minutes

Apples, Pears, Persimmons, Quinces & Sapotes. See diagram, page 156.

Fresh Apricot Crisp

Use sugar according to the sweetness of your apricots. Serve warm with ice cream or whipped cream.

1/2 to 2/3 cup sugar
1 tablespoon cornstarch
1/2 teaspoon ground cinnamon
1/4 teaspoon ground nutmeg
1/4 cup water
4 cups sliced ripe apricots,
    peaches, nectarines or pears,
    peeled, if desired
2 teaspoons lemon juice
1/2 cup rolled or quick-cooking
    oats
1/3 cup packed brown sugar
1/4 cup all-purpose flour
1/2 teaspoon cinnamon
1/3 cup slivered almonds
1/4 cup butter or margarine

Preheat oven to 350F (175C). In a large saucepan, combine sugar, cornstarch, cinnamon and nutmeg. Add water and apricots. Cook, stirring occasionally, over medium heat until mixture comes to a boil. Reduce heat; cover and simmer 2 minutes. Stir in lemon juice. Pour mixture into an 8" x 8" x 2" or 9" x 9" x 2" baking pan. For topping, stir together oats, brown sugar, flour, cinnamon and almonds. Using a pastry blender, cut in butter or margarine; sprinkle over apricot filling. Bake 35 to 45 minutes or until golden-brown and bubbly. Serve warm or cooled. Makes 6 to 8 servings.

Preparation time: 15 minutes

APRICOTS

In Latin, the apricot's name means "precocius," a label earned because it ripens earlier than other summer fruits. China deserves the credit for discovering and cultivating this richly sweet fruit over 4000 years ago. Hundreds of centuries later, the Spanish missionaries carried apricots to California, where today nearly 97% of this country's crop is grown. Israel, Morocco, Japan, Australia and Spain also produce large crops of apricots.

From late May through August, you can enjoy several varieties of fresh apricots. It's particularly important to be fussy about the apricots you buy, because appearance is a strong indicator of good flavor.

Buying Tips: Buy apricots on the firm side, since they'll ripen well at home. Fruit should be smooth-skinned and blemish-free. Color ranges from a pale yellow to a healthy golden-yellow color; watch out for traces of green, indicating the fruit is unripe.

Storage: Ripen fruit at room temperature; refrigerate when ripe. When the fruit is soft to the touch, it's ready to eat.

Basic Preparation: Peeling is not necessary. Halve fruit and remove the pit or eat fruit around the pit, if desired. Slice, chop or purée for recipes. To remove the skin for recipes, plunge fruit in boiling water for 30 seconds, then in cold water. Skins should slip off easily.

Serving Ideas: Use apricots as you would peaches, plums or nectarines. Slice for desserts, salads, fruit compotes or sauces. Chop to add to breads or muffins, cakes or cookies. Excellent puréed for sauces.

Yield: Allow 2 or 3 apricots per serving.
10 to 12 apricots = 2 cups sliced fruit.
10 to 12 apricots = 1 lb.

Nutrition Facts: 3 apricots provide about 50 calories or about 18 per fruit. An excellent source of vitamin A (60% of the U.S. R.D.A.) and potassium and a good source of Vitamin C and iron.

Dried Apricots: Available year-round, whole and chopped, for use in salads, sauces and recipes. They have excellent keeping qualities. Fruit should be soft and tender even when dried.

Roast Chicken with Apricot-Pecan Stuffing

If fresh apricots are out of season, substitute snipped dried apricots for the fresh ones.

1 (3-1/2-to 4-lb.) roasting chicken
Salt and pepper to taste
1 tablespoon vegetable oil

Apricot-Pecan Stuffing:
1-1/2 cups cooked rice
1-1/2 cups diced fresh apricots
1/2 cup coarsely chopped pecans
1/2 cup diced celery
1/4 cup raisins
2 tablespoons melted butter or
  margarine
2 tablespoons orange juice
1/2 teaspoon allspice
1/2 teaspoon salt

Preheat oven to 400F (205C). Prepare Apricot-Pecan Stuffing. Discard excess fat from cavity of chicken; rinse bird and pat dry. Sprinkle chicken with salt and pepper to taste; brush with oil. Spoon stuffing into the cavity; pull skin over cavity and secure with skewers. Tie legs together; tuck wing tips under back. Place on a rack in a shallow roasting pan. Roast chicken, uncovered, for 1-1/4 to 1-1/2 hours or until juices run clear when bird is cut between breast and thigh; baste occasionally with pan juices. Let stand 5 minutes. Carve and spoon out stuffing. Makes 6 servings.

Apricot-Pecan Stuffing:
In a medium bowl, stir together rice, apricots, pecans, celery and raisins. In a small dish, stir together melted butter or margarine, orange juice, allspice and salt. Drizzle over rice mixture and toss to combine. Makes 4-1/4 cups.

Preparation time: 20 minutes

Apricot Margaritas

This recipe works well with nectarines, peaches, papaya, berries and bananas. (photo on page 145.)

1 lime, quartered
Sugar or salt
1 lb. apricots, peeled, pitted,
  sliced
1/2 cup tequila
1/4 cup orange liqueur
3 tablespoons lime juice
3 tablespoons sugar
2 cups cracked ice or 12 ice cubes
Fresh mint sprigs, if desired

Rub rims of 4 long-stemmed glasses with lime; dip rims in sugar or salt to coat. In a blender or food processor fitted with a metal blade, process peeled apricots to a purée. Add tequila, liqueur, lime juice and sugar; process until blended. Through hole in lid of blender or feed tube of processor, add ice cubes 1 at a time until mixture is slushy. Pour into prepared glasses; garnish with mint sprigs, if desired. Makes 4 drinks.

Preparation time: 5 minutes

Apricot-Passion Fruit Sauce

Use this sauce over ice cream, plain cake or brownies or over breakfast pancakes.

4 to 6 ripe wrinkled passion fruit
1/4 cup sugar
1 tablespoon cornstarch
1-1/2 cups apricot or peach nectar

Halve passion fruit. In a blender or food processor fitted with a metal blade, process passion fruit pulp with sugar until blended. Strain out seeds; transfer mixture to a small saucepan. In a medium bowl, stir cornstarch into apricot nectar; add to saucepan. Cook and stir over medium heat until mixture thickens and bubbles. Cook 2 minutes more. Cool. If preparing ahead, cover and refrigerate sauce up to 1 week. Makes 1-3/4 cups.

Preparation time: 10 minutes

Apricot Butter Cookies

This dough makes a soft, rich cookie.

1/3 cup softened butter or
  margarine
1/4 teaspoon almond extract
1/2 cup sugar
1 egg
1-1/2 cups all-purpose flour
1/2 teaspoon salt
1/4 teaspoon baking powder
1/2 teaspoon baking soda
1/2 cup dairy sour cream
2 cups chopped fresh apricots
  (6 to 7 apricots)
Sliced almonds

Almond Icing:
1 cup powdered sugar
2 tablespoons butter or margarine,
room temperature
1/4 teaspoon almond extract
1 tablespoon milk

Preheat oven to 400F (205C). Generously grease several baking sheets. In a large bowl, cream 1/3 cup butter or margarine and 1/4 teaspoon almond extract. Gradually beat in sugar. Add egg and beat well. In a medium bowl, stir together flour, salt, baking powder and baking soda. Add dry ingredients to creamed mixture alternately with sour cream, beating until blended. Stir in chopped apricots. Drop dough by rounded teaspoonfuls onto greased baking sheets. Bake 8 to 10 minutes or until light golden-brown. Prepare Almond Icing; drizzle over cookies. Garnish with sliced almonds. Makes 3 dozen cookies.

Almond Icing:
In a small bowl, stir together powdered sugar, 2 tablespoons butter or margarine, 1/4 teaspoon almond extract and milk until blended. Makes about 2/3 cup.

Preparation time: 20 minutes

AVOCADOS

Avocado Varieties:

Bacon & Zutano: Look-alikes available in winter. Pear-shaped but squattier than a Fuerte with the same semi-smooth green skin.

Cocktail Avocados: A newer variety of miniature avocados, without seeds. Halve and remove meat to use like larger varieties or as a conversation-piece appetizer.

Fuerte: A winter variety; elongated and pear-shaped with smooth, dark green skin that is pebbled.

Hass: Its pear shape is less distinctive than the Fuerte variety, and the skin is dark green with a pebbled texture. Skin turns black when the fruit is ripe. Available May through November.

Avocado 'n Cheese BLT's

Pita bread offers a neat serving solution for this West Coast sandwich.

1 cup shredded lettuce
1/2 ripe avocado, diced
4 strips crisp-cooked bacon,
   crumbled, or 4 thin slices
   turkey, cut into bite-sized strips
1 small tomato, chopped
2 slices Swiss or Muenster cheese,
   diced
2 to 3 tablespoons mayonnaise,
   salad dressing or Thousand
   Island dressing
2 pita bread rounds, slit

In a medium bowl, toss together shredded lettuce, avocado, bacon or turkey pieces, tomato and cheese. Add mayonnaise and toss until coated with dressing. Spoon mixture into pita pockets and serve. Makes 2 sandwiches.

Preparation time: 10 minutes

Spanish conquistadors called the avocado "abogado," derived from an Aztec term that means "butter from the wood." Central and South Americans have appreciated the deliciousness of this creamy, soft-textured fruit since three centuries before Christ, as evidenced by their pictorial writings. In the 1800's, the Spaniards brought avocados to the U.S. Today several varieties of avocados are grown in California, Florida, Africa and the Mediterranean countries, so the fruit is available in produce markets all year.

It's essential to use them at the proper stage of ripeness to enjoy their fullest flavor. Avocados are easily digested, high in vitamins and minerals and contain no cholesterol, so they are appropriate for a number of special diets.

Buying Tips: Some avocados have smooth, green skin; others have thick, pebbly, dark green skin, but all should be free of bruises or damaged spots. Buy according to when it will be used: if using within 1 day, buy fruit that is soft to the touch, but not mushy. If using in several days, purchase the harder fruit; it will ripen within 2 to 3 days.

Storage: Refrigerate soft, soon-to-be-used fruit up to 5 days. Let harder fruit stand at room temperature, or place in a paper bag or fruit ripening bowl to speed ripening. Check fruit daily. Here's one method: insert a wooden pick at the stem end of an avocado; if it can be easily inserted and removed, the fruit is ready to eat.

Basic Preparation: Cut into fruit just before using or serving. With a sharp paring knife, cut the avocado in half lengthwise, around the seed. Twist the two halves in opposite directions to separate them. Slide a spoon beneath the seed to remove it, or carefully strike a knife blade into the seed, then rotate the knife to lift out the seed. The skin should pull off easily, or use a paring knife to slip it off. Fruit discolors quickly when cut; dip halves or slices into a lemon juice and water mixture, or stir a little lemon juice into the mashed fruit.

Serving Ideas: One of the most popular uses for avocados is mashed for guacamole, or as a topping for Mexican dishes. Slice avocados for salads, sandwiches or to top a pizza. Dice the fruit for omelets, fruit compotes or a seafood salad. Use avocado halves as containers for chicken salad, or to enjoy with just a squeeze of lemon or lime juice.

Yield: 2 small avocados = about 1 cup mashed fruit.
2 small avocados = about 1 lb.

Nutrition Facts: One avocado half has about 180 calories. Low in sodium, with twice as much potassium as a banana, avocados are also high in vitamins A, C and E. People on low-cholesterol or low-sodium diets, or those who are coronary or geriatric patients, often find avocados useful in their restricted diets.

Appetizer Tostadas with Guacamole

This appetizer is bound to be a hit with your guests.

3 (12-inch) flour tortillas
1/4 cup vegetable oil
1 recipe Guacamole, page 23
1 cup finely shredded cooked chicken
1/2 cup diced tomatoes
1 cup shredded Monterey Jack or Cheddar cheese (4 oz.)
Toppings: salsa, sour cream, sliced ripe olives or cilantro sprigs

Preheat oven to 350F (175C). With kitchen shears, cut each tortilla into 8 triangles. Heat oil in a 12-inch skillet. Fry tortilla pieces, a few at a time, just until crisp and bubbles form. Drain well on paper towels. Place tortillas on a large ungreased baking sheet. Using 1/2 of Guacamole, spoon a dollop on each tortilla wedge. Sprinkle with chicken, tomato and cheese. Bake 8 to 12 minutes or until heated through. Garnish with remaining Guacamole and desired toppings. Makes 24 appetizers.

Preparation time: 20 minutes

Avocado & Tomato Salad Vinaigrette

The dressing also makes a great marinade for chilled vegetables.

Lettuce leaves
2 medium-ripe avocados, peeled, seeded, thinly sliced
2 large tomatoes, sliced 1/4-inch thick
1/2 cup finely chopped red onion
1 hard-cooked egg, chopped

Vinaigrette Dressing:
1/2 cup vegetable oil
1/4 cup white wine vinegar
2 tablespoons lemon juice
1/4 teaspoon dry mustard
1 garlic clove, mashed
1/4 teaspoon salt
1/8 teaspoon pepper
Dash hot-pepper sauce

Prepare Vinaigrette Dressing. Line a large salad platter with lettuce leaves. Arrange avocado and tomato slices, alternating slices over lettuce. Sprinkle chopped onion and egg down center of salad. Drizzle dressing over salad as needed and serve. Makes 6 servings.

Vinaigrette Dressing:
In a shaker jar, combine oil, wine vinegar, lemon juice, mustard, garlic, salt, pepper and hot-pepper sauce. Cover and shake well to mix. Makes 2/3 cup.

Preparation time: 20 minutes

California Omelet

This omelet is a favorite of brunchers at the beach.

9 eggs
1/4 teaspoon salt
1/8 teaspoon pepper
1/8 teaspoon hot-pepper sauce, if desired
3 tablespoons butter or margarine
1 small avocado, peeled, diced
1 (6-oz.) can flaked crabmeat, drained
1 to 1-1/2 cups shredded Monterey Jack, Swiss or Cheddar cheese (4 to 6 ozs.)
1 green onion, thinly sliced
Homemade Salsa, page 97, or bottled salsa

In a medium bowl, whisk together eggs, salt, pepper and hot-pepper sauce, if desired. For each omelet, in a small skillet or omelet pan, melt 1 tablespoon butter or margarine. Pour in 1/3 of beaten egg mixture. Stir gently with fork for 30 seconds, then cook without stirring until edges begin to set. With a small spatula or knife, lift edges of omelet to allow uncooked egg mixture to flow underneath. When omelet is nearly set, sprinkle 1/3 of avocado, crab, cheese and onion over bottom half of omelet. With spatula fold top of omelet over filling, slide onto a serving plate. Repeat for 2 more omelets. Serve immediately with Homemade Salsa or bottled salsa spooned over. Makes 3 servings.

Preparation time: 15 minutes

Fruit-Stuffed Avocados

This colorful salad gets its own delicious serving container.

Lettuce leaves
2 avocados, halved, pitted
1/2 cup sliced strawberries or whole berries such as blueberries, raspberries or blackberries
1 orange, tangerine or tangelo, peeled, sectioned
1/2 cup chopped peaches, papaya or pineapple

Sour Cream-Honey Dressing:
1/4 cup dairy sour cream
1 teaspoon honey
1 tablespoon milk

Prepare Sour Cream-Honey Dressing. Arrange lettuce leaves on a large platter or 4 individual salad plates. Place avocados cut side up on lettuce. Sprinkle berries, orange sections and cut-up fruit in centers of avocado halves. Serve dressing with salads. If preparing in advance, refrigerate dressing, covered, up to 24 hours. Makes 4 servings.

Sour Cream-Honey Dressing:
In a small bowl, stir together sour cream, honey and milk until well blended. Makes about 1/3 cup.

Preparation time: 15 minutes

Guacamole

Use guacamole with fresh vegetable dippers, too.

2 ripe avocados, mashed
1/3 cup Homemade Salsa, page 97, or bottled salsa
1 tablespoon lemon juice

In a medium bowl, stir together mashed avocado, salsa and lemon juice until well blended. Makes about 1 cup.

Preparation time: 10 minutes

Apple 'n Cheese Hors d'oeuvres, page 17; Fruit-Stuffed Avocados, above.

BABACO

(Bab-a-coh) Looking like a bright yellow Zeppelin, with soft ridges running lengthwise along the fruit, a babaco is a sweet, juicy delight from the papaya family. Super-sized, a babaco averages 6 to 10 inches long and 4 inches wide. Slice into it to enjoy the peach-colored fruit with its melon-like taste and the sweetness of strawberries or pineapple. The fruit has no seeds and there's no need to peel it. Slices of babaco resemble softly-shaped stars.

Ecuador's high altitude and climate provided ideal conditions for the first babacos cultivated. Now both New Zealand and California growers produce the fruit which grows in clumps on heavy tree-like vines.

Buying Tips: A ripe babaco will be a healthy yellow color with smooth, unblemished skin. Avoid fruit that is very soft which indicates over-ripeness.

Storage: Keep green babacos at room temperature to ripen, then refrigerate when ripe. Use within 3 to 4 days. Fruit begins to ferment if stored too long.

Basic Preparation: Wash fruit; do not remove skin since it is completely edible. There are no seeds. To serve, slice thinly, cut into chunks or halve lengthwise like a melon.

Serving Ideas: This very juicy fruit can be used like berries or melon in compotes, fruit salads or as a breakfast fruit. Purée the fruit for sorbet, ice cream or a fruit smoothie. Arrange slices on a fruit tart or serve with apples and cheese for an appetizer.

Yield: 1 babaco = 2 or 3 servings.
1 (10-inch) babaco = about 32 thin slices.

Nutrition Facts: Babacos are high in vitamins, especially vitamin C, and low in calories.

Babaco & Berries Romanoff

When babaco cannot be found, you can substitute fresh figs or melon chunks.

1 medium babaco, halved lengthwise, or 12 fresh figs, quartered, or 1 small cantaloupe, cubed
1-1/2 cups sliced strawberries
1/2 cup blueberries, raspberries or blackberries
1 tablespoon sugar
2 tablespoons raspberry or orange liqueur
1/2 cup whipping cream, whipped

Slice babaco 1/4-inch thick. In a medium bowl, toss together babaco slices with strawberries and blueberries. Spoon into 4 goblets or dessert dishes. In a small bowl, fold sugar and raspberry or orange liqueur into whipped cream. Top fruit with flavored whipped cream. Makes 6 servings.

Preparation time: 10 minutes

Babaco Cooler

This drink is a refreshing boon to dieters, and offers a day's supply of vitamin C.

3 cups cubed unpeeled babaco or peeled melon chunks
Ice cubes
Chilled carbonated water or club soda
Lime wedges

In a blender or food processor fitted with a metal blade, puree babaco or melon chunks until very smooth. Pour into 3 tall glasses. Add ice cubes; fill with carbonated water. Garnish each drink with a lime wedge. Makes 3 drinks.

Preparation time: 5 minutes

Unusual Banana Varieties:

Burros: Looks like a squatty yellow banana. The fruit is creamy white. Peel should be yellow with black spots when ripe. Tangy lemon-banana flavor.

Manzano: Also called Apple bananas. This short banana will turn completely black when ripe and ready to eat. The white fruit inside tastes like a cross between a strawberry and a banana.

Red: Sweeter than yellow bananas with a slight raspberry flavor. Their red skin turns to a purplish-red as they ripen; the fruit has a pale pink hue.

Roasted Bananas with Bacon

Serve this intriguing side dish with pork or chicken.

4 strips bacon, chopped
4 to 6 firm-ripe bananas*, peeled, quartered
1 teaspoon brown sugar
1 tablespoon orange juice
1 tablespoon grated orange peel

In a large skillet, fry bacon until crisp. Drain bacon on paper towels, reserving 1 tablespoon drippings in skillet. Add bananas to drippings; sauté over medium-high heat 2 minutes, turning gently to brown all sides. Stir in brown sugar, orange juice and orange peel with cooked bacon. Cook 2 minutes more or until heated through. Makes 4 servings.

*Number depends on type of banana used.

Preparation time: 15 minutes

BANANAS

Alexander the Great discovered bananas growing in India around 300 B.C. Word spread quickly after that, via traders who carried the plants to East Africa and Polynesia. Today we enjoy a constantly abundant supply of bananas from Central America, Africa and Indonesia.

Bananas grow not on trees, but on tall plants about 25 feet high. Each stem or shoot from the trunk of the plant produces about 10 "hands" with about 12 "fingers" or bananas on each. The entire stem, which only produces fruit once, is trimmed off and the individual hands are packaged for shipping.

Beyond the familiar yellow Cavendish variety, there are several varieties of sweet bananas that look and taste somewhat different. (For information on plantains, see page 136.)

Buying Tips: Manzanos should be black when ripe. Red bananas should be purplish-red when ready to eat. Purchase Burro bananas when the yellow skin has black spots and is slightly firm.

Storage: Store as you would yellow bananas, at room temperature until ripe. Refrigerate, if desired, when ripe for up to 3 or 4 days.

Basic Preparation: Peel like a regular banana; slice or enjoy whole. All bananas will discolor a few minutes after cutting. Use a lemon juice and water mixture to dip slices for salads or pies.

Serving Ideas: Use these unusual bananas as a breakfast fruit, in a fruit compote, mixed into a fruit salad or dipped in chocolate and rolled in coconut. Bananas can be mashed and puréed for shakes, pies, cakes and cookies just like regular bananas. Or sauté these bananas for a vegetable side dish, seasoned with spices like curry, mint or basil.

Yield: 1 banana = 1 serving.
2 to 3 bananas mashed = about 1 cup.

Nutrition Facts: These bananas are very high in potassium and low in sodium. They contain very little fat and are easily digestible. One banana contains about 80 calories.

Banana Beignets (Ben-yays)

Traditional beignets are an old New Orleans favorite—pillow-shaped dough-nuts smothered in powdered sugar. This version looks like a fritter.

1 cup all-purpose flour
3 tablespoons sugar
1 teaspoon baking powder
1/4 teaspoon salt
1/4 teaspoon ground nutmeg
1/4 teaspoon ground cinnamon
1 cup milk
1 egg
1 teaspoon vanilla extract
Vegetable oil for shallow-fat
   frying
3 medium or 6 small ripe
   bananas, peeled, cut into 2-inch
   chunks
Powdered sugar

In a medium bowl, stir together flour, sugar, baking powder, salt, nutmeg and cinnamon. In a small bowl, beat together milk, egg and vanilla until blended; stir into dry ingredients until smooth. Pour oil in a deep skillet to a depth of 2 inches. Heat to 375F (190C). For each beignet, use tongs to dip 2 pieces (or 3 pieces if using small bananas) of banana into batter to coat. Fry 2 to 3 minutes or until golden-brown, turning to brown all sides. Drain on paper towels. Roll each beignet generously in powdered sugar to coat. Repeat with remaining bananas and batter. Serve warm. Makes about 12 to 16 beignets.

Preparation time: 15 minutes

Banana Date Shake

This nutritious favorite is a southern California tradition.

1-1/2 cups milk
1 cup ripe banana chunks
1 teaspoon vanilla extract
1/2 cup chopped dates
2 large scoops vanilla ice cream

In a blender or food processor fitted with a metal blade, process 1/2 of milk, banana chunks, vanilla and dates until smooth. Add 1/2 of ice cream; process again until thick. Pour into a tall glass. Repeat with remaining ingredients. Makes 2 shakes.

Preparation time: 5 minutes

Chocolate-Dipped Bananas

Try this easy dessert idea with other fruits such as strawberries, papaya, pineapple and dried fruits. Do not substitute semi-sweet chocolate morsels for the chocolate.

Lemon juice
3 to 4 bananas, peeled, quartered
1/2 cup semi-sweet chocolate,
   chopped

Sprinkle lemon juice over bananas. In a double boiler, melt chocolate over simmering water. Or microwave on 100% (HIGH) 2 minutes, stirring once during cooking. Dip each banana piece into chocolate to coat; place on a waxed paper-covered wire rack. Refrigerate dipped pieces until set. Serve same day. Makes about 12 to 16 pieces.

Preparation time: 10 minutes

Summer Fruit Salad

The almond fruit dressing is a super low-cal topping for any fresh fruit compote or salad.

Lettuce leaves
1 cantaloupe or 1/2 honeydew
   melon, seeded
1 banana, quartered
4 kiwifruit, peeled, quartered
1/2 cup whole strawberries,
   hulled
1/4 pound seedless red or green
   grapes, cut in clusters
1 tablespoon toasted flaked
   coconut

Almond Fruit Dressing:
3/4 cup lemon, peach or
   strawberry-flavored yogurt
1/2 cup cottage cheese
1/2 teaspoon almond extract

Prepare Almond Fruit Dressing. Line a serving platter with lettuce leaves. Cut melon in thin wedges, slice off skin. Arrange melon wedges, banana quarters, kiwifruit, berries and grapes on lettuce. Place dressing in a serving boat to pass with salad. Sprinkle toasted flaked coconut over salad. Makes 2 servings.

Almond Fruit Dressing:
In a blender or food processor fitted with a metal blade, process yogurt, cottage cheese and almond extract until nearly smooth. Makes 1-1/4 cups.

Preparation time: 15 minutes

Berry Varieties:

Blackberries: Like a black raspberry, these succulent berries are fairly large and sweet when ripe. Color ranges from black to purplish-black.

Boysenberries: This juicy, sweet, large purplish-black berry is a cross between the blackberry, raspberry and the loganberry.

Gooseberries: About the size of large currants, green gooseberries must be cooked and sweetened to eat in pies or sauces. When berries turn pink, they become sweet enough to eat by themselves.

Loganberries: A cross between red raspberries and blackberries resulted in this red tart berry. It's suited to making jams and jellies.

Marionberries: Like large, oval blackberries, these berries are a close relative. They have a soft texture and a rich berry flavor.

Ollalieberries: A cross between two blackberry hybrids, this sweet black berry is shiny and black when fully ripe.

Red Currants: These tiny red berries grow on crawling vines. Their flavor is extremely tart, so they're used mainly for jams, jellies and sauces. Other varieties are white and black.

Yellow Cape Gooseberries (Physalis): Also referred to as a Cape Gooseberry or Ground Cherry, this berry comes from Peru. A round, golden-yellow berry encased in a papery husk, this gooseberry eats like a grape and has a sweet taste. Eat out-of-hand or use in jams and jellies.

Yellow Raspberries: Identical in size and shape to a raspberry, but a soft yellow color. These are very sweet, small berries that become softer as they ripen.

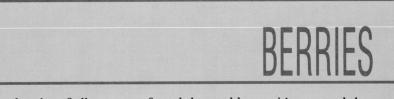

BERRIES

Since berries of all types are found the world over, it's assumed that they first grew wild and were then cultivated by Europeans and Asians. When the Pilgrims came to the New World, they found the Indians enjoying cranberries, blueberries and strawberries. Strawberries as we know them today were cultivated from a cross made between a Chilean strawberry and wild berries found growing in West Virginia.

Indians taught the early American settlers to dry blueberries to add to their winter soups and stews. Along with blueberries, cranberries are one of the truly native North American fruits. Since cranberries require acid peat soil, sand and water to grow, they are cultivated in "bogs" or peat swamps.

Berry producers in Europe, New Zealand and the U.S. are bringing us more types of berries than ever before. Each year the supplies increase, so it's wise to sample them all to find your personal favorites. These varieties are found from late May through July or early August, but may also be found as a winter import.

Buying Tips: Check Varieties information for appropriate color characteristics. Avoid very soft berries that show signs of mold or bruises. Buy berries to use within a day or two for best flavor. Look for firm, plump berries with a healthy color.

Storage: Store berries unwashed in the refrigerator, covered with paper towels to use within a couple of days. To freeze berries, place them whole, unwashed, in freezer containers. Freeze for up to 4 months.

Basic Preparation: Wash and hull berries, if necessary, just before using them. Slice strawberries or serve other varieties whole. (For Yellow Cape Gooseberries, peel off husks, then wash). Sprinkle berries with sugar if desired or top with lightly sweetened whipped cream. Sugaring berries a few minutes before serving will draw out some of the sweet berry juice.

Serving Ideas: Use sweet varieties of berries in all types of chilled and refrigerated desserts, mixed into fruit salads and compotes or puréed for sauces or drinks. Use berries as pretty garnishes for a main dish platter, over avocado slices for a salad or dipped into melted chocolate and allowed to set. Tart varieties can be used in recipes for jams, chutneys and preserves or in pies.

Yield: 1 lb. fresh berries = about 1 quart or 4 cups.
1 pint fresh berries = 4 servings or about 2 cups.

Nutrition Facts: Berries are wonderfully low in calories, averaging about 45 calories per 1/2 cup serving. Berries are high in Vitamin C, calcium and minerals.

Berry Tart à la Crème

Putting dry beans and foil in the unbaked crust will keep it from bubbling up during baking.

1 10-inch unbaked pastry shell
1 cup dry beans, if desired
3 tablespoons apple or currant jelly, melted
3-1/2 cups fresh (hulled, sliced if necessary) berries
1/2 cup whipping cream
1 tablespoon sugar

Preheat oven to 450F (230C). Lay pastry in a 10-inch tart pan with removeable bottom. Press into pan and on sides; trim crust even with top of pan edge. Prick crust well with fork. If desired, place a piece of aluminum foil inside crust; pour beans into foil. Bake 5 minutes; remove foil and beans. Bake 3 to 5 minutes more or until light golden-brown. Cool on a rack. Brush bottom of tart crust with melted jelly. Pour 1/2 of the berries into crust, arranging evenly. In blender or food processor fitted with a metal blade, process remaining berries to a purée. If necessary, strain berry purée to remove seeds. In a medium bowl, beat cream until stiff. With rubber spatula fold in berry puree and sugar until blended. Spoon or pipe mixture around edge of fruit in tart. If preparing ahead, cover and chill pie in refrigerator up to 24 hours. Makes 1 (10-inch) tart.

Preparation time: 30 minutes

Tip:
Larger strawberries are not necessarily the sweetest. If you choose bright red, plump berries with fresh, bright green caps, they'll probably be sweet and delicious, no matter what size.

Fish with Port Wine-Berry Sauce

Fresh berries, orange juice and port combine for a sweetly elegant sauce.

1-1/4 lbs. fresh or frozen fish fillets, thawed
Olive oil or vegetable oil
1-1/2 cups sliced strawberries or whole blueberries, raspberries, ollalieberries, blackberries, boysenberries or Marionberries
2 tablespoons butter or margarine
3 shallots, peeled, sliced
1/4 cup port wine or sweet red dessert wine
1/4 cup orange juice
Dash salt
Dash pepper

Preheat broiler. Place fish fillets on oiled broiler pan; brush lightly with oil. Broil 4 inches from heat about 5 minutes per inch of thickness, turning once. Meanwhile, in a blender or food processor fitted with a metal blade, process 1/2 of berries to a purée. In a large skillet, melt butter or margarine; sauté shallots 2 minutes or until translucent. Add wine and juice; bring to boiling. Simmer 1 minute. Stir in berry purée, remaining berries, salt and pepper. Heat 1 minute more. Spoon sauce over each serving of fish. Makes 3 to 4 servings.

Preparation time: 15 minutes

Berry Seafood Salad

Use light mayonnaise in the dressing if you're watching calories.

2 cups shredded crabmeat, drained canned flaked tuna or flaked canned salmon, bones removed
1 cup sliced strawberries or whole blueberries, raspberries, ollalieberries, boysenberries, blackberries or Marionberries
1 cup melon chunks
1/2 cup halved red or green seedless grapes
2 cups shredded lettuce or red cabbage

Lemon-Chive Dressing:
2 tablespoons lemon yogurt
2 tablespoons mayonnaise or salad dressing
1 tablespoon chopped chives

Prepare Lemon Dressing. In a large bowl, toss together crabmeat, tuna or salmon, berries, melon chunks and grapes. Spoon dressing over salad and toss gently to coat. Serve over shredded lettuce or cabbage. Makes 2 or 3 servings.

Lemon-Chive Dressing:
In a small bowl, stir together yogurt, mayonnaise or salad dressing and chives until well blended. Makes about 1/4 cup.

Preparation time: 15 minutes

Berries. Clockwise from top: Strawberries, blackberries, blueberries, raspberries.

CHERIMOYAS/ATEMOYAS

(SHARE-a-MOY-ahs) (ah-teh-MOY-ahs) Sheathed in a green alligator-like skin, the heart-shaped cherimoya is about the size of your fist. Though not glamorously packaged, this fruit (a favorite of Mark Twain's) is one of heaven's gifts when perfectly ripe. Slice into the gleaming white interior and you'll find large, watermelon-like black seeds embedded in the fruit. Spoon out the soft fruit and enjoy a sweet mix of flavors resembling bananas, pineapple and papaya. The texture is close to sherbet which is why cherimoyas are often called "custard apples."

The atemoya, another hybrid of the cherimoya, weighs almost a pound or more. Its green skin has a shingled texture, but the flavor and texture are very close to the cherimoya.

Cherimoyas and atemoyas originated in Peru and Ecuador. Today they're grown in Spain, Portugal, France, Central and South America, Florida and Southern California. Cherimoyas and atemoyas can be found from late February through June.

Buying Tips: Both fruits begin to split at the stem end and turn a darker green or greenish-brown color when perfectly ripe. Look for fruit that's slightly soft to the touch and free of bruises or large soft dented spots.

Storage: Allow bright green fruit to stand at room temperature until the skin darkens and texture softens. Refrigerate ripe fruit for up to several days. Chopped or puréed fruit can be frozen for up to several months.

Basic Preparation: Halve fruit; use a spoon to remove seeds. Enjoy fruit as is, spooned from the shell or cube or mash fruit for use in recipes. Fruit will discolor like bananas do when cut; use a lemon juice-water mixture for cubes or chunks to be used in salads or recipes.

Serving Ideas: Purée the fruit for beverages, sauces or fruit fillings. Cube fruit to add to fruit or seafood salads, to sprinkle with orange or raspberry liqueur or to top ice cream. Use chopped cherimoyas or atemoyas over pancakes or waffles as a breakfast fruit, too.

Yield: 1 medium cherimoya = 2 servings.
1 medium atemoya = 3 to 4 servings.

Nutrition Facts: About 3-1/2 ounces of the fruit provides 94 calories. Both fruits are generous in vitamin C, carbohydrates and minerals.

Cherimoya-Pineapple Sorbet

This easy sorbet has naturally sweet flavor and a custard-like texture. (photo on page 76.)

4 ripe cherimoyas or 2 atemoyas
2 cups chopped fresh pineapple

Berry Sauce:
1 cup raspberries, Marionberries or strawberries, hulled
1 to 2 tablespoons sugar

Halve cherimoyas. Scoop out pulp; remove seeds. In a blender or food processor fitted with a metal blade, process pulp until smooth. Fold in pineapple; turn mixture into a 9" x 9" x 2" baking pan. Cover; place in freezer several hours or until almost firm. Break up frozen mixture with fork; place in a chilled medium bowl. Beat mixture just until frothy; turn back into pan. Cover and freeze several hours or until almost firm. Prepare Berry Sauce; spoon some sauce over each serving of sorbet. Makes 3 cups.

Berry Sauce:
In a blender or food processor fitted with a metal blade, place raspberries or strawberries and sugar to taste. Cover and process until smooth. If using raspberries, press mixture through strainer to remove seeds. Makes about 1 cup.

Preparation time: 10 minutes

Queen Anne Sunday Omelet

The lightly sweetened fresh fruit sauce is great on waffles, pancakes and ice cream.

12 extra large eggs
2 tablespoons water
1/2 teaspoon salt
1/4 teaspoon pepper
1/4 cup butter or margarine
1/4 cup dairy sour cream

Cherry-Fruit Sauce:
3 tablespoons sugar
1 tablespoon cornstarch
1 cup water
1-1/2 cups pitted Queen Anne or bing cherries, stemmed, pitted, halved
1 cup chopped fresh peaches, nectarines, plums or starfruit
1/2 cup red or green seedless grapes, halved
2 teaspoons lemon juice

Prepare Cherry-Fruit Sauce; keep warm. In a large bowl, whisk together eggs, water, salt and pepper until blended. For each omelet, in a small skillet or omelet pan melt 1 tablespoon butter or margarine. Pour 1/4 of egg mixture into skillet. Cook over medium-high heat, stirring, until mixture begins to set around edges. Use a small metal spatula or table knife to lift omelet at edges, allowing uncooked portion of egg to flow underneath. When omelet is nearly set, spoon 2 tablespoons of the Cherry-Fruit Sauce onto bottom half of omelet. Use a spatula to flip top portion of omelet over; turn out onto plate. Spoon more sauce over omelet; top with a dollop of sour cream. Repeat with remaining egg mixture and sauce to make 4 individual omelets. Makes 4 servings.

Cherry Fruit Sauce:

In a medium saucepan, combine sugar and cornstarch; stir in water. Heat mixture to boiling; boil 2 minutes. Add cherries, chopped peaches or nectarines and grapes; heat through but do not boil. Stir in lemon juice. Makes 3-1/2 cups.

Preparation time: 20 minutes

CHERRIES

When fresh cherries appear in markets, it's wise to enjoy them while you can, from the end of May through July. The ancient Chinese first cultivated cherries, but it was the Greeks and Romans who perfected the fruit. Today this fruit is grown in nearly every temperate region of the world along with the Western and Eastern United States.

Cherries grow on large trees with heavy foliage. Picking them is difficult because not all of the fruit ripens at the same time. Japanese cherry trees do not produce the sweet variety found in produce markets; the trees are grown primarily for their beautiful blossoms. Legend says that a fifth-century Japanese emperor came to revere the cherry blossoms when they floated into his sake cup as he was boating on a lake one day. He decided to enjoy his sake beneath the cherry trees daily after that. Even today, the Japanese annually celebrate spring in the blossoming cherry orchards.

Buying Tips: Look for plump, shiny-skinned cherries with stems still attached for maximum freshness. Color should be healthy for the variety. Taste for flavor and sweetness, if possible. Avoid bruised, very soft fruit without stems.

Storage: Refrigerate fresh cherries, loosely covered, for up to 2 or 3 days. Or arrange cherries on a paper towel-lined tray; cover with paper towels or plastic wrap. Pitted and stemmed cherries can be frozen in freezer containers for up to several months.

Basic Preparation: Just before serving, remove stems and pits. Use a cherry-pitter, available at kitchen supply shops, or the tip of a vegetable peeler to remove pits. Enjoy the fruit as is or halved and topped with whipped cream.

Serving Ideas: Aside from the classics like cherries jubilee and cherry pie, the fruit is versatile in almost any dessert recipe. Arrange halved cherries over pastry for a fruit tart or toss with other cubed or sliced fruit for gelatin salads, breads and dessert combos. Or try making a mildly sweet cherry sauce for pork, chicken or Cornish game hens. Cherries also do well in preserves and pickles.

Yield: 1 lb. cherries = 2-1/4 to 2-1/2 cups pitted cherries. 1/4 lb. cherries = 1 serving.

Nutrition Facts: One-quarter pound of cherries, about one serving, has 65 calories. Cherries are bursting with vitamin A, calcium and phosphorus.

Varieties:

Bing/Lambert: These are the two most popular fresh sweet cherry varieties. Both are dark red to reddish-black.

Queen Anne: Also called *Ranier* and *Golden Bing,* this variety is a beautiful yellow tinged with a red blush. Some may appear almost white. These are large and sweet.

Black Forest Decadence

Decadence in this case means a rich but light chocolate cake that uses just a little flour. The quick frosting comes from melted candy bars.

6 (1-oz.) squares semi-sweet
   chocolate
2/3 cup butter or margarine
3 tablespoons all-purpose flour
5 egg yolks
5 egg whites
1/2 teaspoon cream of tartar
1/2 cup sugar
3 (1.65-oz.) plain chocolate candy
   bars
2 cups pitted red bing cherries
2 to 3 tablespoons kirsch (cherry
   liqueur) or orange liqueur
Whipped cream

Preheat oven to 350F (175C). Lightly grease bottom of an 8-inch springform pan. In a small saucepan, melt chocolate and butter over very low heat, stirring constantly until melted. Remove from heat; stir in flour. Beat egg yolks slightly; stir 2 tablespoons of chocolate mixture into yolks. Stir chocolate-yolk mixture into remaining chocolate mixture until well mixed. In a large bowl, beat egg whites with cream of tartar to soft peaks. Gradually beat in sugar until mixture forms stiff peaks. Using a rubber spatula, fold egg whites into chocolate mixture until no streaks of white remain. Pour into prepared pan. Bake 30 to 35 minutes or until a wooden pick inserted half-way between center and edge comes out clean. Cool in pan 10 minutes; turn out onto a wire rack. Unwrap chocolate bars; place on warm cake. Spread over top and sides of cake when melted. Arrange pitted cherries over cake; sprinkle with liqueur. Serve cake with whipped cream. Cut into wedges. Makes 8 servings.

Preparation time: 30 minutes

Tip:
To melt chocolate and butter for the cake in a microwave oven, place in a medium bowl and cover with waxed paper. Microwave on 100% (HIGH) 1 minute or until melted, stirring once.

Black Forest Decadence, above.

New Varieties:

Blood Oranges: Beautiful reddish-orange pulp gave this fruit its name. Outer skin is orange with a bright red blush. Flavor is more intense than an orange.

Kumquats: Like a miniature orange, these have the same bright orange skin and sweet fruit inside. This citrus fruit can be eaten, skin and all, for a sweet-tart taste.

Lavender Gems: Also called Wekiwas, this fruit is a cross between a tangelo and a white grapefruit. The fruit is both sweet and tart with a pink-tinged rind.

Limequats: A cross between a kumquat and a lime, these are like miniature limes, football-shaped, with medium green peel. They have a tart taste like limes.

Mandarin Oranges: Clementine and Dancy are 2 types of Mandarin oranges. Both are light orange with orange flesh that contains seeds. Flavor is sweet and mild.

Minneola Tangelo: This variety looks like a large orange with a knob-like formation at the stem end. Because it's a cross between a tangerine and a grapefruit, the flavor is sweet and tart.

Oro Blanco Grapefruit: This new grapefruit is a cross between a grapefruit and a pummelo, see below. Though it looks and tastes like a grapefruit, it is nearly as sweet as an orange.

Pummelo: Actually a forerunner of the grapefruit we know today, this variety has slightly bumpy skin with light pink to red fruit. Flavor is both sweet and tart. The fruit is large and seedless; some weigh up to 1-1/2 pounds each!

Ugli Fruit: From Jamaica comes a grapefruit variety parented by a grapefruit and a tangerine. With greenish, heavily russeted skin, the meat inside is bright orange and sweeter than a grapefruit.

CITRUS FRUITS

Crusaders touring the Middle East discovered a tangy, juicy bright orange fruit whose popularity quickly spread to Spain, the rest of Europe and, through Columbus, to the New World. As early as 1750, it was discovered that citrus fruits could prevent and cure scurvy. Oranges, grapefruit and tangerines became standard cargo on ships that crossed the seas, preventing thousands of scurvy deaths.

Beyond the familiar citrus fruits, a mind-boggling array of new varieties have recently come to market. Giant grapefruits called pummelos, tiny oranges named kumquats and blushing red-tinged blood oranges can be found now. Plentiful and versatile, citrus fruits are grown in most temperate areas of the world including Florida, Texas and California. Most of these varieties are at their best through the winter months until May.

Buying Tips: Purchase citrus fruits with good color for their variety without any signs of mold. Some surface blemishes are common, but avoid fruit with soft spots. Citrus fruit skins vary in thickness depending on weather conditions; actually, the thicker the skins, the higher the concentration of nutrients in the fruit.

Storage: Citrus fruit can be stored at room temperature for up to 10 days, or store in the refrigerator crisper in a plastic bag. The juice and grated peel can be refrigerated or frozen, but do not attempt to freeze whole citrus fruits.

Basic Preparation: Kumquats and limequats should be thinly sliced or quartered for eating or garnishing recipes. All other citrus fruits can be peeled by hand. Remove any white pith, which has a bitter flavor, and separate fruit into sections. Squeeze cut halves to release juice or grate the colored section of the outer peel to add to recipes. If desired, sprinkle cut or sectioned grapefruit varieties with a little sugar to sweeten.

Serving Ideas: Broil any variety (except kumquats and limequats) topped with honey or brown sugar for a breakfast treat. Section fruits to mix with avocado and kiwi slices for a salad or chop to add to muffins or pancake batter. Use fruit in parfaits, salads, warm fruit compotes and beverages. The fruit slices can be used for garnishing desserts, roasts, fish and poultry dishes. Use slices of blood oranges and kumquats to accent a fruit platter, drinks or seafood.

Yield: 1 grapefruit = 2 servings.
1 orange-type fruit = 1 serving.
1 medium orange-type fruit = 1/3 cup juice or 4 teaspoons grated peel.
1 medium grapefruit variety = 2/3 cup juice or 3 to 4 tablespoons grated peel.

Nutrition Facts: Of course, all citrus fruits are high in vitamin C, but they also contain vitamin A and some potassium.

Orange & Mushroom Salad with Honey Dressing

You can also make this salad with a vinaigrette dressing, such as the one featured in Avocado & Tomato Salad Vinaigrette, page 22.

3 blood oranges, lavendar gems, mineolas or tangelos or 1 pommelo or 2 Oro Blanco grapefruit
1/2 lb. fresh mushrooms, sliced
1/2 cup thinly sliced red onion
1/4 cup dark raisins
Lettuce leaves

Honey Dressing:
1/3 cup vegetable oil
1/4 cup orange juice
2 tablespoons honey
1/4 teaspoon paprika
1/4 teaspoon salt

Prepare Honey Dressing. Peel and section fruit to make 1-1/2 to 2 cups sections, reserving peels. In a salad bowl, toss together orange sections, mushrooms, onions and raisins. Remove white pith from some of reserved peel. Sliver peel to make 1/3 cup. Sprinkle peel over salad. Pour dressing over salad. Toss well to coat with dressing. If preparing ahead, cover and chill up to 24 hours. Serve over lettuce. Makes 6 to 8 servings.

Honey Dressing:
In a shaker jar, combine oil, juice, honey, paprika and salt. Cover and shake well to mix. Makes 2/3 cup.

Preparation time: 20 minutes

Poached Fish in Orange Sauce

Try this delicious combination with boned, skinned chicken breasts, too. Poach the chicken for about 20 minutes or until it is no longer pink in the center.

4 tangelos, blood oranges or tangerines
1-1/2 cups sauterne or sweet white wine
1 cup julienne-sliced carrot
1 cup julienne-sliced celery or celery root
2 lemon slices
1/4 teaspoon peppercorns
1 bay leaf
1-1/2 lbs. fresh or frozen fish fillets, thawed
Parsley or watercress sprigs for garnish

Peel tangelos, reserving peel from 1 tangelo. Squeeze juice from fruit; measure juice (should have about 1 cup). Add enough sauterne or wine to measure 3 cups. Pour mixture into a large deep skillet or Dutch oven. Add carrots, celery, lemon slices, peppercorns and bay leaf. Bring mixture to boiling; reduce heat to just below simmering. Add fish fillets. Poach 5 minutes or until fish flakes easily. Meanwhile, remove white pith from reserved tangelo peel; cut into thin julienne strips. With a slotted spoon, remove fish and vegetables from pan; arrange on a platter. Spoon some of poaching liquid over fish. Garnish with tangelo peel and parsley or watercress sprigs. Makes 4 servings.

Preparation time: 20 minutes

Hot Citrus Compote

If desired, reserve the citrus shells to use as serving containers.

2 large grapefruit or Oro Blanco grapefruit or 1 pommelo or 4 oranges or tangerines or 4 or 5 blood oranges or 3/4 lb. kumquats
2 tablespoons butter or margarine
1/4 cup slivered almonds
1/4 teaspoon ground cinnamon
1/8 teaspoon ground nutmeg
3 tablespoons packed brown sugar
1/2 cup chopped dates or dried apricots

Peel and section desired citrus fruit to make about 2 cups. In a large skillet, melt butter or margarine. Stir in almonds, cinnamon and nutmeg. Sauté mixture 2 minutes. Add sugar, citrus fruit sections and dates or apricots. Sauté fruit, tossing gently, about 3 to 5 minutes or until warmed through. Makes 4 servings.

Preparation time: 15 minutes

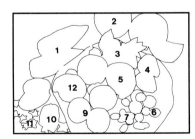

1.Babacos. 2.Pummelos. 3.Mandarins. 4.Mineola tangelo. 5.Oro Blanco grapefruit. 6.Limequat. 7.Preserved kumquats. 8.Mandarins. 9.Blood oranges. 10.Fresh starfruit. 11.Dried starfruit. 12.Texas Rubyred grapefruit.

Grapefruit Ice Cream

Use any grapefruit variety for this scrumptiously rich ice cream.

4 egg yolks
1 cup fresh grapefruit juice
1-1/2 cups sugar
3 tablespoons grated grapefruit peel
3 whole eggs
3 cups half and half
1 cup whipping cream
Grapefruit peel slivers, if desired

In a medium bowl, beat egg yolks 5 minutes or until thick and lemon-colored. In a large saucepan, whisk together grapefruit juice, sugar, grapefruit peel and whole eggs until blended. Whisk in beaten yolks. Cook over medium heat, whisking constantly, until mixture becomes very thick and begins to simmer. Remove from heat. Whisk in half and half. Cover surface of mixture with waxed paper or plastic wrap. Chill in refrigerator about 20 minutes or until cold. Beat whipping cream until thick; stir into chilled grapefruit mixture. Freeze in ice cream maker according to directions. Makes about 1-1/2 quarts.

Freezer method: Pour mixture into a shallow baking pan; cover tightly. Freeze several hours or until nearly firm. Break up frozen mixture with a fork. Working with 1/2 of mixture at a time, turn into a blender or food processor fitted with a metal blade. Process until fluffy. Immediately return beaten mixture back to pan; cover and freeze until firm. To serve, garnish with grapefruit peel slivers, if desired.

Preparation time: 20 minutes

Citrus Fruit. See diagram, opposite page.

COCONUTS/COQUITOS

(co-KEET-ohs) Coconut palms are probably one of the oldest and most versatile plants known. Between the fronds at the crown grow the coconuts which contain both milk and fruit. Dried coconut pulp can be pressed for its oil which is used in cooking and for making soap. The coconut shells, wood and leaves of the palms are used in making furniture, hut walls and roofs, tools and flooring materials. Roots from the tree, once ground, are used to make tea.

Baby coconuts, called coquitos, are cultivated from Chilean palm trees. Sold without their husks, coquitos have smooth, dark brown shells the size of an acorn.

Buying Tips: Coconuts are sold both in the husk (a tan-colored thick outer shell), and removed from the husk (with a fibrous dark brown shell). Either form of coconut should feel heavy and you should be able to hear the juice sloshing inside when the fruit is shaken. To buy a coconut without the heavy husk, check to be certain that the shell and its three "eyes" or soft spots are dry, not moldy or wet. Coquitos should appear dry on the surface without cracks in their shells.

Storage: Store coconuts in the refrigerator for up to several weeks. Check frequently for milk content; as coconuts age, the milk will dry out. Refrigerate drained coconut milk and use within 1 day. Store the chunks of pulp or grated coconut in an airtight container in refrigerator for 2 weeks or freeze for up to several months. Store coquitos for up to 2 months in the refrigerator.

Basic Preparation: Coconuts in the husk can be used as they are as a decoration by carving a face or other design on the surface. Or ask a butcher to saw the husk in half so the coconut inside can be used. Serve coquitos whole to enjoy like nuts, or crack in half to serve in a cocktail.

To remove the shell of a coconut: Heat a husked coconut in a 350F (175C) oven for 15 minutes. Let stand until cool enough to handle; wrap in a kitchen towel. Crack into pieces with a hammer. If you want to save the milk, try this method: with a skewer, pierce the 3 soft spots on the shell. Drain off the milk. Then tap the shell several times with a hammer until it cracks apart.

Serving Ideas: Use chunks of fresh coconut to enjoy as is for a snack or dessert. Use shredded, grated or thinly sliced coconut to top dessert pies or frosted cakes, cupcakes or brownies. Add shredded coconut to pancake or waffle batter, creamy pie fillings or puddings. Add sliced coconut to a fruit or meat platter for an exotic touch. Use the milk and shredded coconut in curry dishes, stir-frys and creamed sauces.

Nutrition Facts: About 3-1/2 ounces of coconut meat has 340 calories. High in fiber, the meat also contains some B and C vitamins.

Fresh Coconut Cream

Use this whenever coconut milk or coconut cream is called for in a recipe.

1 fresh coconut
3 cups warm water

To extract coconut meat, pierce eyes of coconut with a skewer. Preheat oven to 300F (150C). Using a hammer, crack shell of coconut in 4 places. Discard coconut milk or save for later use. Arrange pieces, shell side up, on a baking sheet. Bake 15 minutes. Pry meat from shells, peeling away brown skin from meat. Cut meat into 1/2-inch cubes. In a blender or food processor fitted with a metal blade, process 1/2 of cubes with 1/2 of water until finely ground. Repeat with remaining coconut meat and warm water. Line a medium bowl with cheesecloth; pour in coconut mixture. Bring up ends of cheesecloth and twist together. Squeeze out as much of liquid as possible. Discard pulp. Let stand 30 minutes. The creamy substance on top is coconut cream, the milky bottom layer is coconut milk. Makes about 2-1/4 cups.

Preparation time: 15 minutes

Tip:
To use coconut meat: Hold a piece of coconut by the shell and shred with a hand grater. Or use a small sharp paring knife to remove the outer shell; cut meat into 1/2-inch chunks and place in food processor or blender fitted with a metal blade. Process until finely grated.

To use coconut milk: Drink the coconut milk as is or mix with regular milk. To make coconut cream, see recipe for Fresh Coconut Cream, page 36.

Coconut-Almond Crusted Fish

Use this crunchy tropical coating on chicken breasts, too.

6 (3-oz.) fish fillets
1/2 cup melted butter or
    margarine
1/3 cup all-purpose flour
1 egg
1 tablespoon water
1 cup shredded fresh coconut
1 cup toasted chopped almonds

Lemon-Parsley Sauce:
1/3 cup melted butter or
    margarine
1 tablespoon lemon juice
1 tablespoon minced parsley

Preheat oven to 425F (220C). Place fish fillets on waxed paper; brush with melted butter or margarine. In a shallow bowl, measure flour. In another shallow bowl, stir together egg and water. In a third bowl, stir together coconut and almonds. Dip fish fillets first in melted butter or margarine, then in flour to coat, shaking off excess. Dip in egg until moistened, then roll in coconut-almond mixture until well coated. Place in a shallow baking pan. Bake 15 minutes or until fish flakes easily when tested with a fork. Prepare Lemon-Parsley Sauce; drizzle over fish. Makes 6 servings.

Lemon-Parsley Sauce:
In a small bowl, stir together butter or margarine, lemon juice and parsley. Makes about 1/2 cup.

Preparation Time: 15 minutes

Twenty-Minute Coconut Custard Pie

It takes just 20 minutes to bake this pie— and it goes together in a snap.

1 (9-inch) unbaked pastry crust
2-1/2 cups milk
4 eggs
1/2 cup sugar
1/4 teaspoon salt
1 teaspoon vanilla extract
1/2 cup whipping cream, whipped
1 tablespoon sugar
1 cup toasted fresh coconut
    shreds, see tip, opposite

Preheat oven to 425F (220C). Bake pie shell 5 minutes; remove from oven. Adjust oven temperature to 475F (250C). In a small heavy saucepan, heat milk just until bubbles form around sides of pan (do not boil). Remove from heat. In a small bowl, whisk together eggs, sugar, salt and vanilla until blended. Slowly stir in hot milk until mixed. Place pie shell on oven rack; pour in custard mixture. Bake 5 minutes. Reduce oven temperature to 425F (220C). Bake 10 minutes more or until a knife inserted just off-center comes out clean. Cool. Combine whipped cream and sugar; spread over pie. Sprinkle on coconut. Chill until serving time. Makes 1 (9-inch) pie.

Preparation time: 10 minutes

Tip:
If desired, use the milk that comes from fresh coconut along with regular milk to measure 2-1/2 cups for this pie.

King Kong Brownies

The mashed banana adds moistness and flavor to these chocolatey brownies, and makes them good keepers.

1/2 cup butter or margarine
2 (2-oz.) squares unsweetened
    chocolate
1/2 cup granulated sugar
1/2 cup packed brown sugar
1 egg
2/3 cup mashed banana
1 teaspoon vanilla extract
1-1/4 cups all-purpose flour
1/2 cup shredded coconut
1 (1-oz.) square semi-sweet
    chocolate, melted
Sifted powdered sugar

Preheat oven to 350F (175C). Grease an 8-inch square baking pan. In a medium saucepan, melt butter with unsweetened chocolate. Remove pan from heat; stir in granulated sugar and brown sugar until blended. Stir in egg until blended, then stir in mashed banana and vanilla. Stir in flour and coconut and mix well. Spread batter in greased baking pan. Bake about 30 minutes or until brownies are set on top; cool. Sprinkle brownies with sifted powdered sugar. Melt semi-sweet chocolate and drizzle over powdered sugar. Chill brownies 15 minutes to set chocolate, then cut into squares. Makes 12 to 15 brownies.

Preparation time: 20 minutes

Tip:
For toasted coconut shreds, trim shells from a broken coconut. With a sharp paring knife, slice meat thinly. Arrange on a baking sheet. Bake in a 300F (150C) oven for about 20 minutes or until golden brown, stirring occasionally. Cool; sprinkle with salt for a snack or leave plain to sprinkle on ice cream, fruit or desserts. Store in a tightly covered container.

DATES/JUJUBES

(JOO-joo-bees) The food of nomads and desert travelers for centuries, dates were originally cultivated in the Middle East as early as 3500 B.C. With the Spanish migration into the New World, dates were brought to California, Texas, Florida and Mexico. Today, in North Africa, the Near East and even the Southern Soviet Union, dates are a vital fruit crop.

Date palms, which must be grown in coastal areas that offer more moisture, are prolific producers. Up to several hundred pounds of dates can be harvested from a single tree. This sweet and natural candy can be found fresh and dried at produce counters.

Jujubes, or Chinese dates, strongly resemble the common date, but technically are not dates. China is credited for cultivating this fruit, although it probably originated in Syria. Jujubes have the same shape and coloring as a date with shiny reddish-brown skin. Their texture is crisp and they taste like a mildly sweet apple. Jujubes have a large pit in relation to the fruit. Europeans eat them with honey while the Chinese use them in pastries, preserves and mincemeat.

Buying Tips: The quality of dates sold in markets is so uniform that it's no problem to choose. Dates that are strung are usually the semi-dry type, ideal for eating and cooking. Dates can also be purchased pitted and chopped for ease in recipes.

Storage: Dried dates can be kept almost indefinitely at room temperature. Other types of dates can also be kept for that long, if stored in an air-tight container. Refrigerate them for several months or freeze for a year or more. Store dried jujubes like dates; fresh ones can be covered and refrigerated for up to 2 weeks.

Basic Preparation: Slit unpitted dates lengthwise to remove the slender pit, then sliver or chop the fruit to use in recipes. Or enjoy dates as they are, a sweet fresh fruit. If dates become hard, place them in hot water or fruit juice to plump them. Enjoy jujubes as they are, eating the fruit around the pit.

Serving Ideas: Chopped or slivered dates can be used just like raisins in all types of cakes, quickbreads, cookies and bars. Or stir date pieces into a rice pilaf, poultry stuffing, or trail mix. Combine dates with other fresh fruits for parfaits, puddings or salads. Stir dates into peanut butter for a healthful spread or purée with peaches and papaya for an ambrosial drink. Stuff whole pitted dates with whole almonds or cream cheese for an appetizer or snack. Use jujubes in fruit fillings, preserves, sauces and meat and poultry dishes.

Yield: 8 oz. dates = about 24 medium dates.
20 medium dates = about 1 cup chopped.

Nutrition Facts: One medium date has about 24 calories. Dates are an excellent source of iron, and a good source of copper, calcium and phosphorus.

Date Varieties:

Dried: Often sold as pressed blocks of the fruit, the most common variety is called Thoory. They are very light golden-brown in color. Not a sticky date, their low moisture content means they'll keep for a year.

Semi-dry: These are actually fresh dates and excellent eating dates. They're most commonly found in markets and are usually of the Deglet Noor or Zahidi variety. Zahidi dates are light golden-brown; the Deglet Noor are darker and slightly larger. Both are pleasantly sweet.

Soft: These dates are dehydrated, ready to eat and use in recipes. The most common soft date varieties include Royal Medjool, a large, plump date and Honey Ball Barhi, a smaller, light-colored date with a spherical shape.

Carrots Indienne

For extra elegance, substitute baby carrots for the carrot sticks.

2 cups julienne-sliced carrots
3 tablespoons butter or margarine
2/3 cup chopped dates
1/3 cup slivered almonds
1/2 teaspoon brown sugar
1/4 to 1/2 teaspoon curry powder
1/8 teaspoon pepper

In a steamer basket over simmering water, steam carrot pieces about 8 minutes or until crisp-tender. Remove from heat. Remove steamer basket from pan; discard cooking liquid. In same pan, melt butter or margarine. Add dates and almonds; saute 2 minutes. Stir in sugar, curry and pepper. Add carrots and toss to coat well. Cook 1 minute more to heat through. Makes 4 servings.

Preparation time: 10 minutes

Date-Pineapple Cheese Spread

Use this healthful spread on breakfast toast, in sandwiches or on crackers. It's delicious spread on a thick slice of pear or tart apple.

1 cup chopped dates or jujubes
1/2 cup chopped dried apricots or golden raisins
Water
1 (8-oz.) pkg. cream cheese, room temperature
2 tablespoons milk
1 teaspoon brown sugar
1 teaspoon vanilla extract
1/2 cup finely chopped pineapple

In a medium saucepan, place dates or jujubes and apricots or raisins in water to cover. Bring to boiling; reduce heat and simmer 2 minutes. Drain well. In a blender or food processor fitted with a metal blade, process drained fruit, cream cheese, milk, sugar, vanilla and pineapple in an on-and-off motion until well blended and some fruit chunks remain. Turn into a covered container; refrigerate up to 2 weeks. Makes 2-1/3 cups.

Preparation time: 10 minutes

Old-Fashioned Date Rice Pudding

If you like, layer this treat with sliced fresh fruit in parfait glasses to serve.

4 cups milk
1/2 cup white long-grain rice
1/2 cup sugar
1/4 teaspoon salt
1 egg
1-1/2 teaspoons vanilla extract
1 cup pitted chopped dates or dried apricots, figs or starfruit
1/2 cup whipping cream, whipped
Chocolate syrup, if desired

In a large saucepan, combine milk, rice, sugar and salt. Bring mixture to boiling; reduce heat. Simmer, covered, about 1 hour or until rice is very tender. Remove pan from heat. Beat egg slightly; stir some of rice mixture into egg, then stir rice-egg mixture back into pan. Cook and stir over medium heat 1 minute more. Remove from heat; stir in vanilla. Stir in dates. Cover and chill 30 minutes. Fold in whipped cream. If preparing ahead, cover and refrigerate up to 48 hours in advance. Serve drizzled with chocolate syrup, if desired. Makes 6 servings.

Preparation time: 10 minutes

Breakfast Cereal Mix

Later in the day, use this combination as an instant snack mix, or toss with popcorn for extra crunch.

2 cups plain granola
1 cup oat bran cereal
1 cup chopped dates
2/3 cup chopped dried apricots, prunes, apples or peaches
1/2 cup sliced almonds
1/4 cup shredded coconut, if desired
1/4 cup melted butter or margarine
1/2 teaspoon ground cinnamon

Preheat oven to 300F (150C). In a large bowl, stir together granola, cereal, dates, dried apricots, almonds and coconut, if desired. Stir together melted butter and cinnamon; drizzle over cereal mixture. Turn mixture onto a shallow baking pan with sides. Bake for 15 minutes, stirring once. Cool; store in an airtight container. Makes about 5 cups.

Preparation time: 15 minutes

Granola Date Bread

Try this mildly sweet bread spread with pineapple cream cheese.

1 cup Breakfast Cereal Mix, below
2/3 cup hot tap water
1 cup buttermilk
1/4 cup vegetable oil
1 lightly beaten egg
1-3/4 cups all-purpose flour
1/2 cup sugar
1-1/2 teaspoons baking soda
1/2 teaspoon salt

Preheat oven to 350F (175C). Generously grease and flour a 9" x 5" loaf pan. In a medium bowl, pour Breakfast Cereal Mix. Pour hot water over mix and let stand 5 minutes. Stir in buttermilk, oil and egg until blended. Add flour, sugar, soda and salt. Beat about 40 strokes (batter will be thin). Pour batter into prepared loaf pan. Bake for 55 to 60 minutes or until a wooden pick inserted in center comes out clean. Turn onto a wire rack to cool. Wrap airtight to store. Makes 1 loaf.

Preparation time: 15 minutes

FIGS

Biblical references indicate that figs are probably the world's oldest fruit. Historians tell us that figs most likely existed in the Stone Age. Botanically speaking, a fig is not a fruit but merely a sweet receptacle designed to hold the seeds or "fruits" inside. It is the seeds that are pollinated, so the tree does not blossom. Cultivated throughout the world, fig trees thrive in arid, semi-desert regions and the fruit is harvested all year long.

Figs are small, pear-shaped fruits with soft, edible skins and a sweet, soft interior that is almost like jelly. Some varieties are sold from May through September, while others arrive in markets from November through January.

Buying Tips: Purchase any variety of fresh figs when they are still slightly firm to the touch, plump and well-shaped. If figs are too hard, they will be dry inside; if too soft, they will have a sour taste. Avoid fresh figs that are flattened, bruised or splitting. Handle fresh figs carefully, since the delicate skins bruise easily.

Storage: Use fresh figs within 2 days. Store them in the refrigerator arranged in a single layer on a paper towel-lined plate or tray. Store dried figs in an airtight container for 6 months to 1 year.

Basic Preparation: For dried and fresh figs, trim off the hard portion of the stem end with a sharp knife. California figs are as moist as fresh dates, but imported dried figs may need to be simmered for 2 minutes in boiling water or fruit juice to plump them for use. Enjoy fresh or dried figs, skin and all, as a snack fruit or dessert. Slice or halve fresh figs to serve with cream or a squirt of lemon or lime juice.

Serving Ideas: Dried figs can be used just like any other dried fruit such as raisins, apricots or dates. Add fresh chopped or dried figs to cookies, cakes, baked puddings and chutneys. Poach whole fresh figs in wine and fruit juice for a dessert or breakfast fruit. Stuff whole fresh figs with flavored soft cheeses or wrap in thin strips of ham or proscuitto for appetizers. Add whole figs to fruit platters, slice over ice cream or use to top breakfast cereal.

Yield: 1 lb. fresh figs = 8 large or 14 small figs.
1 lb. fresh figs = 2-1/2 cups chopped.
8 oz. dried figs = 1 to 1-1/4 cups chopped figs.

Nutrition Facts: One medium fresh fig has about 40 calories while 1/2 cup of dried figs has 250 calories. Figs have up to 30 times the calcium of other fruits and are generous sources of potassium, magnesium and B vitamins.

Varieties:

Black Mission: The soft skin is a dark purple color with sweet pink fruit inside. Excellent for eating, preserving and preparing pie.

Brown Turkey: Outer skin is a reddish-brown color; inside, the fruit is purple. Sweet and juicy.

Calimyrna: Largest of all figs, Calimyrnas have a nutty, sweet flavor. The outer skin is greenish-yellow with pale pink fruit. One of the best eating figs.

Dried: May be Calimyrna or Black Mission figs; packaged sun-dried. Available all year.

Kadota: First bright green, then light yellow when ripe, Kadotas have pinkish-purple fruit inside.

French Afternoon Platter

For picnics, an elegant snack or a midnight celebration, try this continental combination. Serve it with a dry white wine or slightly sweet white zinfandel.

Lettuce leaves
10 large fresh Calimyrna or Black Mission figs, halved
4 oz. thinly sliced deli ham or proscuitto
4 oz. thinly sliced salami or smoked turkey
4 oz. Jarlsburg, Swiss or fontina cheese, thinly sliced
4 oz. strawberry-flavored cream cheese, room temperature
French bread slices
Butter or margarine
Dijon-style mustard

Arrange lettuce leaves on a large serving platter. Arrange figs in 1 area; roll meat slices and arrange in a design with cheese slices. Serve with bread and butter or margarine and mustard in condiment dishes. Makes 5 to 6 appetizer servings.

Preparation time: 10 minutes

Fig-Walnut Crumble

If you use dried figs, this dessert square becomes a cookie bar.

**3 cups chopped fresh figs or 1
  cup chopped dried figs**
2 eggs
1/3 cup orange juice
1/2 cup packed brown sugar
2 tablespoons all-purpose flour
2 teaspoons grated orange peel
1/4 teaspoon baking powder
3/4 cup chopped walnuts
Whipped cream or ice cream

Crust:
1 cup regular oats
1/2 cup all-purpose flour
1/4 cup packed brown sugar
1/4 teaspoon salt
2/3 cup butter or margarine

Prepare crust. If using dried figs, place in a small saucepan with water to cover. Boil about 5 to 7 minutes or until soft. Drain well. In a medium bowl, beat eggs until frothy. Add orange juice, brown sugar, flour, orange peel and baking powder; beat about 3 minutes or until slightly thickened. Stir in figs and walnuts. Pour mixture over baked crust. Sprinkle on remaining crumb mixture. Continue baking 30 to 35 minutes more or until mixture is set in center. Cool and cut into squares or bars. Serve topped with whipped cream or ice cream. Makes 9 dessert squares or 16 bars.

Crust:
Preheat oven to 350F (175C). Grease an 8" x 8" x 2" baking pan. In a medium bowl, stir together oatmeal, flour, brown sugar and salt. Using a pastry blender, cut in butter or margarine until mixture resembles small peas. Sprinkle 1/2 of mixture in bottom of greased baking pan; press into pan. Bake crust about 12 to 15 minutes or until lightly browned. Set aside remaining crumb mixture. Makes 1 crust.

Preparation time: 20 minutes

French Afternoon Platter, opposite page.

GRAPES

Grapes have always been an extremely important food to hot Asian nations and ancient Greek and Egyptian cultures dating back to the Bronze Age. Grapes were prized for their sweet flavor and for their juice, which was found to make a heady, delicious drink. Since ancient times, wines have been appreciated as a thirst-quencher in the absence of clean drinking water.

Spanish Mission Fathers transplanted grape vines to California, which flourished commercially by 1860. Today California provides nearly all of the eating grapes enjoyed in the U.S., though grapes grown for wines account for almost 80% of the total crop!

In addition to the familiar green Thompson seedless and purple Concord grapes, there are a dozen other varieties harvested in different seasons. Crops from Mexico and Chile during the winter months make it possible for you to purchase grapes all year.

Buying Tips: Look for full, well-formed bunches that show good color for the variety. Avoid sticky fruit or bunches with brittle stems. Green varieties are sweetest when yellow-green in color. Red varieties should be all-over red and blue/black or purple grapes should have full, lustrous color.

Storage: Store fresh grapes in the refrigerator or the crisper section, wrapped in plastic bags. Use as soon as possible; most varieties will store well up to 1 week. Chilling grapes brings out the best flavor.

Basic Preparation: Simply rinse grapes with cool water to serve. If desired, use kitchen shears to cut bunches into snack-size portions.

Serving Ideas: Freeze grapes to enjoy as a summer snack, to take on picnics or purée for a sorbet. Serve with cheeses and other fruits for a light meal or snack; combine with other fruits for salads, compotes or in sparkling drinks. Use small bunches of grapes to garnish meat or poultry platters or add to bread stuffings for pork. Stir into savory meat sauces or sauté with mild vegetables for interesting side dishes. Use halved grapes to garnish frosted cakes, peanut butter sandwiches or to sprinkle into yogurt.

Yield: 1 lb. grapes = about 2-1/2 cups grapes.

Nutrition Facts: There are about 55 calories per 1/2 cup of grapes, which are a good source of vitamin C.

Grape Varieties:

Almeria: A pale green, large, oval-shaped grape. Mild and sweet contains small seeds.

Beauty Seedless or Black Seedless: A very sweet, deep purple grape, similar in taste to Concord.

Black Corinth, Champagne or Zante Currant: Tiny, deep purple grapes used in making champagne, but also made available for eating. Sweet, heady flavor. Makes a pretty garnish.

Calmeria: Long, oval-shaped green grapes with firm skins and small seeds. Mild, sweet flavor.

Cardinal: Large, purple-red grapes with a grayish cast or bloom. Fruity and a little tart, with seeds.

Christmas Rose: Gorgeous reddish-purple hue; crunchy, juicy and fruity-sweet, with seeds.

Emperor: A red-violet grape that can be almost purplish-black. Mild, pleasant flavor, with seeds. Popular at fall and winter holidays.

Exotic: A deep bluish-purple to blue-black grape; rounded plump berries with a mildly sweet taste.

Flame Seedless: A deep red grape that is round, firm, crunchy and seedless.

Niabell: Bred from American and European varieties, a brilliant blue grape with slippery skins and a Concord grape flavor.

Perlette: Seedless green grapes that are the first of the summer season. Mild, sweet and crisp.

Queen: Available only in August and September; this grape has a reddish-purple cast and a juicy, crisp bite. Flavor is mild and sweet.

Red Globe: A fall and winter grape, bright red in color and mild in taste. Seeds are large and so are the grapes which are nearly the size of a small plum.

Ribier: With a deep, blue-black color, these grapes grow in large, beautiful bunches. Thick skins hold full, mild flavor.

Ruby Red Seedless: Tender red skins house firm, sweet fruit without seeds. Bunches are large and full.

Tokay or Flame Tokay: An Eastern grape, deep red in color with large round grapes. Mild flavor, crisp. Used in brandies.

Shimmering Grape Tart

Red and purple grapes are exceptionally attractive on this tart.

1/2 (17-1/4-oz.) pkg. frozen puff pastry sheet, thawed according to package directions
2 slightly beaten eggs
1 cup milk
2 tablespoons sugar
1/8 teaspoon salt
1 teaspoon vanilla extract
1-1/2 cups any variety seedless grapes, halved
1/3 cup red currant jelly

Preheat oven to 350F (175C). Place thawed pastry on a lightly floured surface. With a small sharp knife, cut 1/2-inch-wide strips from 4 sides of pastry rectangle. Lay strips on top of cut edges of pastry to build up edges for filling. Bake pastry according to package directions. Cool on a wire rack. In a heavy medium saucepan, whisk together eggs, milk, sugar and salt. Cook over medium heat, stirring constantly, until mixture coats a metal spoon. Pour custard mixture into a medium bowl; set inside a larger bowl filled with ice water. Stir in vanilla. When completely cool, spread custard over baked pastry almost to edges. Arrange grapes, cut side down, over custard. In a small saucepan, heat currant jelly until melted; brush over grapes and custard. If preparing in advance, cover and chill tart in refrigerator up to 24 hours. Cut in 3-inch squares to serve. Makes 12 servings.

Preparation time: 30 minutes

Grapes. Clockwise from top right: Tokay grapes, Ribier grapes, Emperor grapes, Champagne grapes, Red Globe grapes and Beauty seedless grapes.

Marsala Fruit Compote

Serve this elegant fruit compote warm or chilled in long-stemmed goblets. (photo on page 63.)

3 cups white grape juice
1 cup marsala or sweet dessert wine
3 cups seedless grapes, halved
3 cups chopped fresh fruit such as melon, apples, pineapple, papaya or pears
1/2 lemon, sliced
1/2 orange, sliced
1 (3-inch) cinnamon stick, broken
1/4 teaspoon ground allspice
Plain yogurt or unsweetened whipped cream

In a large saucepan, stir together white grape juice, marsala, grapes, chopped fruit, lemon, orange, cinnamon and allspice. Bring to a boil; reduce heat to low. Cover and simmer 5 to 10 minutes or until grapes are tender. Cool; transfer to bowl. If preparing in advance, cover and chill in refrigerator up to 2 days. Serve warm or chilled, topped with yogurt. Makes 8 servings.

Preparation time: 20 minutes

Chicken with Grape-Orange Sauce

Try substituting fish fillets for the chicken next time.

1 cup chicken broth
1 cup rosé wine
1 cup orange juice
4 (4-oz.) chicken breasts, skinned
Shredded peel 1 orange
1/2 onion, sliced
4 peppercorns
1 cup halved green grapes
1 cup orange segments
1 tablespoon minced parsley
1/2 teaspoon crushed dried thyme
Salt and pepper to taste
Hot cooked rice

In a deep medium skillet or Dutch oven, pour chicken broth, wine and orange juice. Place chicken breasts in liquid; add orange peel, onion, and peppercorns. Bring mixture almost to a boil; reduce heat and simmer gently, uncovered, 25 to 30 minutes or until chicken is done. Remove chicken to warm platter; cover and keep warm while preparing sauce. Bring liquid to a boil; boil 5 to 10 minutes or until reduced by half. Turn heat to low. Stir in grapes, orange segments, parsley and thyme. Season with salt and pepper to taste. Serve sauce over chicken and rice. Makes 4 servings.

Preparation time: 15 minutes

Autumn Fruit Salad

This combination is an ideal first course or side dish for fall and winter holiday meals.

Lettuce leaves
2 ripe fuyu persimmons or pears, peeled, thinly sliced
1 ripe pear or Granny Smith apple, thinly sliced
1 cup red or green seedless grapes
1/2 cup pomegranate seeds or slivered almonds
2 oz. sharp Cheddar or Swiss cheese, cubed
Creamy French Dressing, page 76 or Parmesan Dressing, page 140

Line a salad platter with lettuce leaves. Arrange persimmon and pear or apple slices over lettuce. Sprinkle on grapes, pomegranate seeds and cheese. Pass with desired dressing. Makes 4 servings.

Preparation time: 10 minutes

Bow-Tie Chicken & Fruit Salad

You can substitute your favorite pasta shapes for the bow ties.

4 oz. bow-tie pasta
3 cooked chicken breasts, boned, skinned, chopped
1 cup halved seedless grapes
1 cup chopped apple, peaches, plums or fresh starfruit
1/4 cup chopped green onion
Lettuce leaves
1 ripe avocado, peeled, pitted, thinly sliced

Cinnamon-Cream Dressing:
1/3 cup sour cream
3 tablespoons white grape juice or orange juice
3 tablespoons vegetable oil
1 tablespoon sugar
1/4 teaspoon ground cinnamon
1/8 teaspoon paprika
Dash salt

Prepare Cinnamon-Cream Dressing. In a medium saucepan, cook pasta according to package directions; drain and rinse with cold water. Drain again. In a large bowl, toss together pasta, chicken, grapes, apple and onion. Toss with dressing until well mixed. On a large platter, arrange lettuce leaves. Spoon salad over lettuce. Garnish with avocado slices. Makes 2 or 3 servings.

Cinnamon-Cream Dressing:
In a small bowl, combine sour cream, grape juice, oil, sugar, cinnamon, paprika and salt. Beat together until mixture is smooth. If preparing ahead, cover and chill in refrigerator up to 24 hours. Makes 1 cup.

Preparation time: 15 minutes

Varieties:

Beaumont Guava: Fruit resembles a pale-colored lemon; its bright pink interior is heady and sweet.

Feijoas or Pineapple Guavas: An oval-shaped fruit that grows from 3/4 to 3-1/2 inches long. The tart skin may be dark green to gray-green and smooth or bumpy, depending on growing conditions. The juicy yellow fruit inside has a sweet, minty, pineapple flavor and usually tastes best peeled. Also has tiny edible seeds.

Guavas: May be round or oval in shape with green to yellow skins. Size ranges from 1 to 4 inches long. The center of the fruit contains many small edible seeds and the flesh may be pink, white or yellow in color. Guavas are a delicious snack fruit.

Lemon Guava: Lemony tropical flavor; very small fruit.

Strawberry Guava: Pinkish interior and a sweet-tart strawberry flavor.

Sautéed Guavas With Ginger

Try this spicy relish-like fruit sauté with barbecued meats or poultry.

2 tablespoons butter or margarine
5 guavas or feijoas, peeled, sliced
1/3 cup sliced green onion
1 tablespoon fresh chopped
  gingerroot
1/3 cup chicken broth
1/4 teaspoon salt
1/8 teaspoon pepper

In a large skillet, melt butter; add guavas or feijoas, onion and ginger-root. Sauté over medium heat about 2 minutes, turning fruit gently. Add chicken broth, salt and pepper; bring to a boil. Cook 1 minute more. Makes 2 or 3 servings.

Preparation time: 10 minutes

GUAVAS/FEIJOAS

(GWA-vah) (fee-JOH-ah) Although guavas and feijoas come from the same botanical family and are often thought to be identical tropical fruits, they actually represent 2 uniquely different species. Part of the confusion stems from the fact that feijoas are also called "pineapple guavas," though they are not guavas at all. However, the two fruits are interchangeable in recipes, being close in size, with tart skins and a similar tangy, tropical fruit flavor.

Both guavas and feijoas are left to ripen on the tree until they literally drop to the ground. That means you are likely to find the fruits at their flavor peak in markets. Mexico, South America, Hawaii, Florida and Southern California are prime producers of guavas, while feijoas flourish in New Zealand, Brazil and California.

Buying Tips: Choose guavas that feel firm to the touch since the fruit ripens easily at room temperature. Color should be good for the variety and the fruit should be undamaged by bruising or soft spots. Feijoas or pineapple guavas are hardier fruit than guavas; skin should feel waxy and appear shiny. The fruit should feel firm when pressed.

Storage: Both feijoas and guavas will ripen at room temperature until they give to gentle pressure. Refrigerate immediately when fruit are ripe. Enjoy guavas as soon as they are ripe; feijoas can be kept refrigerated for up to several weeks.

Basic Preparation: Guavas can be eaten out of hand, seeds and all. Or slice and serve with cream or a sprinkling of sugar. Feijoas usually must be peeled because of the tart skin; spoon out the sweet fruit inside.

Serving Ideas: Guavas make great preserves, jellies, pickles and chutneys. Feijoa pulp combines well with other fruits in pies, sauces and sherbet. Or slice either fruit to accent a fruit platter, frozen dessert or pudding. Both fruits can be stir-fried or sautéed for an accent to a main dish or grilled with poultry, pork or fish.

Yield: 1 medium feijoa or guava = 1 serving.
6 large ripe feijoas or guavas = about 1 cup pulp.

Nutrition Facts: Both fruits are wonderful sources of vitamin C and are high in fiber. Feijoas have fewer calories, about 45 in 1 medium fruit as compared to about 60 in a guava.

KIWANOS/AFRICAN HORNED MELONS

(Kee-WAHN-no) Brilliant red-orange in color, shaped like a hand grenade with ominous spikes over all, is the Kiwano or "African horned cucumber," "horned melon" or "jelly melon." The inside is perhaps the biggest surprise: a bright kelly-green, jelly-like pulp with seeds resembling those of a cucumber. Originally grown in the deserts of Southwest Africa, Kiwanos became popular with New Zealand growers more than sixty years ago. Today, New Zealand's North Island and Florida are the most popular growing areas.

A member of the melon family, Kiwanos grow on melon-like vines. The pulp has a tropical flavor reminiscent of banana and lime. New Zealanders consider Kiwano pulp to be the ultimate thirst-quencher.

Buying Tips: Look for bright orange fruit with no blemishes or soft spots on the skin. Spikes should be intact.

Storage: Kiwanos are good storers; store in a cool, dry place for up to 4 to 6 months. Do not refrigerate.

Basic Preparation: To enjoy the fruit au naturel, halve the fruit lengthwise. Scoop out the pulp (it can be eaten seeds and all). Sprinkle pulp with a little sugar, if desired. Or cut fruit into slices or wedges to eat like melon.

Serving Ideas: Add slices of Kiwano to a fruit platter or salad, or spoon the pulp over ice cream or a fruit compote. Use the pulp in tropical drinks, salad dressing or fruit sauces. If desired, strain out seeds before using; this is easier to do if the pulp is whirled in a blender or food processor first.

Yield: 1 Kiwano yields about 2 servings of pulp.

Nutrition Facts: Kiwano pulp contains about 25 calories per 4-ounce serving. Low in sodium, it also contains significant amounts of potassium and vitamin A.

Kiwano Limeade

Kiwano pulp adds a unique flavor twist to a traditional limeade cooler. Try the lemonade version, too.

1 Kiwano, halved
2/3 to 3/4 cup sugar
2 limes, thinly sliced
4 cups water
Ice cubes

Halve Kiwanos lengthwise; scoop out pulp and seeds. In a blender or food processor fitted with a metal blade, process to a purée. Strain out seeds. Turn strained mixture into a medium saucepan; add sugar to taste, lime slices and water. Bring mixture to a boil; remove from heat. Pour into a heat-safe pitcher or container; cover and chill. To serve, pour over ice into tall glasses. Makes 4-1/3 cups.

Preparation time: 10 minutes

Variation:
Kiwano Lemonade: Substitute 2 lemons for limes.

Kiwano Fruit Sundaes

The Kiwano sauce is also great over ice cream, fresh melon or chocolate cake.

2 Kiwanos
1 tablespoon sugar
1 tablespoon lemon juice
1 cup pineapple chunks
1 cup chopped melon, peaches or pears
1 medium banana

To prepare sauce, halve Kiwanos lengthwise. Scoop out pulp and seeds, reserving shells. In a blender or food processor fitted with a metal blade, process pulp and seeds with sugar and lemon juice to a purée. Strain out seeds; set mixture aside. If preparing ahead, cover sauce and Kiwano shells and refrigerate up to 1 day. Just before serving, in a medium bowl, toss together pineapple and melon, peaches or pears. Peel banana; cut in 1/2-inch slices; add to pineapple mixture. Divide mixture among Kiwano shells. Spoon some of sauce over fruit in shells. Pass sauce. Makes 4 servings.

Preparation Time: 15 minutes

Down-Under Fruits. See diagram, page 156.

KIWI FRUIT

In Southern China, it was called yang tao and highly prized by the court of the great Khans. By the 19th century, the English cultivated it under the name Chinese gooseberry. But it wasn't until the fruit vines were brought to New Zealand that kiwi fruit got its commercial name (taken from the native kiwi bird).

American GIs stationed Down Under during World War II grew fond of the fuzzy brown fruit. It wasn't long before kiwi fruit became a major commerical crop for California as well. Because New Zealand and California have opposite growing seasons, the two countries are able to provide most of the world's crop year-round. Kiwi fruit is easily found in American markets today.

If you haven't tried kiwi fruit, you're in for a marvelous taste treat. About the size of a jumbo chicken egg, the fuzzy brown fruit hides a dazzling jade green interior and is sprinkled throughout with tiny edible black seeds. Kiwi fruit tastes like a strawberry, a peach and a melon rolled into one and has a sweet, juicy flavor. Though a newcomer just a few years ago, it looks like kiwi fruit is here to stay.

Buying Tips: Look for firm, round or oval-shaped fruit, free from bruises and skin breaks. Kiwi fruit are ripe when the skin gives slightly when pressed. It's easy to ripen fruit at home if the kiwi fruit is very firm when purchased.

Storage: Ripen fruit at room temperature if very firm; refrigerate as soon as the fruit is ripe for up to several days. Store refrigerated kiwis away from other fruits as the kiwi fruit quickly overripens when exposed to the gases from others. Do not freeze.

Basic Preparation: With a small paring knife, trim off stem ends of kiwi fruit. Use a vegetable peeler to trim off the thin brown skin. Quarter, slice, purée or chop the fruit to enjoy as is or top with whipped cream or use in recipes.

Serving Ideas: Kiwi fruit makes a stunning garnish for fresh fruit platters, poultry dishes, salads and desserts. Use it to top a cheesecake, ice cream, sherbet or a brownie. Layer the fruit in peanut butter sandwiches or add it to fruit compotes, a fruit trifle or turkey salad. Kiwi fruit has an enzyme that acts as a meat tenderizer; rub the fruit over steak just before grilling. Do not use kiwi fruit in gelatin molds as the same enzyme will prevent the gelatin from setting up.

Yield: 1 kiwi fruit = 1 serving.
1 kiwi fruit = about 1/2 cup cut up fruit.

Nutrition Facts: Kiwi fruit is low in calories, about 45 per fruit. It's bursting with vitamin C, enough in 1 fruit to take care of a day's requirement. There's more fiber in 1 kiwi fruit than a serving of bran flakes and more potassium than in one banana.

Kiwi Fruit Meringues

This dessert is an easy make-ahead.

1 quart vanilla, peach or strawberry ice cream
4 kiwifruit, peeled, halved, sliced
1/2 cup chocolate syrup

Meringue Shells:
4 egg whites
1/2 teaspoon cream of tartar
Dash salt
1 cup sugar
1 teaspoon vanilla extract

Prepare Meringue Shells. If preparing in advance, cover with waxed paper and store at room temperature up to 24 hours. Spoon 8 generous scoops of ice cream onto a wax paper-lined baking sheet; store in freezer up to 24 hours in advance. To assemble desserts, place 1 meringue shell on each dessert plate. Place a scoop of ice cream in center of each meringue shell. Top with pieces of kiwifruit; drizzle with chocolate syrup. Makes 8 servings.

Meringue Shells:
Preheat oven to 300F (150C). Grease 2 baking sheets. In a medium bowl, beat egg whites with cream of tartar and salt until soft peaks form. Gradually beat in sugar until stiff glossy peaks form (mixture should feel smooth, not grainy, when rubbed between 2 fingers). Beat in vanilla. Spoon mixture into 8 mounds on greased baking sheets. With back of spoon, spread each mound in a nest shape about 4 inches wide. Bake 50 to 60 minutes or until lightly browned. Turn oven off; let meringues stand in oven 1 hour longer to dry. Makes 8 individual meringues.

Preparation time: 15 minutes

Kiwi-Berry Cheesecake Pie

Next time, try a chocolate cookie crumb or graham cracker crust for this easy pie.

1 (9-inch) unbaked pastry shell
2 cups sliced strawberries or whole raspberries, boysenberries, blackberries, ollalieberries, Marionberries or blueberries
2 (8-oz.) pkgs. cream cheese, softened
1 cup dairy sour cream
1/3 cup sugar
2 teaspoons grated orange peel
1 teaspoon vanilla extract
4 kiwi fruit, peeled, thinly sliced

Lay pastry in a 9-inch pie pan. Press into pan and on sides; flute edge. Prick crust well with fork. If desired, line crust with aluminum foil and pour dry beans into foil. Bake 5 minutes; remove foil and beans. Bake 5 to 7 minutes more or until light golden-brown. Cool on a wire rack. Sprinkle 1-1/2 cups of berries into bottom of pastry crust. For filling, in a food blender or food processor fitted with a metal blade, place cream cheese, sour cream, sugar, orange peel and vanilla. Process until smooth. Spoon 1/2 of cream filling over berries to cover, smoothing top. Arrange half of the kiwi fruit slices over filling. Spoon remaining filling mixture over kiwi fruit, mounding top. Arrange remaining kiwi slices and berries in a circular design over top of pie. Cover pie and chill at least 4 hours before cutting and serving. Makes 1 (9-inch) pie.

Preparation time: 25 minutes

Curried Turkey Fruit Salad

Serve the salad in melon shells or on red cabbage leaves. Next time, substitute Dijon-style mustard for the curry in the dressing.

Lettuce leaves
2 cups cooked turkey, chicken or ham strips
3 kiwi fruit, peeled, quartered, sliced
1 cup melon chunks or sliced strawberries
1 cup sugar snap peas or stringed pea pods, halved crosswise
1/3 cup sliced almonds, peanut halves or sliced waterchestnuts
1 green onion, thinly sliced

Orange Curry Dressing:
1/4 cup mayonnaise or salad dressing
2 tablespoons orange juice
1/2 teaspoon curry powder

Arrange lettuce leaves on a serving plate or 3 individual plates. In a medium bowl, toss turkey strips with kiwi fruit, melon chunks, peas, almonds and onion. Prepare dressing. Spoon over salad and toss gently to coat with dressing. Spoon onto lettuce-lined platter. Cover and chill up to 24 hours in advance or serve immediately. Makes 3 servings.

Orange Curry Dressing:
In a small bowl, stir together mayonnaise or salad dressing, orange juice and curry until blended. Makes about 1/3 cup dressing.

Preparation time: 20 minutes

Tip: Recipe can be doubled.

Roast Duck & Kiwis l'Orange

A 3-1/2- to 4-pound roasting chicken or four Cornish game hens can also be used in place of the duck.

1 (5-lb.) oven ready duck
1 onion, quartered
2 tablespoons butter or margarine
1/3 cup minced onion
1 cup chicken broth
1-1/2 tablespoons cornstarch
1/2 cup marsala wine
1 orange, peeled, halved, thinly sliced
3 kiwi fruit, peeled, halved, thinly sliced
2 tablespoons slivered orange peel
1/2 teaspoon salt
1/8 teaspoon pepper

Preheat oven to 450F (230C). Wash duck; pat dry. Trim fat from cavity; remove giblets and heart. Place quartered onion inside cavity; skewer cavity shut. Place duck, breast side up, on a rack in a shallow roasting pan. Place pan in oven; reduce temperature to 350F (175C). Roast about 1-3/4 hours or until juices run clear when leg is pierced. Remove from oven; cover and let stand while preparing sauce. In a medium saucepan, melt butter or margarine; saute minced onion until tender. Stir together chicken broth and cornstarch; add to onion mixture. Stir with a wire whisk until mixture thickens and bubbles; reduce heat to simmering. Stir in wine; add orange and kiwi fruit pieces, orange peel, salt and pepper. Stir gently 1 minute more, taking care not to break up fruit. Carve duck; serve with fruit sauce. Makes 4 servings.

Preparation time: 20 minutes

LYCHEES/LONGANS

(LEE-cheese) (LONG-ganz) In the first-ever published work on the subject of fruit, a Chinese scholar in 1059 A.D. wrote in praise of the lychee. Asians have a special reverence for fresh fruit and lychees have retained enormous popularity through 2000 years of oriental cuisine. A pearl-like fruit the size of a walnut, lychees will remind you of green grapes with a sweeter fruit flavor and a soft, juicy texture. Covered with a thin red shell the color of Chinese lacquer, lychees can be peeled easily to enjoy the cream-colored fruit inside. Watch out for the large dark pit; it's worth the trouble to enjoy the delicate, perfumed taste of this fruit.

Longans, in contrast, come in a small round shell that turns a medium brown shortly after the fruit is picked. Longans (sometimes called Dragon's Eye) and lychees are very close relatives. The grape-like fruit of the longan looks the same and tastes like a lychee which makes these fruits easily interchangeable in recipes. Both fruits are available not only from Asia, but also New Zealand, Australia, Brazil, Mexico, Hawaii and Florida in late May to mid-August.

Buying Tips: Fresh lychees are available either as individual berries or as clusters on the stem. Look for fruit with shells intact; avoid cracked fruit. Lychee shells turn from bright red to reddish-brown after harvest; do not purchase if shells are shriveled and dull brown in color.

Storage: Lychees keep well for up to 1 week at room temperature. Lychees can also be refrigerated for up to 3 weeks, tightly wrapped in plastic bags. Longans, however, keep for shorter periods; refrigerate and plan to use within 2 to 3 days.

Basic Preparation: It's easy to crack the shells of lychees and longans, then remove the center pit to enjoy the fruit. You can chop or halve the pulp to add to recipes or fruit mixtures.

Serving Ideas: Both lychees and longans pair off well with any type of citrus fruit, in compotes and salads, spiced with mint. Drop pieces of the fruit in sparkling wine or champagne for an aperitif; combine with pineapple and papaya chunks for dessert. Add the fruit to cold chicken salad, a fruit slaw or to a mildly sweet fruit sauce for chicken or fish.

Yield: 1 lb. longans or lychees = about 35 to 40 pieces. 1/4 - 1/3 lb. fruit = 1 serving.

Nutrition Facts: Both fruits are very good sources of vitamin C, potassium and trace minerals. Ten pieces of these fruits contain about 65 calories.

Sparkling Oriental Compote

Serve as an elegant first course or as the finale to a far-eastern meal with almond cookies.

1/2 honeydew melon, seeded, cut in balls or 1-inch chunks
1 (1-oz.) can mandarin oranges, drained
12 lychees or longans, peeled, seeded, halved
Sparkling wine or apple cider
8 unblanched whole almonds

In 6 long-stemmed goblets, spoon chunks of honeydew, mandarin oranges and lychees, dividing evenly. Fill with sparkling wine or apple cider. Drop 2 almonds into each glass and serve. Makes 6 servings.

Preparation time: 10 minutes

Lychee & Orange Cups

For a light lunch or side-dish salad substitute cottage cheese for the frozen yogurt and serve the cups on lettuce.

2 oranges
6 to 8 lychees, longans or loquats, peeled, pitted, quartered
1/2 cup sliced fresh berries, bananas or peaches
4 scoops frozen lemon yogurt or sherbet
2 to 4 tablespoons kirsch (cherry liqueur)

Halve oranges; scallop edges, if desired, and remove fruit from shells. Reserve shells for serving containers. Remove white pith from orange pulp; chop fruit. In a medium bowl, toss together orange pieces, lychees and desired sliced fruit; spoon into orange shells. Top each orange half with a scoop of frozen yogurt or sherbet; drizzle on kirsch. Serve at once. Makes 4 servings.

Preparation time: 15 minutes

Mango-Topped Gingerbread

This richly spicy gingerbread has a heavy texture that's every bit as rewarding as grandma's version.

1-3/4 cups all-purpose flour
1 tablespoon minced fresh gingerroot
1 teaspoon baking soda
1 teaspoon allspice
1/2 teaspoon salt
1/3 cup butter or margarine, softened
1/4 cup dark-brown sugar
1 egg
3/4 cup dairy sour cream
3/4 cup dark molasses
1 small mango or 1 large peach

Preheat oven to 350F (175C). Grease and lightly flour a 9" x 9" x 2" baking pan. In a medium bowl, stir together flour, gingerroot, soda, allspice and salt. Set aside. In a medium bowl, beat butter or margarine and brown sugar until fluffy. Beat in egg, sour cream and molasses until mixed. Stir dry ingredients into molasses mixture until blended. Pour into prepared pan. Bake 40 to 45 minutes or until a wooden pick inserted in center comes out clean. Cool cake in pan 10 minutes; invert onto plate. Pit, peel and slice mango or peach. Serve cake warm topped with fruit slices. Makes 9 servings.

Preparation time: 15 minutes

Tip:
Mango flowers are an easy serving idea and make attractive centerpieces for fruit platters. To make, cut off two lengthwise slices from each side of mango, removing a slice from each side of the long seed. With a sharp knife, score each slice by making first lengthwise, then crosswise cuts, 1/4 inch apart on each slice, cutting to the skin but not through it. Then, turn mango inside out by pushing the skin up from underneath so fruit pops forward, fanning itself out. Squeeze fruit with lemon or lime juice.

MANGOES

(MAY-ng-oh) Mangoes are a relatively new tropical fruit in American markets, but the people of India have been enjoying the fruit and its beautiful yellow flowers for over 4000 years. Later brought to South Africa, Brazil, Israel, South America and Florida, mangoes now reach their peak market season in June. Many areas provide the fruit from January through August.

With an oval shape about the size of a large apple, mangoes have greenish-yellow skin that blushes red all over when ripe. Inside, the orangy-yellow fruit surrounds a large, slender white seed. Mangoes will remind you of peaches and pineapple, but spicier and more fragrant. Mangoes can be substituted in any recipe that calls for peaches, papayas or nectarines.

Buying Tips: Figure on 1 mango per serving. Mangoes are harvested unripe because they ripen easily off the tree. Look for fruit with reddish-yellow skin that is fairly firm with gentle pressure. Some mangoes turn yellow all over when ripe. Mangoes will smell fruity and fragrant when ready to eat; a few brown spots on the skin are normal indicators of ripeness. Avoid very soft, bruised or green mangoes.

Storage: Store mangoes at room temperature if texture is very firm. Once the fruit becomes soft to the touch, refrigerate. Do not cut fruit until ready to serve. Store ripe fruit in refrigerator up to 1 week.

Basic Preparation: Peel fruit and slice lengthwise around the oval seed. Enjoy the fruit as is or sprinkle with lemon or lime juice. Top with lightly sweetened cream, chop or purée for recipes.

Serving Ideas: Mangoes are a beautiful addition to fruit platters, main dishes and compotes. Use the long, slender slices to garnish roast chicken or duck, on fruit tarts or to serve with grilled fish. Purée the fruit to use in tropical drinks. Pair mango slices with avocado and coconut for an exotic first course or arrange around a holiday ham.

Yield: 1 medium mango = 1 serving.
1 medium mango = 3/4 - 1 cup puréed fruit.

Nutrition Facts: Rich in vitamins A and C, mangoes also provide a healthy boost of potassium, calcium and phosphorus. There are about 140 calories in one medium mango.

Grilled Flank Steak with Mangoes

The marinade is superb on chicken and fish, too.

1-1/2 lbs. flank steak
1/4 cup red wine vinegar
1/4 cup soy sauce
1/4 cup honey
1/4 cup sherry
2 cloves garlic, minced
1 tablespoon fresh minced
    gingerroot
1/2 small onion, quartered
2 medium-ripe mangoes, peeled,
    pitted, cut in 8 wedges
Vegetable oil
2 tablespoons lime juice

In a shallow nonmetal dish, place flank steak. In a small bowl, stir together vinegar, soy sauce, honey, sherry, garlic and gingerroot. Pour over steak; turn steak over to coat both sides with marinade. Add quartered onion to dish; cover and marinate 3 hours or overnight. To cook steak, lightly oil a broiler pan. Drain off marinade; reserve. Place flank steak on oiled broiler pan; broil 4 inches from heat 10 to 14 minutes, turning once and brushing frequently with reserved marinade. Meanwhile, brush mango wedges with oil; sprinkle with lime juice. Add to broiler pan during last 5 minutes of cooking time, turning once. Slice steak thinly across grain; serve with mango wedges. Makes 4 to 6 servings.

Preparation time: 15 minutes

Fresh Mango Sauce

Here's a lightly sweetened sauce that's just as good on chicken or pork as it is on ice cream or pound cake.

3 tablespoons butter or margarine
2 medium-ripe mangoes, peeled,
    pitted, quartered, thinly sliced
2 tablespoons packed brown sugar
1/3 cup orange juice
1 teaspoon cornstarch
1 tablespoon rum, if desired

In a large skillet, melt butter. Add mango pieces and brown sugar. Sauté 2 to 3 minutes, stirring frequently. In a small bowl, stir together orange juice and cornstarch; stir into skillet. Cook and stir until mixture thickens and bubbles. Cook 1 minute more. Stir in rum, if desired; remove from heat. Serve hot or chilled. If preparing in advance, cover and chill in refrigerator up to 1 week. Makes 3 cups.

Preparation time: 10 minutes

Spirited Mangoes

Try this quick dessert idea with papayas, peaches and nectarines, too.

2 ripe mangoes, peeled, seeded,
    thinly sliced
2 tablespoons packed brown sugar
2 tablespoons rum
2 tablespoons toasted coconut
Whipped cream or vanilla or
    peach ice cream

Arrange mango slices on a serving platter or 4 dessert plates. Sprinkle with brown sugar, then rum. Cover and chill at least 30 minutes to allow flavors to blend. If preparing ahead, cover and chill up to 6 hours. To serve, sprinkle with coconut; top with whipped cream or ice cream. Makes 4 servings.

Preparation time: 5 minutes

Paradise Fruit Trifle

This dessert tastes more full-flavored when given at least four hours to mellow.

1 (10-3/4-oz.) frozen poundcake,
    thawed
1/4 cup sherry, orange liqueur,
    brandy or orange juice
1 cup chopped peeled mango or
    peaches (1 medium mango)
2 kiwi fruit, peeled, halved
    lengthwise, sliced
1 cup chopped papaya, plums,
    apricots or nectarines
1 cup fresh berries, hulled, sliced
    if necessary
2 eggs
1 cup milk
2 tablespoons sugar
Dash salt
1 teaspoon vanilla extract
1-1/2 cups whipping cream,
    whipped
2 tablespoons powdered sugar
2 tablespoons toasted sliced
    almonds

Slice poundcake lengthwise into 3 layers; stack layers and cut crosswise into 1/2-inch-wide sticks. In a 2-quart glass bowl, arrange poundcake sticks to cover bottom of bowl, then arrange like bricks around sides of bowl to top. Sprinkle with liqueur or orange juice. Sprinkle fruit and berries in poundcake shell. To make custard filling, in a small saucepan, lightly beat eggs. Whisk in milk, sugar and salt. Cook, whisking constantly, over medium heat until mixture thickens and coats back of a metal spoon. Remove from heat; set pan in a bowl of ice water. Stir custard about 5 minutes until it cools. Remove pan from ice water; stir in vanilla. Pour custard over fruit layer. Fold powdered sugar into whipping cream; spoon over top and smooth to cover cake and custard. Sprinkle with almonds. Cover with plastic wrap; chill at least 4 hours before serving. Spoon into dessert dishes. Makes 8 to 10 servings.

Preparation time: 30 minutes

Newer Melon Varieties:

Casaba: A deep yellow, globe-shaped melon with a slightly pointed stem end and ridges on its rind.

Crenshaw: An oval, light yellow melon with lightly ribbed rind tinged with green. The fruit is a bright salmon-pink color that is sweet and spicy-fragrant.

French Afternoon: From European seeds and much sweeter than French Breakfast, this cantaloupe-like melon has a canary yellow rind with no netting. The fruit is orange and very sweet.

French Breakfast: The size of a cantaloupe, with pale yellow-orange lightly netted rind. Fruit inside is light green and tastes like a sweet honeydew.

Galia: An Israel import, named after the daughter of the grower. Galias are large, round, light green melons with a strong aroma. The green fruit is the most fragrant of melons and medium-sweet.

Honeydew: In varieties of green, orange, gold and pink, this versatile melon may have white, golden, pink or pale orange rind with fruit in pastel colors. Regular honeydew is sweet with a honey aroma; pink has a slightly different sweetness tinged with honey. Orange honeydew has a papaya-like flavor and golden honeydew is very similar to cantaloupe.

Honeyloupe: A cross between a honeydew and cantaloupe with a large, rounded shape and pale yellow, smooth rind. The fruit is pale orange and medium-sweet in flavor.

Juan Canary: This football-shaped, large melon has a bright yellow rind with creamy white fruit tinged with pink. The flavor is very sweet and fragrant.

MELONS

Thirst-quenching melons are more than 90% water; small wonder that tropical areas in Africa, Asia, India and the Middle East have cultivated and enjoyed these fruits for thousands of years. Cantaloupes, christened after the town of Cantalupa in Italy, and watermelons have the longest history; other types of melons like honeydew are actually very recent hybrids.

Succulent new varieties of melons with romantic names, like French Afternoon, seem to be proliferating in markets as rapidly as melon vines. As many as 20 different melons can be found at produce stands and in stores, extending availability all through the year. So even though a brilliant red watermelon is a classic summer staple, a rainbow of other melons can be enjoyed during every other season.

Buying Tips: All melons, no matter what the variety, should feel heavy for their size, be free of dents and bruises and have dry rinds. Outer color and shape should be uniform. If there is netting on the rind, it should stand out in bold relief all over outer surface. Select a cantaloupe by smelling the soft stem end; sweetness means ripeness. Watermelon varieties should have pale yellow bottoms and dull, not waxy skin. Thumping a watermelon is not a good indicator of ripeness. For other melon varieties, look for a slightly soft stem end and a fruity aroma. Cut melons should have firm, well-colored meat without dryness, mealyness or stringyness.

Storage: If slightly unripe, keep melon at room temperature for 1 to 2 days. Refrigerate ripe melons to use within a few days. Store cut melons tightly wrapped in the crisper section of refrigerator.

Basic Preparation: With a large sharp knife, slice melon in half. Scoop out seeds (except for watermelon varieties); cut into wedges to serve. Sprinkle melon with lime juice or top with ice cream or whipped cream. Cube melon, cut into balls with a melon-baller or purée for recipes.

Serving Ideas: Melons make a natural dessert or snack, alone or in combination with any other fruits. Hollow out melon shells to use as serving containers for cold soups, chicken salad or a fruit compote. Fill a melon half with seafood, fresh berries, cottage cheese or a fruity sorbet. Grill melon wedges to serve with main dishes of poultry or chicken. Purée melons for sauces or tropical beverages. Wrap a slice of melon in ham or proscuitto and serve with a strong cheese such as blue cheese or Cheddar for an appetizer or first course.

Yield: 1 lb. melon = about 1 cup cut up fruit.
1 lb. melon = about 1 serving.

Nutrition Facts: Calorie counts are low for every variety averaging 50 calories per cup of cubed fruit. Varieties with orange or salmon-colored fruit offer lots of vitamin A; most are high in vitamin C.

Mickey Lee/Minnie Lee: These baby watermelons average between 6 and 8 pounds each, bred to be sweeter than larger water melons. Also called icebox melons.

Pepino: Very different, small, oval-shaped melon with a pale yellow skin streaked with purple. Inside, the golden-yellow fruit has a sweet, typical melon flavor.

Persian: Like a super-sized cantaloupe, this large round melon may be green or golden on the outside with salmon-colored fruit. Tastes like a mildly sweet cantaloupe; fragrant.

Santa Claus or Christmas Melon: Shaped like a small watermelon with a deep green rind that's streaked with gold. Flesh is greenish-yellow; flavor is mildly sweet with a fruity tang.

Saticoy: Named for the California area where it's grown, this melon has an oblong shape that's thickly netted, with a beige cast on the outside. Very juicy, bright orange fruit inside; sweet.

Sharlyn: Rind is netted with a green or orange cast. Oval shape, white fruit tinged with orange. Sweet mixture of honeydew and cantaloupe flavors.

Seedless Watermelon: A smaller version of red watermelon with none of the black seeds. Flavor is identical to seeded watermelon.

Yellow Watermelon: In varieties that are seeded and seedless, this variety looks like a red watermelon on the outside with golden yellow, very sweet fruit on the inside.

Melons in Berry Sauce

Simple yet elegant, this rainbow of melons makes a grand finale.

4 thin wedges orange melon (such as cantaloupe, Crenshaw, honeyloupe, Saticoy or French Afternoon), peeled
4 thin wedges green melon (French breakfast, Galia, pepino, Santa Claus or honeydew), peeled
4 thin wedges red or yellow watermelon, peeled
Fresh sliced or whole berries

Berry Sauce:
1 cup raspberries, sliced strawberries or blueberries
1 to 2 tablespoons sugar
2 tablespoons Cassis or orange liqueur

Prepare Berry Sauce. On 4 dessert plates, arrange 1 slice of each melon, overlapping slices. Spoon some sauce over each serving. Garnish each serving with a few berries. Makes 4 servings.

Berry Sauce:
In blender or food processor fitted with a metal blade, process berries to a purée. Add sugar and liqueur to taste; process until blended. If using raspberries, strain purée to remove seeds. If preparing in advance, cover and refrigerate sauce up to 2 days. Makes 1-1/4 cups.

Preparation time: 10 minutes

Grilled Melon with Herbs

Grill these alongside your sizzling meat, poultry or fish.

8 wedges firm ripe melon, cut 2 inches thick (do not use watermelon)
1/4 cup vegetable oil
2 tablespoons red or white wine vinegar
1 tablespoon snipped chives
1 tablespoon minced fresh basil
1/4 teaspoon salt
1/8 teaspoon pepper

Remove rind from melon, if desired. Place melon on a lightly oiled broiler pan or grill. In a shaker jar, combine oil, vinegar, herbs, salt and pepper. Brush mixture liberally over melon. Broil 4 inches from heat about 5 minutes or until heated through, turning once and brushing liberally with marinade during cooking. If desired, heat remaining marinade and spoon over hot melon to serve. Makes 4 servings.

Preparation time: 5 minutes

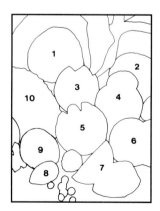

1.Seedless watermelon. 2.Casaba. 3.Crenshaw. 4.Casaba. 5.Persian. 6.Sharlyn. 7.Persian melon. 8.Pepino melon. 9.Honeyloupe. 10.Yellow watermelon.

Melons. See diagram, opposite page.

Melon Angel Pie

You can make this pie with a nine-inch baked pastry shell, too.

2 cups chopped peeled melon (such as French afternoon, French breakfast, crenshaw, cantaloupe, honeyloupe, Persian or saticoy)
1/2 cup sugar
2 (1/4-oz.) envelopes unflavored gelatin (2 tablespoons)
1 teaspoon grated orange peel
3 egg whites
1/4 cup sugar
1/2 cup heavy cream, whipped
Mint leaves, if desired

Coconut Crust:
2 cups sweetened flaked coconut
3 tablespoons butter or margarine, melted

Preheat oven to 325F (165C). Prepare Coconut Crust. To prepare filling, in a blender or food processor fitted with a metal blade, process melon until puréed. Place purée in a medium saucepan with 1/2 cup sugar, gelatin and orange peel. Cook over medium heat, stirring constantly, just until mixture comes to a boil. Place pan in refrigerator 30 to 45 minutes, stirring occasionally, until mixture mounds when dropped from a spoon. Using a rubber spatula fold whipped cream into melon mixture (do not stir). In a large bowl, beat egg whites until foamy; gradually beat in 1/4 cup sugar until mixture is stiff and glossy. Fold melon mixture into meringue until no streaks of white remain. Turn into pie shell. Chill several hours or until set. To serve, garnish with mint leaves, if desired. Makes 1 (9-inch) pie.

Coconut Crust:
In a small bowl, stir together coconut and melted butter or margarine. Spray a 9-inch pie pan lightly with cooking spray. Press coconut mixture onto bottom and sides of pan, building up top edge slightly to hold filling. Bake 20 to 25 minutes or until light golden brown. Cool before adding filling. Makes 1 (9-inch) crust.

Preparation time: 25 minutes

Watermelon-Jicama Salad

Reserve the leftover Mint Vinaigrette to accent another fruit salad.

1-1/2 cups jicama julienned sticks
1-1/2 cups 1/2-inch watermelon cubes
Lettuce leaves
Fresh mint sprigs, if desired

Mint Vinaigrette:
1/4 cup red or white wine vinegar
1/3 cup vegetable oil
2 tablespoons chopped fresh mint
1 teaspoon sugar

Prepare Mint Vinaigrette. In a medium bowl, toss together jicama and watermelon pieces. Pour vinaigrette over jicama mixture. Cover and refrigerate 30 minutes to 24 hours. With a slotted spoon, serve jicama mixture on lettuce-lined plates. Garnish with fresh mint sprigs, if desired. Makes 4 salads.

Mint Vinaigrette:
In a shaker jar, combine red or white wine vinegar, oil, mint and sugar. Cover and shake well to mix. Makes about 2/3 cup.

Preparation time: 15 minutes

Proscuitto & Melon Appetizer Balls

Serve these in a lettuce-lined melon shell or basket.

1/4 lb. proscuitto, deli ham or black forest ham
2 cups melon balls, such as cantaloupe, honeydew, casaba, honeyloupe, canary or crenshaw melon
Frilled party picks

Lime Mustard Dressing:
1 cup mayonnaise or salad dressing
2 tablespoons lime juice
1 teaspoon Dijon-style mustard
1 teaspoon brown sugar
1/4 teaspoon pepper

Prepare Lime Mustard Dressing. Julienne proscuitto in 4" x 1/2" strips. Wrap 1 or 2 strips of ham around each melon ball, securing with a party pick. If preparing in advance, cover and chill up to 6 hours in refrigerator. Serve with Lime Mustard Dressing for dipping. Makes about 40 appetizers.

Lime Mustard Dressing:
In a small bowl, stir together mayonnaise or salad dressing, lime juice, mustard, brown sugar and pepper until well mixed. Cover and chill up to 24 hours. Makes about 1 cup dressing.

Preparation time: 20 minutes.

Tip:
A medium cantaloupe yields about 2 cups melon balls.

Summer Fruit Slaw

A vinegar-oil dressing is used in this fresh fruit cole slaw. Great for summer picnics.

3 cups coarsely shredded red or green cabbage
1 cup chopped fresh plums
1 cup chopped nectarines, peaches, papayas or mangoes
1/2 cup raisins

Walnut Dressing:
1/2 cup vegetable oil
1/3 cup cider vinegar
1 teaspoon brown sugar
1/2 cup finely chopped walnuts

In a large salad bowl, toss together the cabbage, plums, nectarines or other fruit and raisins. Prepare Walnut Dressing; pour over salad and toss well to coat. Cover and chill or serve as is. Makes 6 servings.

Walnut Dressing:
In a shaker jar, combine oil, vinegar, sugar and walnuts. Cover and shake well to mix. Makes 1-1/4 cups.

Preparation time: 15 minutes

Nectarine Daiquiris

Garnish this refreshing tropical sipper with fresh strawberries or orange slices.

1 cup chopped nectarines, peaches, cherimoya, papayas or mango
1 (6-oz.) can lemonade or limeade concentrate
1/2 cup light rum
1/4 cup triple sec or orange liqueur
2 tablespoons sugar
2 cups crushed ice

In a blender or food processor fitted with a metal blade, process 1/2 of cherimoya, lemon or limeade concentrate, rum, liqueur, sugar and ice until thick and smooth. Pour into 2 long-stemmed glasses. Repeat with remaining ingredients and serve. Makes 4 drinks.

Preparation time: 10 minutes

NECTARINES

So close botanically are the peach and the nectarine that a peach pit can produce a nectarine tree (and the opposite is also true). Nectarines are often mistakenly thought to be a peach-plum cross or a specially cultivated fuzzless peach. In truth, the fruit was discovered growing wild in Asia over 2000 years ago, so as a fruit, the nectarine stands sweetly on its own. With a name derived from the Greek "nekter," it's obvious that even in ancient times the fruit was thought to be heavenly.

With a blushing golden-red, smooth skin and rounded shape, a nectarine does resemble a peach or an overgrown apricot. Nectarines have a more sophisticated, richer flavor than peaches and are a perfect, natural package for out-of-hand eating. They're at their peak between mid-May and late September.

Buying Tips: There are over 100 varieties of nectarines available during the season; some are smaller with fruit that clings to the pit (called semi-freestone). Later, larger fruit with a deeper red color called freestone (fruit does not adhere to the pit) is available. Nectarines should be a uniform shape, with a creamy yellow skin and no green at the stem end. The rose-colored blush on the skin varies with nectarine type, so it not indicate ripeness. Choose fruit that yields to gentle pressure.

Storage: To ripen nectarines at home, place in a brown paper bag or in a bowl with apples or other fruit. Check fruit daily. When ripe, refrigerate and use within a few days.

Basic Preparation: Peel nectarines if desired; eat out-of-hand, around the center pit. Best flavor is at room temperature. Or slice, chop or purée fruit for recipes. Treat fruit pieces with a lemon juice and water solution to prevent discoloration if fruit will be left standing before serving.

Serving Ideas: Use sliced nectarines to top cereal, garnish a tropical drink, decorate a roast or stuff a melon or avocado. Use nectarines as you would peaches, plums and apricots in recipes for desserts, salads, main dishes, fruit sauces, compotes and pies. Make a nectarine milk shake with the puréed fruit, a sundae with ice cream or frozen yogurt or use as a sweet topper for pancakes.

Yield: 3 medium nectarines = about 1 lb.
1 medium nectarine = 1 serving.
1 lb. nectarines = 2 cups sliced, 1-3/4 cups diced.

Nutrition Facts: A medium nectarine weighs in at 65 calories. Ideal for low-sodium, low fat and cholesterol-reduced diets. Good source of potassium and fiber.

Lila's Nectarine Ice Box Pie

Lighter than cheesecake, this dessert can be made with peaches or plums, too.

6 ripe nectarines, peaches or large plums, peeled, pitted, sliced
6 eggs, separated
1/2 cup sugar
2 (1/4-oz.) envelopes unflavored gelatin (2 tablespoons)
1/3 cup orange juice
1/2 cup sugar
2 nectarines, pitted, thinly sliced
Whipped cream

Vanilla Cookie Crust:
1 (11-oz.) pkg. vanilla wafers, crushed
1/4 cup melted butter or margarine

Prepare Vanilla Cookie Crust. In a blender or food processor fitted with a metal blade, process 6 nectarines to a purée. In a small heavy saucepan or top of a double boiler, whisk together egg yolks and sugar. Stir in nectarine purée. Cook and stir over medium heat about 5 minutes or until mixture thickens. Remove from heat. Sprinkle gelatin over orange juice; let stand 5 minutes. Place over medium-low heat; stir until dissolved. Stir into egg yolk mixture; cool 10 minutes. In a large bowl, beat egg whites at high speed until frothy; gradually beat in remaining sugar till stiff peaks form. Fold into nectarine mixture; turn into crust. Refrigerate 6 hours or overnight until firm. To serve, top with sliced nectarines and whipped cream. Cut into wedges. Makes 10 servings.

Vanilla Cookie Crust:
In a large bowl, stir together crushed wafers and melted butter or margarine until well moistened. Pat mixture into bottom of a 10-inch springform pan. Cover and chill until needed or up to 24 hours if preparing ahead. Makes 1 (10-inch) crust.

Preparation time: 30 minutes

Nectarine-Glazed Pork Ribs

Pork loin ribs are best for this recipe; though more expensive, these ribs have more meat on them.

4 lbs. pork spareribs, cut in 2- or 3-rib sections
1 teaspoon salt
1/4 teaspoon pepper

Nectarine Glaze:
6 ripe nectarines, peaches or large plums, peeled, pitted, chopped (2-1/2 cups)
2 tablespoons butter or margarine
1/2 cup sliced green onion
1 cup orange juice
2 tablespoons brown sugar
2 tablespoons lemon juice
1 tablespoon cornstarch
1/2 teaspoon salt
1/2 teaspoon allspice
1/8 teaspoon pepper

Preheat oven to 450F (230C). Sprinkle ribs with salt and pepper. Place ribs, meaty side down, in a shallow roasting pan. Bake, uncovered, 30 minutes. Remove from oven; drain off fat. Turn ribs meat side up. Lower oven temperature to 350F (175C); bake 1 hour more. Drain off fat. Prepare Nectarine Glaze. Pour sauce over ribs. Bake 20 to 30 minutes more or until meat and fruit are tender. Spoon sauce from pan over ribs to serve. Makes 4 servings.

Nectarine Glaze:
In a blender or food processor fitted with a metal blade, process 1/2 of nectarines to a purée. In a medium saucepan, melt butter. Sauté green onion 2 minutes. Stir in orange juice, brown sugar, lemon juice, cornstarch, salt, allspice and pepper. Cook and stir until mixture thickens and bubbles; stir in nectarine purée and remaining chopped nectarines. Cook 2 minutes more.

Preparation time: 20 minutes

Fruited Saffron Rice

One cup of chopped dried apricots can be substituted for the nectarines.

2-1/3 cups water
1/8 teaspoon powdered saffron or saffron threads
1/2 teaspoon salt
1 cup converted rice
2 tablespoons butter or margarine
3 nectarines or peaches or 6 apricots, pitted, chopped
1 tablespoon minced fresh parsley
2 tablespoons minced green onion
1 teaspoon grated lemon or orange peel

In a medium saucepan, place water, saffron and salt. Bring to a boil; stir in rice. Cover tightly and simmer 18 to 20 minutes or until all water is absorbed. Transfer hot rice from pan to serving bowl. In same pan, melt butter; add nectarines, parsley, onion and orange peel. Sauté 3 minutes or until heated through. Stir mixture into rice; serve hot. Makes 4 to 6 servings.

Preparation time: 10 minutes

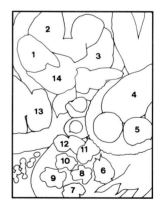

1. Red bananas. 2. Coconuts. 3. Burro bananas. 4. Mexican papaya. 5. Mangoes. 6. Tamarindos. 7. Deglet noor dates. 8. Dayri dates. 9. Mission figs. 10. Calimyrna figs. 11. Brown turkey figs. 12. Kadota figs. 13. Hawaiian papaya. 14. Manzano bananas.

Tropical Fruits. See diagram, opposite page.

PAPAYAS

(PUH-pie-ahs) Papaya's exotic fruit flavor was delectable enough to be called "food of the angels" by Columbus when he discovered the tropical treasure in the Caribbean. Sommerset Maughn, another fan of papaya, was inspired to write, "When you have used it, you acquire a passion for it." Papaya lovers through history have not only eaten the fruit, they also used it to clean and soften their skin, ease indigestion and tenderize meat. Even today, island cooks add chunks of green (unripe) papaya to a stewing chicken to make it tender. In the U.S. papain, the tenderizing enzyme in papaya, is used in commercial meat tenderizers.

Sometimes incorrectly called pawpaws, papayas are shaped like an elongated pear, about 5 to 6 inches long, with one bulbous end that holds a cavity with round black seeds and juicy orange fruit. The seeds are easily scooped out, so you can enjoy the creamy tropical fruit. Papayas have the taste of a rich, sweet melon with peachy overtones. Available nearly year-round, papayas are grown in all tropical areas with Hawaii and Florida supplying most of the U.S. crop.

Buying Tips: Select papayas that are at least half yellow (the rest of the skin will be green) and yield to gentle pressure. Look for bruise-free fruit with smooth, unwrinkled skin. Avoid very soft or bruised fruit with a fermented aroma.

Storage: Green papayas will ripen at home in 3 to 5 days if kept at room temperature, out of sunlight. Fruit is ripe when soft and almost fully yellow. Refrigerate ripe fruit to use within 1 week.

Basic Preparation: Halve fruit lengthwise and scoop out the seeds and strings. Spoon fruit from the skin or peel skin and slice fruit thinly to serve. Enjoy au natural or with a squirt of lemon or lime juice. Dice or purée fruit for use in recipes.

Serving Ideas: Like kiwi fruit and pineapple, papaya cannot be used in gelatin salads or gelatin-based desserts because the papain enzyme will prevent gelling. But papaya, sliced, puréed and chopped, can be used in all other fresh fruit recipes like peaches or nectarines. Papaya is also delicious with meats, turkey, chicken and fish. Grill papaya along with salmon or red snapper, brushing with barbecue sauce. Add papaya to sparkling wine, ice cream drinks or fruit sauces. Use papaya in jams or jellies, stuffed with chicken or shrimp or layered in a fruit salad.

Yield: 1 large papaya = about 2 servings.
2 medium papayas = about 1 lb.
1 medium papaya = about 3/4 cup cut up fruit.

Nutrition Facts: Papayas have about 65 calories per medium half. They provide double the vitamin C needed for a day's requirement and 70 percent of the U.S. RDA for vitamin A.

Varieties:

Kapoho Solo: A Hawaiian-grown papaya with golden-colored fruit that is the most familiar. Very sweet and juicy; ripe when yellow.

Mexican: A very large papaya that can weigh up to 12 pounds, shaped like a large football. The fruit becomes a pinkish-orange when ripe.

Sunrise Solo: Pear-shaped variety with a pinkish-orange flesh and mostly green skin.

Papaya-Shrimp Salad

Another time, try this refreshing combo with flaked crabmeat.

Lettuce leaves
1 cup shredded cucumber
1 cup shredded carrot
2 papayas, peeled, seeded, thinly sliced
1 pound peeled deveined shrimp, cooked

Honey-Almond Dressing:
1/3 cup mayonnaise or salad dressing
1/3 cup plain yogurt
1 tablespoon milk
1 tablespoon honey
1/4 cup sliced almonds, toasted

Prepare Honey-Almond Dressing. On 4 dinner plates, arrange lettuce leaves. Sprinkle 1/4 of shredded cucumber and carrot over lettuce on each plate. Fan 1/4 of papaya slices and shrimp over each plate. Drizzle Honey-Almond Dresssing over salads. Makes 4 servings.

Honey-Almond Dressing:
In a medium bowl, stir together mayonnaise or salad dressing, yogurt, milk and honey until well blended. Stir in almonds. Makes 1-1/2 cups.

Preparation time: 10 minutes

Passion Fruit-Strawberry Mousse

Serve this exotic but light dessert after a heavy meal.

4 ripe wrinkled passion fruit
1-1/2 cups sliced fresh
   strawberries or chopped
   peaches, nectarines or papaya
1 (1/4-oz.) envelope unflavored
   gelatin (1 tablespoon)
1/3 cup sugar
1/3 cup water
2 egg whites
2 tablespoons sugar
1 cup heavy cream, whipped
2 ripe wrinkled passion fruit, if
   desired

Halve 4 passion fruit; spoon out pulp and seeds. In a blender or food processor fitted with a metal blade, process passion fruit pulp and seeds with strawberries to a purée. Strain out seeds. In a medium saucepan, mix gelatin and 1/3 cup sugar. Add fruit purée and water; cook and stir over medium heat until mixture comes to a boil. Remove from heat. Refrigerate, stirring occasionally, about 20 minutes or until mixture mounds when dropped from a spoon. Beat egg whites to soft peaks; gradually beat in sugar until stiff. Fold into passion fruit mixture with whipped cream until blended; do not stir. Spoon into 8 dessert dishes; chill 4 hours or until set. If desired, process pulp from remaining 2 passion fruits; spoon purée over each serving. Makes 8 servings.

Preparation time: 25 minutes

PASSION FRUIT

Any other fruit with puckered, moldy skin would be ready for the garbage bin—not so with the exotic passion fruit! This purple fruit, about the size of an egg, is picked when the skin is smooth and reaches its peak of ripeness when its skin wrinkles. Inside the hard shell is juicy, pinkish-green pulp filled with edible black seeds. Passion fruit tastes both sweet and sour and the aroma is tropical and perfumy. The pulp is luxurious over ice cream, fruit sorbets, in drinks or in cake fillings.

Passion fruit got its name when Spanish missionaries, who found the plants in the jungles of South America, saw symbols of the Crucifixion in the plants' flowers. Today, the fruit is grown in Australia, Africa, South America and California. Supplies of passion fruit become available from February through the summer months.

Buying Tips: Purchase wrinkled fruit to use within a few days; smooth-skinned fruit will ripen at home in 3 to 5 days. For the best-tasting, ripe fruit, look for wrinkled skin that may show signs of mold.

Storage: Store smooth-skinned passion fruit at room temperature until wrinkled. Refrigerate wrinkled fruit up to several days or freeze whole fruit or pulp if desired for up to 6 months.

Basic Preparation: Halve fruit and spoon out the pulp to eat as is or sweeten with a little sugar. Use the pulp to spoon over ice cream or other fruits mix it into whipped cream or purée the pulp for use in drinks or recipes. The seeds are completely edible but can be strained from the puréed pulp if desired.

Serving Ideas: Spoon the pulp over fresh raspberries, melons or banana chunks. Purée the pulp, straining out seeds if desired, to add to sauces, fruit salad dressings, pie fillings or puddings. Combine the pulp with a favorite fruit juice or punch or process with sherbet and other fruits for a tropical smoothie. Passion fruit pulp makes an exotic addition to banana cream pie, rice pudding and dessert soufflés.

Yield: 1 to 2 passion fruits = 1 serving.
6 passion fruits = 1/2 cup juice.
4 - 5 passion fruits = 1/3 cup purée.

Nutrition Facts: Passion fruit is generous in vitamin C, iron and niacin. One fruit contains about 90 calories.

PEACHES

China grew the "tao," or peach, over 2500 years ago, revering the fruit as a symbol of longevity and immortality. Peaches quickly became popular throughout Greece, Persia and Europe and were brought to the New World by the Spaniards, the French and the English. Today the U.S. produces one-fourth of the total world supply of peaches, which rank as one of the 4 most popular American fruits (others being apples, bananas and oranges).

Peach connoisseurs describe the delicious fruit flavor and texture of a perfectly ripe peach as "melting." Not all peaches have this characteristic because early-season types are cultivated for canning and preserving. Later-season varieties have the softer texture and sweet, aromatic flavor that make peaches so popular. Mechanical "de-fuzzers" remove some of the characteristic peach fuzz before shipping, so you can enjoy peaches without peeling them.

Buying Tips: The best characteristic to look for is a creamy or overall golden yellow undercolor. The rosy blush doesn't indicate ripeness and varies between varieties. Avoid peaches with traces of green, wrinkles, blemishes or brown spots. Peaches ripen easily at home, so purchase them on the firm side. Press fruit gently between two palms; when the fruit feels slightly soft, peaches are ready to eat.

Storage: Store firm fruit at room temperature in a brown paper bag or fruit ripening bowl until they begin to soften. Refrigerate soft fruit to use within a few days. Chopped, sliced or puréed fruit can be frozen if treated with a lemon juice and water mixture and tightly wrapped.

Basic Preparation: Enjoy peaches as they are, without peeling at room temperature for best flavor. Slice, chop or purée the fruit for recipes. Peaches discolor when cut, so treat fruit with a lemon juice-water mixture for use on fruit tarts, salads, etc.

Serving Ideas: Use peaches for a double-crust pie or tarts, in fruit parfaits, over breakfast cereal, on shortcake and in muffins or quick-breads. Purée the fruit for homemade ice cream, milkshakes, tropical drinks and sauces and to enjoy over roast duck, chicken or pork. Fold peach slices into whipped cream or yogurt, sprinkle with fruity liqueurs for dessert or stuff with sharp cheese for an appetizer. Use in trifles or wrapped inside pancakes or crepes.

Yield: 1 peach = 1 serving.
1 lb. peaches = 2 large or 3 medium peaches.
1 lb. peaches = 2 cups peeled, sliced peaches.
1 lb. peaches = 1-2/3 cup diced, 1-1/2 cups puréed.

Nutrition Facts: A medium-size peach contains about 50 calories. Low in sodium, fat and cholesterol, peaches are a good source of potassium and fiber.

Varieties:

Clingstone: A type of peach with firmer fruit that "clings" to the pit; very good flavor. Excellent for canning and preserving are May-crest, Springcrest and Flavorcrest.

Freestone: The "melting" peach, with a loose stone that separates easily from the soft, sweet fruit. Varieties to look for are Elberta, Angelus, O'Henry, Fairtime and Carnival.

Semi-Freestone: This peach type has softer fruit with a semi-loose stone in the center. Good for preserving and in recipes. Varieties include June Lady, Redtop and Elegant Lady.

Fresh Peach Chutney

Serve this delightful chunky fruit condiment over salads, meat and fish.

1 tablespoon vegetable oil
1/2 cup chopped onion
1 clove garlic, finely chopped
1/4 cup white wine vinegar
1/2 cup packed brown sugar
1 tablespoon lime juice
1 tablespoon minced gingerroot
1/4 teaspoon ground nutmeg
1/4 teaspooon dry mustard
1/3 cup dark raisins
2 large fresh peaches or nectarines or 5 to 6 plums, pitted, chopped (1-1/3 cups)

In a large skillet, heat oil; sauté onion and garlic 2 minutes. Stir in vinegar, brown sugar, lime juice, ginger, nutmeg and dry mustard until well mixed. Stir in peaches, nectarines or plums; cook just until mixture is heated through. Serve warm or at room temperature. Store tightly covered in refrigerator for up to several weeks. Makes 1-2/3 cups.

Preparation time: 15 minutes

Peaches & Cream Shortcake

Enjoy this easy favorite year-round by substituting in-season fruits for the peaches.

2 cups all-purpose flour
1/4 cup sugar
1 tablespoon baking powder
1/2 teaspoon salt
1/2 cup vegetable shortening
1 cup milk
1 teaspoon vanilla extract
1 tablespoon melted butter or margarine
4 medium peaches or nectarines, 8 plums or 2 mangoes or papayas, peeled

Cream Filling:
1 cup whipping cream
2 tablespoons sugar
1 teaspoon vanilla extract

Preheat oven to 450F (230C). Grease a 9-inch round cake pan. In a large bowl, stir together flour, 3 tablespoons of sugar, baking powder and salt. Using a pastry blender, cut in shortening until mixture resembles small peas. In a glass measure, whisk together milk and vanilla. With a fork, stir milk and vanilla into dry ingredients just until moistened. Spread dough in greased pan. Brush top of dough with melted butter; sprinkle with remaining 1 tablespoon of sugar. Bake 25 to 30 minutes or until golden brown. Turn out onto rack to cool 10 minutes. If preparing in advance, wrap cooled cake tightly in plastic wrap; store at room temperature up to 24 hours. Prepare Cream Filling. Split cake horizontally. Place 1 layer cut side up on a serving plate. Pit and slice peaches. Top cake layer with 1/2 of peach slices and 1/2 of filling. Top with remaining cake layer, cut side down. Spread with remaining peach slices and filling. Cut in wedges to serve. Makes 8 servings.

Cream Filling:
In a medium bowl, beat whipping cream until stiff. Stir in sugar and vanilla. Cover and chill in refrigerator up to 24 hours. Makes about 2 cups.

Preparation time: 20 minutes

Peaches & Cream Shortcake, above; Marsala Fruit Compote, page 44.

PEARS/ASIAN PEARS

From the familiar Bartletts to the exotic Asian varieties, pears (or "butter fruit" as they are sometimes called) can now be found in stores at nearly any time of year. No longer are pears grown only in America or Europe; Asian countries are now producing a number of varieties of apple pears or Asian pears.

The traditional pear has a long history dating back to the Stone Age, when pears were first enjoyed. Later, pears were further cultivated by the ancient Greeks. French horticulturists developed many varieties of pears, as did the English, and in 1630 a pear tree was planted on American soil. Pear trees are so hardy that they can produce fruit for a century or more.

Buying Tips: Like bananas, American varieties of pears are not tree-ripened; they are typically sold when firm and must be ripened at home. Avoid pears with soft spots near the stem or bottom end and those with heavy bruises. Asian pears should be firm like an apple, never soft.

Storage: For very firm fruit, use a fruit-ripening bowl or store at room temperature until pears are soft to the touch (exceptions: Asian apple pears and Stark Crimson Bartletts soften from the inside out and should be firm for eating). Store ripened pears in the refrigerator; use within a few days. Asian pear varieties keep up to 2 weeks at room temperature or 3 months refrigerated.

Basic Preparation: For eating out of hand, there's no preparation needed. Or peel if desired, core like an apple and cut into slices or wedges. For use in salads or cooking, dip pear pieces or slices in a lemon juice or ascorbic acid mixture to prevent discoloration of the fruit.

Serving Ideas: Pears can be eaten raw or sautéed, poached, baked, steamed or microwaved. Asian pears are good mixed with apples in pies, in poached mixtures or sautéed. Pears served with soft or hard cheeses are a popular dessert or appetizer. Substitute pears for apples in a Waldorf salad or poach pears to serve around a holiday turkey or as a dessert, laced with chocolate sauce.

Yield: 1 lb. pears/Asian pears = about 3 medium pears, 2-1/2 cups diced or 2-1/3 cups slices or 1-3/4 cups purée.

Nutrition facts: High in fiber, pears and Asian pears are low in sodium, cholesterol and fat. They're a good source of calcium and potassium. An average pear is about 100 calories.

Pear Varieties/American:

Anjou: Good eating pear; light green to yellow-green color. Egg-shaped with a short stem.

Bosc: Russet-colored skin and an elongated, slender shape. Tender and buttery in flavor. Perfect for cooking, baking or poaching, and eating fresh.

French Butter: A delightful but delicate variety of pear; resembles the standard green Bartlett pear. Sweet pear flavor with a touch of lemon. Very soft fruit.

Red Bartlett: A red-skinned version of the green Bartlett. A super eating pear; also perfect for canning. Sweet and juicy with a traditional pear shape.

Stark Crimson Red: A brilliant red skin covers luscious fruit. Rich flavor. Eat while still firm since they are mealy when soft. Available during August and September.

Asian Pears:

These varieties are the result of numerous cross-breedings between apple and pear varieties. They are also called apple pears or oriental pears. They have the mellow, sweet flavor of a pear with the crispness of an apple. Don't wait for them to soften as pears do; they should be hard like an apple for the best eating.

Chajuro: Russet-colored skin, apple-shaped with a distinctive perfume-like flavor and aroma.

Hosui: Apple shape; golden-brown skin with a delicate flavor. Best for eating.

Kikusui: Greenish-yellow skin; a very popular variety. Has a sweet flavor that is a little tart. Widely available.

Nitaka: Mottled brown skin, very mild flavor. Crisp, juicy texture.

Shinko: Has russet-orange skin and a more pronounced flavor. Firm texture; good for cooking.

Shinsaki: A tarter variety of apple pear but flavor is rich and texture is juicy. Thin, tender pale green skin.

Tsa Li: More pear-shaped than the others with green skin and very mild flavor. Flavor is better when cooked.

Ya Li: Like Tsa Li, it's more pear-like with a yellowish-green skin and a delicate flavor.

Pear-Brie Melt

Serve this as a uniquely elegant appetizer, or a sophisticated dessert.

1 very ripe pear (such as Anjou, Bosc, or French Butter) cored, chopped
1 tablespoon butter or margarine
1 (8-oz.) round ripe brie or Camembert cheese
1 tablespoon dark raisins
1 tablespoon chopped walnuts or pecans
Crackers, French bread slices or shortbread cookies

Preheat oven to 350F (175C). In a small skillet, sauté chopped pears in butter or margarine for 4 to 5 minutes or until almost tender. Lightly oil an 8-inch pie plate or cake pan. Place cheese in center of pan (do not peel coating from cheese). Spoon chopped pears over cheese. Bake uncovered 5 to 10 minutes or until cheese is soft and partially melted. Sprinkle raisins and walnuts or pecans over melted cheese. Serve at once as a spread for crackers, French bread or shortbread cookies. Makes 4 appetizer or dessert servings.

Preparation time: 10 minutes

Curried Chicken & Pear Salad

Any type of ripe pear will enhance this salad.

3 ripe pears (American or Asian varieties), peaches or large plums, cored, thinly sliced
2 cups cooked chicken or turkey strips
1 cup shredded red cabbage
1 cup diced green bell pepper
1/3 cup toasted shredded coconut
1/3 cup peanut halves
1/3 cup raisins
Lettuce leaves

Chutney Dressing:
1/3 cup mayonnaise or salad dressing
1/4 cup chutney, finely chopped
1 teaspoon curry powder
About 1 to 2 tablespoons milk

Prepare Chutney Dressing. In a large bowl, toss together pears, chicken, cabbage, bell pepper, coconut, peanuts and raisins. Toss salad ingredients with dressing until well mixed. If preparing ahead, cover and refrigerate up to 2 hours. Spoon salad onto lettuce-lined plates. Makes 3 or 4 servings.

Chutney Dressing:
In a small bowl, stir together mayonnaise or salad dressing, chutney and curry powder. Add milk, 1 tablespoon at a time, until dressing is consistency of bottled salad dressing. Makes about 2/3 cup.

Preparation time: 15 minutes

Variation:
Curried Chicken & Pear Sandwiches: Prepare mixture as directed, except chop pears and chicken in 1/4-inch pieces. Spread on bread. Makes about 4 sandwiches.

Tip:
Coconut can be toasted easily in a toaster oven. Place coconut on a piece of aluminum foil; toast about 5 minutes or until golden.

Pear-Streusel Muffins

Always welcome at breakfast, these hearty muffins also partner well with salads and soups.

2 cups all-purpose flour
1/3 cup sugar
2-1/2 teaspoons baking powder
1/2 teaspoon salt
1 cup milk
1/4 cup vegetable oil
1 egg
1 teaspoon vanilla extract
1-1/4 cups finely chopped ripe pear, such as Bartlett, Bosc, Anjou, or French Butter pears (1 large pear)

Streusel Topping:
3 tablespoons packed brown sugar
2 tablespoons all-purpose flour
1/4 teaspoon ground cinnamon
3 tablespoons chilled butter or margarine
1/4 cup sliced almonds

Preheat oven to 400F (205C). Line a 12-cup muffin tin with paper muffin cups. In a large bowl, stir together flour, sugar, baking powder and salt. In a small bowl, whisk together milk, oil, egg and vanilla. Stir egg mixture into flour mixture just until moistened (batter will be lumpy). Stir in pears. Spoon batter into muffin cups. Prepare Streusel Topping; sprinkle mixture evenly over batter. Bake 20 to 25 minutes until golden brown and a wooden pick inserted in center comes out clean. Immediately remove muffins from pan; serve warm. Makes 12 muffins.

Streusel Topping:
In a small bowl, stir together sugar, flour and cinnamon. Cut in butter or margarine until mixture resembles small peas. Stir in almonds.

Preparation time: 20 minutes

Pear Pie Lorraine with Custard Sauce

This pie is also superb made with apple varieties such as Braeburn, Cortland, Gala and Grannysmith. Do not use Asian apple-pears in this pie.

**6 cups thinly sliced ripe pears
  (about 2 lbs.)**
1 tablespoon lemon juice
3/4 cup sugar
1/2 cup sliced toasted almonds
1/4 cup golden raisins
2 tablespoons all-purpose flour
1/2 teaspoon ground cinnamon
Dash ground nutmeg
1 tablespoon butter or margarine

Rich Pie Pastry:
2 cups all-purpose flour
1 teaspoon salt
3/4 cup vegetable shortening
4 to 5 tablespoons cold water

Custard Sauce:
1 lightly beaten egg
1/2 cup sugar
Dash salt
2 cups milk
2 tablespoons cornstarch
1 teaspoon vanilla extract

Preheat oven 375F (190C). Sprinkle pear slices with lemon juice. In a large bowl, stir together sugar, almonds, raisins, flour, cinnamon and nutmeg. Add pears to sugar mixture; toss well to coat fruit. Prepare pie pastry. On a lightly floured surface, roll 1/2 of Rich Pie Pastry to 12-inch circle; transfer to 8- or 9-inch pie pan. Trim pastry even with rim of pan. Fill pastry-lined pie pan with pear mixture; dot with slivers of butter or margarine. Roll remaining pastry to a 12-inch circle; place on top of filling. Trim pastry to 1/2-inch beyond rim of pan; fold under bottom edge. Flute edge if desired. Cut slits in crust for escape of steam. Bake 45 to 50 minutes or until crust is golden-brown and pears are tender. Cool on a wire rack. Prepare Custard Sauce. Serve pie warm or cool with Custard Sauce. Makes 1 (8- or 9-inch) pie.

Rich Pie Pastry:
In a medium bowl, stir together flour and salt. With a pastry blender, cut in shortening until mixture resembles small peas. Sprinkle 1 tablespoon of cold water over mixture; gently toss with fork. Add remaining water by tablespoons, mixing with a fork until mixture forms a ball. With lightly floured hands, shape dough into a ball.

Custard Sauce:
In a medium saucepan, stir together egg, sugar, salt and 1-3/4 cups of milk. Cook over medium heat, stirring with a wire whisk, until mixture forms bubbles around sides of pan. Remove from heat. In a small bowl, stir together remaining 1/4 cup milk and cornstarch; whisk into hot mixture. Return pan to heat; cook over medium heat until mixture thickens and bubbles, stirring constantly. Remove from heat; stir in vanilla. Makes about 2 cups.

Preparation time: 45 minutes

Poached Pears & Persimmons

Use the crisp Fuyu persimmon; it cooks up well in this sweetly spiced breakfast treat, side dish or ice cream topper.

3 Fuyu persimmons
**2 firm-ripe pears, such as Bartlett,
  Anjou, or Bosc**
3/4 cup orange juice
1/2 cup sugar
3 tablespoons lemon juice
1/4 teaspoon ground allspice

Peel and remove stems from persimmons. Slice into 1/2-inch-thick slices; discard any seeds. Core pears; slice 1/4-inch thick. In a large saucepan, place sliced fruit, orange juice, sugar, lemon juice and allspice. Bring to boiling; reduce heat. Simmer, uncovered, about 20 to 25 minutes or until tender. Uncover; bring to boiling. Cook over high heat until liquid is reduced by half, about 10 minutes. If preparing ahead, cover and refrigerate. Serve warm or chilled. Makes 6 servings.

Preparation time: 15 minutes

Ginger Pear Butter

Enjoy this scrumptious spread on toast, fruit breads and pancakes or as a condiment for pork. Do not use Asian apple-pears in this recipe.

**3 pounds ripe pears, peeled,
  cored, quartered (8 cups)**
1 cup water
1 cup apple juice
1/2 cup sugar
1/2 cup honey
3 tablespoons lemon juice
1 tablespoon grated lemon peel
**1 tablespoon chopped gingerroot
  or 1/2 teaspoon ground ginger**
1 teaspoon ground cinnamon
1/2 teaspoon ground nutmeg

In a large saucepan or Dutch oven, combine pears and water; bring to a boil. Reduce heat and simmer, partially covered, about 30 minutes or until tender. In a blender or food processor fitted with a metal blade, process pear mixture to a purée. Return to pan. Add apple juice, sugar, honey, lemon juice, lemon peel, gingerroot, cinnamon and nutmeg. Bring mixture to a boil; reduce heat and simmer over medium heat 1-1/2 hours or until thickened, stirring frequently. Cool; turn into freezer or refrigerator containers and cover tightly. Freeze up to 3 months or refrigerate up to 1 month. Makes 4 cups.

Preparation time: 20 minutes

Varieties:

Dried persimmons: Ripe, firm persimmons are used for drying. Use like any dried fruit.

Hachiya: The leading variety, a Japanese type, is large, oblong in shape, with one pointed end and a deep orange-red skin color. Must be soft-ripe to enjoy.

Fuyu: Neat to eat like an apple, fuyus have a crisp texture that makes the fruit good for slicing, preserving and for use in recipes. Same bright color, but shape is flattened.

Persimmon Clafouti

This version is like a cross between a fruit-filled cake and a custard.

**3 medium firm-ripe hachiya or
    fuyu persimmons, peeled,
    thinly sliced
1 cup milk
3 eggs
1/4 cup orange juice
2/3 cup all-purpose flour
1/3 cup packed brown sugar
2 teaspoons vanilla extract
1/2 teaspoon ground cinnamon
1/4 teaspoon ground nutmeg
1/8 teaspoon salt**

Preheat oven to 350F (175C). Generously grease a 10-inch quiche dish or pie plate. Arrange persimmon slices in dish. In a blender or food processor fitted with a metal blade, process milk, eggs, orange juice, flour, brown sugar, vanilla, cinnamon, nutmeg and salt until smooth. Pour batter evenly over persimmons. Bake 60 to 70 minutes or until a knife inserted halfway between center and edge comes out clean. Place a 10- or 12-inch platter over dish; invert cake onto platter. Cool 15 minutes; cut into wedges. Serve warm or cool with whipped cream or ice cream. Refrigerate leftovers. Makes 8 servings.

Preparation time: 10 minutes

PERSIMMONS

Nicknamed "the apple of the Orient," persimmons were first harvested in Asia. A welcome sight in the autumn season, this brilliant orange fruit is rich and sweet when ripe, smooth enough to spoon directly from the skin. Unfortunately, since the outer skin reaches its full color before the fruit is ripe, many people bite into a persimmon too soon when the taste is astringent and bitter. Since the fragile fruit must be picked when firm, it's up to the consumer to ripen the fruit to sweet perfection at home.

About the size of a tomato, persimmons are available from October through January with dried persimmons available almost year-round in some markets.

Buying Tips: Look for persimmons with smooth, brilliant orange skins with no breaks, cracks or soft spots. The green cap should be attached. Buy soft persimmons to use immediately; purchase while still firm to ripen at home.

Storage: Store ripe persimmons refrigerated; use as soon as possible. To ripen, allow firm, unripe persimmons to stand at room temperature up to 1 week. Persimmon pulp sprinkled with lemon juice to prevent browning may be frozen in airtight containers. You can also freeze whole persimmons, tightly wrapped, for future use.

Basic Preparation: Bite into a crisp Fuyu persimmon like an apple or slice or purée if fruit is soft. It's messier to bite into a Hachiya persimmon. Instead, cut an "X" in the pointed end of the fruit with a sharp knife, peel back the skin and spoon out the soft pulp inside. Cut into slices or purée the pulp for use in recipes. Substitute dried persimmons in recipes calling for dried fruit or enjoy as is.

Hachiya persimmons acquire an unpleasant astringent taste when used in cooking or baking unless the pulp is first combined with baking soda. In recipes for puddings, cakes and cookies, stir together the pulp and soda before adding remaining ingredients.

Serving Ideas: Hachiya pulp is perfect for baking, in puddings, cakes, cookies, quickbreads, even muffins and pancakes. Slice fuyus for fruit platters, as a garnish for ham, pork or duck or for fruit or chicken salads. Persimmons make great jams and preserves and are a taste treat in combination with grapefruit sections or avocado slices. Dried persimmons can be sprinkled into salads or breakfast oatmeal.

Yield: 1 persimmon = 1 serving.
1 persimmon = 3/4 to 1 cup pulp.
1 lb. persimmons = 3 to 4 medium persimmons.

Nutrition Facts: A 3-1/2-ounce serving of persimmon pulp has between 75 and 120 calories, depending on variety. An excellent source of vitamins A and C, persimmons also provide some potassium, calcium and phosphorus.

PLUMS/PRUNES

Jack Horner had nothing on the Asians and Europeans who discovered this sweet, easy-to-eat fruit about 2000 years before Mother Goose. When the pilgrims landed, American Indians were enjoying plums along the New England coast to Florida. Today more than 150 varieties of plums and prunes are cultivated in this country, the majority in California.

Because only 3 or 4 of every 100 plum blossoms bear fruit, the growers import bees into the orchards to aid in fertilization. When the fruit is harvested, pickers use standarized color cards to match with the plum's color; this insures that grading standards are met.

Prune plums, which are the purple European variety, are the only plums used for drying and shipping as prunes. They are harvested late in the season in late August and September. The eating plums are available from May through late September.

Buying Tips: Choose firm, plump fruit that are slightly soft at the tip end. The bloom or cloudy gray cast on the skin's surface is natural and has no bearing on the quality of the fruit. Plums finish ripening off the tree, so fruit can be purchased ready to eat or slightly firm for ripening at home. Avoid fruit with broken skin, bruises or brown spots.

Storage: Refrigerate ripe, soft fruit. Let firm fruit stand at room temperature to ripen; transfer to chilled crisper when ripe. Use ripe fruit within a few days; unripe fruit will become ripe within 3 to 5 days.

Basic Preparation: Enjoy plums au natural, enjoying the sweet-tart skin and fruit that surrounds the center pit or slice the fruit. Purée peeled fruit for use in recipes or canning or preserving. To neatly pit plums, use a small sharp knife to cut along the seam all around the pit. Twist fruit halves in opposite directions to separate, then cut away the pit.

Serving Ideas: Slice plums to top a fruit tart, shortcake, waffles or cereal. Sprinkle sliced plums with spices like cinnamon, nutmeg or ginger and top with whipped cream or ice cream. Plums bake well in pies, turnovers and cookie bars. Use them on a fruit platter, to take on picnics or for a low-calorie dessert with lightly sweetened yogurt.

Yield: 1 to 2 plums = 1 serving.
1 lb. plums = About 6 plums.
1 lb. plums = 2-1/2 cups sliced or 1-3/4 cups purée.

Nutrition Facts: There are just 33 calories in a single medium plum with a healthy dose of potassium and high fiber to boot.

Varieties:

Early-season: These varieties appear earliest; Red Beaut (red skin), Black Beaut (black-red skin), Santa Rose (purplish-red skin) and Burmosa (red blush).

Italian plums: This variety is most often used for drying as prunes. High in sugar, this plum is blue-black in color with fruit that separates easily from the pit.

Late-season: At the end of summer, look for these; Friar (black skin), Kelsey (unusual apple-green skin), Casselman (red skin) and Standard (dark blue skin).

Mid-season: These varieties appear mid-summer; Black Amber (black skin), El Dorado (black-red skin), Laroda (red skin) and Simka (purple skin).

Turkey Kabobs with Plum Sauce

Use the plum sauce as a marinade/basting sauce for pork chops and chicken breasts, too.

1 pound turkey tenderloins
1 small onion
1/4 fresh pineapple, peeled, cut into 1-1/2-inch chunks
2 zucchini, cut into 1-inch slices

Plum Sauce:
4 plums, peeled, pitted, sliced
1/3 cup vegetable oil
2 tablespoons lime or lemon juice
2 tablespoons honey
2 tablespoons chili sauce
1 clove garlic, minced
1 tablespoon sesame seed

Prepare medium-hot coals on grill, or preheat broiler. Slice turkey tenderloins in half lengthwise, then cut each piece crosswise into 6 sections. Thread pieces on skewers. Peel onion; halve and cut each half into quarters. On separate skewers, thread onion, pineapple and zucchini chunks. Prepare Plum Sauce; brush generously over all kabobs. Place turkey kabobs on grill 4 inches above coals or on broiler pan 3 inches under broiler. Broil 9 to 12 minutes, turning once and basting frequently with sauce. Add vegetable-fruit kabobs during last 5 minutes of cooking, basting frequently and turning once. Serve any remaining sauce with kabobs. Makes 4 servings.

Plum Sauce:
In blender or food processor fitted with a metal blade, process plums until smooth. Add oil, lemon or lime juice, honey, chili sauce, garlic and sesame seed; process until blended. Makes 2/3 cup.

Preparation time: 20 minutes

Peaches, Plums & Nectarines. Clockwise from top right: Queen Anne plums, Elberta peaches, Italian prune plums, Elberta peaches, Nectarines, Friar plums.

POMEGRANATES

(*POM-ah-GRAN-ets*) The early Persians enjoyed not only cultivating and eating this intriguing fruit, but also using the rich, red juices as a dye for their hand-made rugs. Translated literally, the name pomegranate means "apple with many seeds," about 613 of them, according to lore. Pomegranates are a colorful fall fruit about the size of an apple with hard, leather-like deep red skin. Inside is a labyrinth of shiny red kernels or seeds embedded in a spongy white membrane. The deep red juice is used as the basis for grenadine syrup, an ingredient widely used in drinks and drink products.

Enjoying the seeds and juice of a pomegranate is a messy proposition, especially since the juice can permanantly stain clothing. But the flavor is sophisticated and pleasantly sweet and sour. The crunchy kernels are a pretty addition to fruit salads or platters.

Buying tips: Look for the largest pomegranates; they'll have more kernels and will be juicier. Fruit should be shiny, not shriveled, and heavy for its size.

Storage: Store in refrigerator crisper to use within 1 week. The kernels can be frozen for year-round use in recipes; store in an airtight container.

Basic Preparation: With a serrated knife, cut off the top of the pomegranate, just above the seeds. Score the shell into small segments, so the skin can be peeled back for neater eating. Suck out the seeds and juice to enjoy; do not eat the membrane, since it's bitter. Another way to extract the juice is to roll the fruit over a hard surface to crush the kernels inside; then cut a small plug out of the thick skin and suck out the juice. Both the seeds and juice can be processed in a blender or food processor until pulverized, then strained to use as juice in recipes.

Serving Ideas: Add pomegranate seeds to poultry stuffings, tossed green salads or sprinkle over sliced fruit to add color. Pomegrante juice can be used in drink recipes, fruit sauces, meat marinades or mixed into softened ice cream for an exotic flavor.

Yield: 1 pomegranate = 1 serving.
3 pomegranates = about 1 lb.
4 pomegranates = about 1 cup juice

Nutrition Facts: One pomegranate yields about 100 calories and contains small amounts of potassium and other mineral nutrients.

Pomegranate Juice

Add the juice to sweetened fruit juice drinks, tropical drinks, salad dressings or stir into softened French vanilla ice cream. To obtain the most juice, first roll the fruits on a hard surface until you hear the seeds cracking. If you decide to use a juicer, be sure it's a nonmetallic one since the juice will discolor metal.

1-1/4 lbs. pomegranates (about 4)
Cheesecloth

Slice off stem end of pomegranates. Working over a blender or food processor fitted with a metal blade, split fruit into segments and scoop out seeds, discarding the white membrane. Process the seeds until liquified. Strain mixture through a double thickness of cheesecloth into a nonmetal bowl. Bring cheesecloth up around seeds and squeeze to release more juice. Store in a tightly covered jar in refrigerator for up to 1 week or freeze for up to 6 months. Makes about 1 cup juice.

Preparation time: 15 minutes

Variation:
Use this sweet red syrup in drink recipes that call for grenadine.

Pomegranate Syrup: Place 1 cup pomegranate juice and 1/2 cup sugar in an enameled saucepan. Bring to boiling; reduce heat. Simmer, uncovered, for 3 minutes. Skim off froth; remove from heat. Cool. Strain through cheesecloth if a clearer consistency is desired. Chill in a tightly covered jar in refrigerator for up to several weeks or freeze for up to 6 months. Makes about 1 cup.

Varieties:

Green: Lime green on the outside, this variety has a greenish-white interior, sweet flavor.

Orange: The sweetest variety with peachy-orange flesh and a pale orange skin.

Purple: These have purplish skins with deep violet-red flesh and a sweet flavor.

Red: These have a reddish-colored outer skin with crimson-red fruit inside. Less sweet than other varieties available.

Prickly Pear, Avocado & Ham Salad

2 prickly pears
Lettuce leaves
1/4 fresh pineapple, peeled, thinly sliced
1/2 lb. boiled sliced ham, thinly sliced
1 small avocado, pitted, peeled, thinly sliced

To peel prickly pears, wear protective gloves. Using tongs to hold fruit, slice off both ends of fruit. Slit fruit lengthwise and lift out pulp. In a blender or food processor, purée pulp. Arrange lettuce leaves on a large platter. Arrange pineapple on lettuce. Roll ham slices; add to platter with avocado slices. Spoon purée over salad. Makes 3 to 4 servings.

Preparation time: 15 minutes

PRICKLY PEARS

It's amazing how anyone ever discovered the taste of this fruit from the Nopal cactus. Lodged among the prickly thorns and covered with its own, the prickly pear is a very interesting fruit that must literally be treated with gloves to be enjoyed. Fortunately for us, most of the fruit found in markets has been de-spined. Prickly pears have a sweet juicy flavor reminiscent of watermelon. Once peeled, the fruit may be golden or deep red inside, depending on variety, and filled with small edible seeds.

Prickly pears are also called "tuna fruit" "cactus fruit" and "Indian figs." American Indians appreciated prickly pears both for their food value and for medicinal use. The roots were ground for a healing poultice and used to make a diuretic tea. They also used the pads of the nopal cactus; today they are a popular ingredient in southwestern cooking (see Cactus Leaves, page 93). Prickly Pears from California and Mexico are available from September through December and again from March to May.

Buying Tips: Though most of the thorns have been removed during harvest, handle the fruit with caution (most fruit in markets is partially wrapped in tissue for this reason). Fruit should be a uniform egg shape with few blemishes and no soft spots. Fruit should be firm, but not rock-hard, with bright, fresh-looking skins.

Storage: Ripen hard fruit at room temperature; refrigerate slightly softened fruit in crisper for up to several days.

Basic Preparation: Handle fruit with tongs to avoid prickles since the tiniest spikes are difficult to see. Slice off ends of fruit, then slit skin lengthwise. Peel back the skin or remove completely and discard. Enjoy the pulp as is, slice or purée, straining out the seeds. (Note: remove any prickles that become embedded in your skin with tweezers or sticky tape.)

Serving Ideas: Prickly pear pulp is often used in jams and jellies or puréed for fruity sauces. The sliced fruit is attractive on fruit platters or fruit salads. Sprinkle the fruit with lime juice or purée to mix in with whipped cream or ice cream. Add chopped pieces to a fruit compote or toss into a cabbage slaw.

Yield: 1 to 2 prickly pears = 1 serving.
1 lb. prickly pears = about 3 fruits.

Nutrition Facts: There are about 42 calories in a 3-1/2-ounce serving of prickly pear. The fruit is high in potassium and low in sodium.

Tropical Prickly Pear Mousse

Use only canned pineapple juice in this recipe since the fresh juice will prevent the gelatin from setting up.

1 (1/4-oz.) envelope unflavored gelatin (1 tablespoon)
3/4 cup pineapple juice or water
4 prickly pears
1/3 cup sugar
1/8 teaspoon almond extract
Dash salt
1/2 pint heavy cream, whipped (1 cup)

In a medium saucepan, sprinkle gelatin over pineapple juice or water; let stand 5 minutes. To peel prickly pears, wear protective gloves. Using tongs to hold fruit, slice off both ends of fruit. Slit fruit lengthwise and lift out pulp. Chop pulp. In blender or food processor fitted with a metal blade, process pulp until liquified. Strain out seeds. Stir liquid into gelatin mixture with sugar, almond extract and salt. Cook and stir 5 minutes over medium heat to dissolve gelatin. Place in refrigerator; chill 1 to 1-1/4 hours until mixture mounds when dropped from a spoon. With a rubber spatula or whisk, fold in whipped cream until blended (do not stir). Spoon into 4 dessert dishes or long-stemmed goblets; chill several hours or until firm. Makes 4 servings.

Preparation time: 15 minutes

Tropical Prickly Pear Mousse, above.

Varieties:

Pineapple: This round or pear-shaped variety can be as small as a large apple or as large as a grapefruit. It's pale yellow skin has a wooly or fuzzy surface; fruit is white.

Perfumed: An aromatic variety of quince, shaped like a mini-football with smooth skin. Has a fruity taste when cooked.

Smyrna: Quince with a more irregular pear shape; it often has brown indentations on the blossom end which is a normal characteristic. It has the same white flesh.

Ginger Quince Butter

The ingredients are the same as for the pear version, page 66, but the technique is different because of the natural pectin found in quince.

3 lbs. ripe quince, (5 to 6 quinces) peeled, cored, sliced (8 cups)
1-1/2 cups water
1 cup apple juice
3 tablespoons lemon juice
1/2 cup sugar
1/2 cup honey
1 tablespoon grated lemon peel
1 tablespoon chopped gingerroot or 1/2 teaspoon ground ginger
1 teaspoon ground cinnamon
1/2 teaspoon ground nutmeg

In a large saucepan or Dutch oven, combine quince, water, apple juice and lemon juice. Bring to boiling; reduce heat and simmer, partially covered, about 30 minutes or until tender. Stir in sugar, honey, lemon peel, gingerroot, cinnamon and nutmeg. Cook and stir 5 minutes more. In blender or food processor fitted with a metal blade, process mixture in 2 batches until puréed. Cool; turn mixture into freezer or refrigerator containers and cover tightly. Freeze for up to 3 months or refrigerate up to 1 month. Makes 5 cups.

Preparation time: 20 minutes

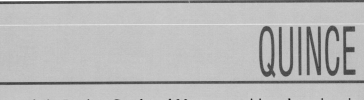

Long a staple in Persian, Greek and Moroccan cuisine, the quince is such an old favorite that one theory pegs it as the original forbidden fruit. Enjoyed before the pyramids were built, quinces were considered a symbol of love and fertility, a gift often exchanged between a bride and groom.

Quinces look like a golden yellow apple or pear, round or pear-shaped, with a knob at one end. But unlike apples or pears, quinces must be cooked or baked to be enjoyed since the fruit is hard and gravelly in texture when raw. Quince contain a natural pectin which makes them ideal for use in preserves and jellies. The fruit turns a beautiful pink color when cooked. Quinces are grown in Mexico, Europe and the U.S. and become available between late August and November.

Buying Tips: Quince should be firm with few blemishes. Most of the fuzz should have been removed. Fruit will be green when unripe, turning to pale yellow all over when ripe.

Storage: Ripen quinces at room temperature (you'll notice they give off a pleasant, fruity aroma). Fruit will turn a pale yellow color, but will not become soft when ripe. Store ripe quinces in the refrigerator to use within a week or 2.

Basic Preparation: Peel and slice quince; remove the seed cavity as you would in an apple or pear. Do not eat raw; cook fruit before eating. Use according to recipes or cook in water to cover until tender, sweetening with honey or sugar as desired.

Serving Ideas: Add raw quince slices to apple pie filling before the pie is baked. Use quince in fruit jellies or preserves. Bake quince whole as you would a pear or an apple; sweeten with brown sugar to use as a dessert or an accompaniment to roast pork. Add quince to meaty stews or use in meat fillings to stuff squash. Purée cooked quince to add to puddings, fruit fillings or to use in sauces.

Yield: About 3 quinces = 1 lb.
1 baked quince = 1 serving.
1 lb. quince = 3 to 4 cups sliced fruit.

Nutrition Facts: 3-1/2 ounces of cooked quince has about 55 calories. It is high in vitamin C, calcium, potassium, and phosphorus.

SAPOTES

(suh-PO-tays) Sapotes are one of the most delicious tropical fruits known. Cultivated in South America and Mexico, the "custard apple" as it is often called, has a smooth, creamy pulp that is easily digestible. The sweet, slightly tart taste is a combination of apricot and banana flavors. Soft sapotes mash easily for use in pie fillings, desserts and breads.

The white sapote is the most common variety available. About the size of an apple with an oval shape, the sapote has a smooth, pale green to dark green skin with a brownish hue. The fruit inside is creamy ivory-yellow with several small black seeds in the center. Bite into the soft fruit for a sweet snack or preserve the pulp in a fruit jam. Sapotes also have a superb aroma that will remind you of pears and apricots. Sapotes are available from August through November.

Buying Tips: Sapotes should be plump, free of sunken spots or bruises and tears in the skin. The fruit is harvested while still very firm, but sapotes ripen easily at room temperature. If the fruit is very soft when you buy it, plan to use it within a day or two.

Storage: Ripen sapotes at room temperature until they are as ripe as a soft pear. Refrigerate soft sapotes to use within a few days. Sapotes do not freeze well.

Basic Preparation: Eat a ripe sapote as you would an apple, peeling if desired, and discarding the seed-filled center core. Slice the fruit to use on fruit platters or to top with whipped cream. Or use the soft pulp as you would mashed banana in recipes. Note that cut sapote will turn brown on standing; treat with lemon juice to preserve the color.

Serving Ideas: Enjoy sapote mixed in a compote with citrus fruits, tossed with vanilla-flavored yogurt or spread on bread like an instant fruit spread. Use the pulp in recipes as you would puréed fruit such as in pie or cake fillings, gelatin desserts or blended fruit drinks. Sapote pulp goes easily into jams or preserves for enjoyment all during the year.

Yield: 1 sapote = 1 serving.
About 2 sapotes = 1 cup mashed pulp.

Nutrition Facts: Calorie count is approximately 120 calories for 1 small sapote. The fruit is a fair source of vitamins A and C.

Sharon's Sapote-Fruit Jam

Spread this treat on toast and peanut butter sandwiches or spoon on ice cream.

3 to 4 ripe sapotes
2 cups chopped fresh peaches
1 cup crushed pineapple
1 cup cranberry juice
1 (1-3/4-oz.) box powdered pectin
3 cups sugar
1/4 teaspoon ground cinnamon
1/8 teaspoon ground nutmeg

Peel sapotes; halve fruit and remove pits. Transfer mixture to a large saucepan; stir in cranberry juice and pectin. Bring to boiling. Stir in sugar and spices. Boil 4 minutes, stirring constantly, at a full rolling boil. Remove from heat; allow mixture to settle. Cool 15 minutes, stirring every 5 minutes. Pour into sterilized jars; seal. Makes 3 pints.

Preparation time: 30 minutes

Sapotes Grand Marnier

Very ripe sapotes take on a velvety, sorbet-like texture in this spur-of-the-moment dessert.

4 very ripe sapotes
1/4 cup Grand Marnier or orange liqueur
Fresh mint sprigs, if desired

About 30 minutes to 1 hour before serving, place 1 sapote in each of 4 long-stemmed glasses. With a small paring knife, carefully cut a small circle around top of fruit. Spoon 1 tablespoon Grand Marnier over each sapote. Place in freezer until serving time. To serve, garnish with mint sprigs. Makes 4 servings.

Preparation time: 5 minutes

Varieties:

Dried Starfruit: Sun-dried slices of starfruit taste like raisins and apricots; fruit is very sweet.

Fresh Starfruit: Fruit is deeply grooved and elongated. Outer skin is brilliant golden-yellow; the fruit inside is juicy with a texture similar to plums. Flavor varies from sweet-tart to very sweet.

Exotic Ambrosia Salad

Prepare this salad year-round by substituting in-season fruits.

Lettuce leaves
1 papaya, peeled, seeded, cut into 1-inch chunks
1 starfruit or Kiwano, sliced 1/4-inch thick
2 kiwifruit, peeled, sliced
1 cup halved strawberries or other whole berries

Sour Cream-Coconut Dressing
1/2 cup dairy sour cream
1 to 2 tablespoons honey
1/4 teaspoon ground cardamom or nutmeg
1 to 2 tablespoons toasted shredded coconut

Arrange lettuce leaves on a salad platter. Arrange papaya chunks, starfruit slices, kiwi slices and berries on lettuce. Prepare Sour Cream-Coconut Dressing; pass with salad. If preparing ahead, cover salad and dressing. Refrigerate up to 24 hours. Makes 5 to 6 servings.

Sour Cream-Coconut Dressing:
In a small bowl, stir together sour cream, honey, cardomom or nutmeg and coconut until well mixed Makes about 1/2 cup.

Preparation time: 15 minutes

STARFRUIT/CARAMBOLA

(Care-ahm-BOWL-ah) Northerners who travel to tropical countries are always amazed to see starfruit (also called "carambola" or "star apple") hanging from the trees like Christmas ornaments. This bright, golden-yellow, blimp-shaped fruit is 4 to 6 inches long with a deeply ribbed surface. Starfruit gets its unusual name because when the fruit is sliced crosswise, the slices have a distinctive star shape.

Southern Chinese cultures and India have enjoyed starfruit for centuries. Some varieties of starfruit are sweeter than others; the flavor is a juicy combination of plums, pineapples and lemons. Starfruit makes a beautiful fresh fruit garnish for desserts as well as entrées and can be enjoyed raw or sautéed. Virtually all of the U.S. supply comes from Florida, but the fruit is also cultivated in South Africa, Brazil, Israel and Thailand. Starfruit can be found in markets in late summer, through fall and the holiday season.

Buying Tips: Look for fruit with shiny skins, good shape and firm texture. Starfruit ripens easily at home, so fruit that is tinged with green will turn bright yellow when ripened. Fruit that is glowing yellow is ready to eat.

Storage: Store fruit at room temperature if very firm and slightly green until fruit is golden-yellow overall. Refrigerate yellow, softened fruit to use within 5 days. Do not freeze starfruit.

Basic Preparation: Peeling starfruit is not necessary. Slice fruit crosswise into thin slices to eat as is or to use in recipes. Fruit can be chopped, cut into sticks or puréed. Remove the small seeds in the center; they are inedible. Substitute starfruit for other fruit in recipes.

Serving Ideas: Use starfruit to garnish roast poultry or ham for a holiday touch. Or slit a starfruit slice to slip over the rim of a champagne or cocktail glass to garnish. Sliced starfruit looks beautiful placed on a fruit tart, frosted cakes, cream pies and fruit platters. Chop semi-ripe carambola for chutneys or pickles. Use sweet carambola for preserves or jellies. Or add pieces of starfruit to stir-fried vegetables or chicken.

Yield: 1 medium starfruit = 1 serving.
1 lb. starfruit = 2 large or 3 medium starfruit.
1 large starfruit = about 1 cup sliced fruit.

Nutrition Facts: About 1/2 cup of sliced starfruit is less than 40 calories. It's a great source of vitamin C.

Tortellini New Zealand-Style

Purchase the tortellini either dried or fresh; the fresh is sold in the supermarket dairy case.

8 oz. spinach or egg tortellini
2 cups shredded lettuce
1 cup chopped cooked ham, chicken or shrimp
3 kiwi fruit, peeled, halved, sliced
1 (11-oz.) can mandarin oranges, drained
1 fresh starfruit, if desired, thinly sliced
1/2 cup diced celery

Creamy French Dressing:
1/4 cup bottled French dressing
1/4 cup dairy sour cream

Prepare Creamy French Dressing. In a large saucepan, cook tortellini according to package directions; drain. Rinse in cold water and drain again. On a serving platter or 2 individual dinner plates, arrange shredded lettuce. In a large bowl, toss together pasta, ham, chicken, kiwifruit, oranges, starfruit, if desired, and celery. Toss dressing with salad to coat. Spoon over lettuce and serve. Makes 2 main-dish servings.

Creamy French Dressing:
In a small bowl, whisk together French dressing and sour cream until well mixed. Makes 1/2 cup.

Preparation time: 15 minutes

Starfruit Snack Mix

Sprinkle this mix over breakfast cereal, ice cream, fresh fruit or mix into freshly popped popcorn. Or eat just as it is for a healthy, energizing snack.

1 (4-oz.) pkg. dried starfruit
2/3 cup peanuts or cashews
1 cup slivered dried apricots, pears or apples
1/2 cup flaked coconut

In a medium bowl, toss together dried starfruit, peanuts or cashews, desired dried fruit and coconut until well mixed. Store in a tightly covered container up to 1 month. Makes about 3 cups mix.

Preparation time: 5 minutes

Cherimoya-Pineapple Sorbet, page 30; Tortellini New Zealand-Style, above.

Varieties:

Red Tamarillo: With brilliant red skin and deep-red pulp. Both skin and fruit turns yellow when heated. Slightly acidic, mildly sweet flavor. Red is the most common variety.

Yellow Tamarillo: Has golden-yellow, smooth skin and yellow fruit; flavor is considered milder and sweeter.

Lamb Chops With Tamarillo Relish

Tamarillos are the basis for this piquant fruit relish that will grace pork, beef and ribs, too.

4 tamarillos
1 tablespoon vegetable oil
1/2 cup sliced onions
1 clove garlic, minced
1/3 cup orange juice or water
2 tablespoons vinegar
1/4 cup packed brown sugar
1/2 teaspoon salt
1/8 teaspoon pepper
Dash cayenne pepper, if desired
8 lamb rib chops

Preheat broiler. To peel tamarillos, pour boiling water over fruit; remove skins and stems. Slice fruit. In a large skillet, heat oil. Sauté sliced tamarillos with onions and garlic about 3 minutes or until onions are tender. Stir in orange juice or water, vinegar, brown sugar, salt, pepper and cayenne pepper, if desired. Reduce heat and simmer, uncovered, 10 minutes. Meanwhile, broil lamb chops 4 inches from heat for 9 to 11 minutes for medium-rare, turning once. Spoon tamarillo sauce over chops. Makes 4 servings.

Preparation time: 20 minutes

TAMARILLOS

(TAM-ah-RILL-ohs) With their shiny, brilliant red skins and green stems, these subtropical fruits are sometimes called tree tomatoes, but the comparison ends there. Originally cultivated in South America and Southern Africa, tamarillos are now appearing in markets as a New Zealand import.

The size and shape of a jumbo egg, tamarillos' glossy outer skin hides crimson-red fruit that turns golden when cooked or heated. Along with the red tamarillo, there is a golden-skinned variety with bright yellow fruit. Both types have a soft, pulpy center filled with tiny edible seeds that are arranged like tomato seeds. Tamarillos have a sweet-tart taste of apples and bananas, so most people like to sprinkle them with sugar to enjoy the fruit. Peeling is necessary since the skins are bitter. Tamarillos are available sporadically during the year, but are most often seen in markets between April and October.

Buying Tips: When ripe, a tamarillo should be firm, but will feel slightly soft to the touch. The stem turns from green to brown as the fruit ripens. Skins should be smooth, brilliantly colored for the variety and unblemished.

Storage: Tamarillos will soften if kept at room temperature, like avocados. Store ripe tamarillos in your refrigerator crisper for up to 3 weeks. Tamarillos freeze well if unpeeled and stored as chopped or puréed fruit in an airtight container, for up to 1 year.

Basic Preparation: Tamarillos must be peeled to enjoy the fruit. To remove the peel, pour boiling water over the fruit. Allow fruit to stand 3 to 5 minutes (the skins will turn yellow from the heat) then slip off the peel and remove stems. Slice or chop fruit to eat; sprinkle with sugar or honey to taste. Purée the fruit, sweeten to taste and use in recipes as desired.

Serving Ideas: When sliced or puréed tamarillos are sprinkled with sugar and refrigerated for several hours, the fruit and juice become a delightful sauce. Use it over ice cream or as the basis for a fruit sauce for pork or poultry. Tamarillos can be stewed and baked with a roast or stuffed into cooked vegetables. Use the fruit in jellies, preserves or for pickling. Add to fruity tropical drinks or mix the pulp with mashed banana to add to cake or quickbread batters.

Yield: 1 tamarillo = 1 serving.
1 lb. tamarillos = about 5 medium fruit.
1 lb. tamarillos = 2 cups chopped or sliced fruit.

Nutrition Facts: One tamarillo contains about 36 calories, with as much vitamin A and C as tomatoes and oranges. Tamarillos are also rich in iron, and are an excellent source of fiber.

TAMARINDOS

(TAM-ahr-IN-dohs) A native of the African tropics, India and Southern Asia, the large evergreen tamarind tree has been cultivated since prehistoric times. The tree blooms with beautiful yellow flowers that bear the tamarind fruit, long brown pods filled with large seeds and a flavorful pulp. The flat pods may be 3 to 7 inches long and the shells become brown and brittle as the fruit ripens. During the ripening process, the fruit inside becomes dehydrated and the sticky brown pulp that results is almost date-like in consistency.

Tamarind pods found in markets may be cracked and splitting with the pods and pulp exposed, but once you become acquainted with the flavorful taste of tamarindos, you won't be put off by its appearance. Tamarind tastes strongly of apricots, dates and lemons. The pulp can be eaten raw, but its best use is as a flavorful base for cooling drinks, sauces and chutneys. Latin natives insist that enzymes in tamarindos help counteract the heat. Indians use the pulp frequently to add a fruitful kick to curried dishes. Available all year.

Buying Tips: It's best not to be too fussy about the appearance of the tamarindo; as described above, the shells may be cracked or missing from some of the pulp inside. The pulp will be filled with large seeds and long fibers. Do not buy pods that have mold on them; otherwise, tamarindos last a long time.

Storage: Tamarind pods can be stored at room temperature for up to 1 year, if tightly wrapped. Tamarind pulp can be refrigerated or frozen for 6 months to 1 year.

Basic Preparation: Crack open the brittle shells and peel back from the seeds and pulp. Peel off the long strings or fibers and cut the pulp away from the seeds. The best way to enjoy the pulp is to make a flavorful concentrate from the pulp to add the tamarind character to recipes. For a concentrate, discard the seeds; soak the pulp in very hot water to cover for several hours. Press out all juice from the pulp. Strain the mixture into a bowl. Use this concentrate in recipes or add to fruit juice to flavor. See the suggestions below.

Serving Ideas: Use tamarindo concentrate in recipes for curried meat dishes, in fruit salad dressings, tropical fruit drinks or to pep up lemonade or iced tea. The concentrate can also be stirred into fresh fruit mixtures, ice cream and soft cheeses for a flavor punch. It also makes an excellent marinade for chicken or fish.

Yield: 1/2 lb. tamarindos + 3 cups hot water = 3 cups concentrate

Nutrition Facts: Tamarindos contain higher amounts of calcium than any other fruit. They are also generous in B vitamins and phosphorous.

Tamarindo Chicken With Peaches

Allow time ahead to soak the tamarindo pods and marinate the chicken.

6 tamarindos, shelled
2 tablespoons hot tap water
1/2 cup chicken broth
Dash hot pepper sauce
1 teaspoon cornstarch
About 1/4 cup peanut oil or vegetable oil
4 chicken breasts, skinned, boned, cut into bite-sized strips
1 tablespoon minced fresh gingerroot
1 clove garlic, finely chopped
2 fresh peaches or nectarines, peeled, pitted, thinly sliced
3 green onions, sliced
Dash hot-pepper sauce
Hot cooked rice

Remove strings from tamarindo pulp; place pulp in hot water for 15 minutes. With the back of a spoon, smash pulp in liquid to release juices and loose pulp. Discard skin and seeds. Place chicken pieces in a shallow dish; spoon tamarindo extract over chicken. Cover and chill for 1 to 24 hours. Stir together broth, hot pepper sauce and cornstarch. Set aside. In wok or large skillet, heat 2 tablespoons of oil; stir-fry chicken pieces with gingerroot and garlic about 3 minutes or until plump. Remove from wok. Add a little more oil, if necessary; stir-fry peaches or nectarines with green onions for 2 minutes. Remove from skillet. Stir broth mixture; pour into center of wok. Cook and stir until mixture bubbles. Add chicken and peaches back to pan; toss to coat with sauce. Cover and heat through 1 minute more. Serve with rice. Makes 4 servings.

Preparation time: 20 minutes

VEGETABLES

Vegetables. See diagram, page 156.

ARTICHOKES

This unusual vegetable is actually a very large bud from the thistle-like artichoke plant, harvested before it has a chance to bloom. Lovingly cultivated in the Mediterranean for thousands of years, artichokes were introduced to America by Italians and Spaniards. Once it was discovered that artichokes adapted well to California coastal regions (mainly around Castroville, the artichoke capital of the world), the vegetable became readily available in markets across the U.S. Peak season is in the spring and fall.

Buying Tips: In spring and summer, look for artichokes with an all over green coloring. Avoid bruised or damaged artichokes. In the fall and winter months, frost on the leaves sometimes causes browning or blistering on the leaf tips; however, these artichokes are often considered the most flavorful and tender. Artichokes should be firm, well-shaped and heavy for their size.

Storage: Artichokes store very well for up to a full two weeks. Do not wash artichokes, but sprinkle them with a few drops of water; then seal airtight in plastic bags in the refrigerator.

Basic Preparation: To cook whole artichokes (medium to large sizes), pull off lower outer petals; cut stems to 1 inch. Snip off all leaf tips. Dip all cut edges in a lemon juice and water solution. Boil or steam whole artichokes in lemon juice and water 20 to 40 minutes or until a center petal pulls out easily. Or wrap artichoke in plastic wrap, and microwave on High (100%) power for 6 to 8 minutes, depending on size. Let stand 5 minutes; check for doneness by pulling out one of the petals.

To cook baby artichokes, remove outer lower petals and cut off top third of artichoke, just below green tips of petals. Trim off the dark green areas from the bases of the artichokes. Spoon out any pink or purple leaves, and the small fuzzy chokes. Cook as directed for larger artichokes, or sauté halves or quarters 5 minutes in a small amount of oil.

Serving Ideas: Eat whole large artichokes with a variety of savory dips and dressings, for an appetizer or first course. Stuff the leaves of whole artichokes, or halved artichokes (with the choke removed), with meat, seafood or vegetable mixtures. Marinate any size artichoke in bottled Italian or homemade vinegar-oil-herb dressing, or quarter artichokes and deep-fry in a tempura-style batter.

Yield: 1 medium (1/2-lb.) artichoke = 1 serving.
2 large (1-lb.) artichokes provide 6 to 8 appetizer servings.

Nutrition Facts: 1 medium artichoke, served au natural, has only 25 calories. Artichokes are high in fiber and minerals, and contain about 75 milligrams of sodium per 12-ounce serving.

Varieties:

Baby Artichoke: Sized 2 inches or less in diameter; this miniature artichoke has a very small choke, or fuzzy center, and is completely edible when trimmed. Can be used in entrées or as an appetizer or side-dish.

Globe: This is the name for the American variety, which is available in a very large and a medium size. The larger artichokes are perfect for stuffing, and can weigh as much as a pound. Medium-sized artichokes are a good size for appetizers and side-dish recipes.

Eating Tips:

Artichokes are very simple to prepare, and fun to eat, but they are not a vegetable to be consumed quickly. There is an art to enjoying an artichoke. The stiff leaves of this edible thistle have a small amount of delicious "meat" at their bases. To enjoy it, the eater must draw each leaf between the teeth to remove the soft underside, a slightly nutty, delicately flavored morsel. The rest of the leaf is discarded. Once all the leaves have been eaten, what's left is a purple-tipped cone that covers the heart of the artichoke. Remove and discard the cone portion, with its fuzzy hair-like base. Cut up the heart to enjoy. Usually the leaves and heart are dipped in melted butter, hollandaise sauce or other dips to enhance the flavor.

Shrimp-Stuffed Artichokes

Serve this special-occasion dish as an hors d'oeuvre or main course. (photo on page 83.)

4 medium artichokes, washed
Lemon juice
2 tablespoons vegetable oil
2 leeks, sliced (white part only), or 1/2 medium onion, sliced
2 cups chopped fresh mushrooms
1 green or red bell pepper, chopped
2 garlic cloves, finely chopped
1 lb. cooked baby shrimp, thawed if frozen
1 large tomato, chopped
Salt and pepper to taste
1/3 cup seasoned bread crumbs
1/3 cup grated Parmesan cheese

Cut stems level with bottom of artichokes. Remove small bottom leaves; slice off top quarter of artichokes. Dip tips of artichoke in lemon juice. Stand upright in a nonaluminum or noncast-iron pan with 2 inches of water. Bring to boiling; cover and simmer 30 to 40 minutes or until a leaf pulls out easily. Drain upside down. When cool enough to handle, cut artichokes in half from top to stem. Remove fuzzy choke and heart. Discard choke; chop hearts. In a large skillet, heat oil. Sauté leeks, mushrooms, bell pepper and garlic 3 minutes. Stir in shrimp, tomato, chopped artichoke hearts and salt and pepper to taste. Cook 2 minutes more or until heated through. Preheat broiler. Spoon shrimp mixture into artichoke halves, mounding on top. In a small bowl, stir together bread crumbs and Parmesan cheese; sprinkle over filling. Place under broiler 1 to 2 minutes or until crumbs are golden. Serve hot. Makes 8 appetizer servings or 4 main-dish servings.

Preparation time: 25 minutes

Cheese-Stuffed Artichoke Bottoms

Enjoy these warm or chilled.

6 to 8 artichoke bottoms, cooked
1 (3-oz.) pkg. cream cheese, softened
1/4 cup crumbled blue cheese
2 tablespoons milk
1 tablespoon finely chopped pimiento
1 tablespoon minced green onion
1/8 teaspoon salt
1/8 teaspoon pepper
Pimiento strips, if desired

If serving artichokes warm, preheat oven to 350F (175C). Place artichoke bottoms on a heatproof platter. In a small bowl, beat together cream cheese, blue cheese, milk, chopped pimiento, onion, salt and pepper until well mixed. Spoon 1 to 2 tablespoons mixture into center of each artichoke bottom. If preparing in advance, cover and chill in refrigerator up to 24 hours. If desired, place in oven 10 to 15 minutes or until heated through. Garnish each with a curled pimiento strip, if desired. Makes 6 to 8 appetizers.

Preparation time: 10 minutes

Artichokes with Curry-Mustard Mayonnaise

See "Basic Preparation" for tips on cooking artichokes in the microwave oven.

4 fresh medium artichokes, washed
Lemon juice

Curry-Mustard Mayonnaise:
1 cup plus 1 tablespoon vegetable oil
1 tablespoon curry powder
1/8 teaspoon cumin
1 egg
2 tablespoons lemon juice
1 teaspoon Dijon-style mustard
1/4 teaspoon salt
1/8 teaspoon pepper

Pull off lower petals of artichokes; cut stems to 1 inch or less. Slice off top quarter of each artichoke. Snip off tips of lower petals; brush all cut edges with lemon juice. Place artichokes snugly in a Dutch oven or large saucepan; fill pan with water 3 inches deep. Add 1 tablespoon lemon juice. Cover; bring to boiling. Reduce heat and simmer 25 to 35 minutes or until a petal pulls out easily. Drain upside down on paper towels. Meanwhile, prepare Curry-Mustard Mayonnaise. When artichokes are cool enough to handle, turn upright and serve with mayonnaise. If preparing in advance, cover mayonnaise and wrap artichokes individually in plastic wrap; chill in refrigerator up to 24 hours. Makes 4 servings.

Curry-Mustard Mayonnaise:
In a blender or food processor fitted with a metal blade, process 1 tablespoon of oil, curry, cumin, egg, lemon juice, mustard, salt and pepper until blended. With machine running at high speed, pour in 1 cup of oil in a thin stream until all oil is added. Makes about 1 cup.

Preparation time: 15 minutes

ASPARAGUS

As if to herald the coming of spring, the long, slender stalks of fresh green asparagus appear in markets, as beautiful as they are delicious. Asparagus connoisseurs argue about whether fat or thin stalks of fresh asparagus make better eating. One argument says that fatter stalks are more likely to be tender because they contain more pulp; while others counter that thinner stalks of asparagus are easier to cook properly, and so retain a more tender, flavorful quality. Whatever your preference, you'll find this delicate member of the lily family a royal treat to be savored whenever spring appears.

Buying Tips: Look for firm, straight green or creamy white spears with closed, compact tips or buds. Purchase spears of uniform thickness, either thick or thin, so that asparagus will cook uniformly. Early green asparagus will have purplish buds that turn a brilliant green when cooked.

Storage: It's very important to keep the stem ends moist, so store asparagus upright, if possible, in about 1/2 inch of water in your refrigerator. Or store asparagus lying on the refrigerator shelf, ends wrapped in wet paper toweling, and covered in a plastic bag. Asparagus can be blanched just till green, and frozen in moisture-proof containers for up to 10 months.

Basic Preparation: Cooks often snap off the bottom portion of asparagus and discard the tough stems. But the bottom portion of the stems will cook tender if the stalk is peeled off. Peel just the bottom two inches of the stalks; and place the asparagus in a steamer basket over boiling water, or in a skillet filled with simmering water. It's not necessary to tie the asparagus in bunches; cooking the stalks loose permits even cooking. Cook asparagus just until nearly tender, about 4 to 8 minutes, depending on thickness. To steam fat asparagus, stand the spears upright in a tall saucepan so that the thick stems will cook in about the same time as the buds.

To microwave asparagus, place in a shallow dish with 1/4 cup water. Cover with plastic wrap, leaving one corner uncovered for steam to escape; cook 2 to 4 minutes, turning dish once.

Serving Ideas: Cooked asparagus is typically served drizzled with butter and seasoned with herbs and garlic, or covered in hollandaise sauce or cheese sauce. Asparagus can also be cut up and tossed into stir-fried vegetables and meats, steamed vegetable mixtures, soups and quiches. Purée asparagus for sauces or a creamy bisque. Use chilled cooked asparagus as an appetizer dipper.

Yield: 1 lb. asparagus = 12 to 14 spears.
1/2 lb. asparagus = 1 serving.
1 lb. asparagus = about 2-1/2 cups cut-up.

Nutrition Facts: Asparagus, unadorned with butter, is low in calories, about 55 calories per 1/2 pound serving. Asparagus also offers a generous amount of potassium and vitamin A.

Varieties:

Green: The most common variety of asparagus with medium green stalks and purplish-green tips.

White: Very light green to creamy white spears that turn white when steamed or blanched. A European variety, white asparagus has a more delicate flavor and tender texture.

Asparagus Bundles with Lemon Butter

Use these pretty, delectable bundles to garnish a meat platter.

4 green onions, green stems intact
1-1/2 lbs. fresh asparagus

Lemon Butter:
1/3 cup butter or margarine
2 tablespoons lemon juice
1 teaspoon grated lemon peel
Dash pepper

Cut green stems from onions; reserve white portions for another use. Slit stems lengthwise in 1/4-inch-wide strips. Dip strips in boiling water a few seconds or until limp; drain on paper towels. Break off bottom 2 inches of asparagus stems; discard. Using 1 or 2 of green onion strips, tie 3 stalks of asparagus together. Repeat until all asparagus are used. Place a steamer basket into a 12-inch skillet or wok; add 1 inch of water to bottom of pan. Bring to simmering; add asparagus. Cover and steam 7 to 8 minutes or until tender. Prepare Lemon Butter. Arrange asparagus bundles on platter; drizzle with Lemon Butter. Makes 4 to 5 servings.

Lemon Butter:
In a small saucepan, melt butter with lemon juice, lemon peel, and pepper. Makes about 1/2 cup.

Preparation time: 15 minutes

Asparagus-Pâté Rafts

Prepare these elegant hors d'oeuvres on a moment's notice, or add them to an open-faced sandwich platter.

1 lb. asparagus
5 slices sandwich bread
2 tablespoons softened butter or margarine
1 (4- or 4.5-oz.) can pâté

Break off bottom 1-inch of asparagus spears; cut in 2-inch pieces. Steam asparagus over simmering water 5 minutes; drain. Toast bread slices until golden; cut diagonally in quarters. Arrange on a serving plate or tray. Spread bread triangles with butter or margarine. Spread pâté over each piece. Arrange 2 asparagus pieces on each bread piece. Makes 20 appetizers.

Preparation time: 15 minutes

Pasta with Asparagus & Ham

For an easy main dish, toss in double the amount of ham, or substitute any leftover chopped cooked meat or poultry.

4 oz. linguine, fettucine or spaghetti
1/2 lb. asparagus, cut in 1-inch pieces
1/4 cup butter or margarine
1 garlic clove, finely chopped
1/4 cup dry white wine
2 tablespoons chopped fresh parsley
1/4 teaspoon pepper
1 (4 oz.) pkg. cooked sliced ham, cut in julienne strips
1/2 cup chopped pecans or walnuts
2 tablespoons grated Parmesan cheese

Cook pasta according to package directions and drain. Meanwhile, steam asparagus over simmering water 5 minutes. In same pan used to cook pasta, melt butter. Sauté asparagus and garlic 2 minutes. Stir in wine, parsley and pepper. Bring to a boil; reduce heat and simmer 1 minute. Add cooked pasta, ham and pecans. Toss well to coat with sauce. Serve at once sprinkled with Parmesan cheese. Makes 4 servings.

Preparation time: 20 minutes

Artichokes & Asparagus. Clockwise from top right: Globe artichokes, Shrimp Stuffed Artichokes, page 81, White asparagus, Green asparagus, Baby artichokes.

BABY VEGETABLES

A plethora of miniature vegetable favorites is now available in produce markets and farmer's markets today. These baby vegetables are sometimes harvested simply by picking them in the early developmental stages. Others are genetic hybrids, bred to be true miniatures, as perfectly formed as their full-size counterparts.

Baby vegetables, because they are picked early, have a great fresh flavor and are generally more tender and delicately-flavored than the larger varieties. Most do not need peeling simply because they are so young; even the tender tops and roots, in many cases, are deliciously edible.

First cultivated in France and enjoyed in European restaurants, many varieties of baby vegetables are available for home cooks at different times of year. These attractive miniatures are more expensive than larger vegetables, but should continue to decline in price as supplies increase.

Buying Tips: Baby vegetables as a whole are easily bruised and highly perishable. Buy them in mint condition, plump, firm and with unblemished skins and bright green caps, if applicable.

Storage: Store them in your refrigerator crisper in plastic bags; use within a few days. For freezing, follow instructions given in sections for the adult-sized versions.

Basic Preparation: All vegetables listed above except corn, eggplant, and potatoes can be enjoyed raw, as vegetable dippers or out-of-hand snacks. Steam baby vegetables or simmer gently in boiling water just until tender. Or microwave vegetables in a small amount of water, loosely covered with plastic wrap, just until nearly tender. Serve cooked vegetables drizzled with butter or lemon juice and sprinkled with chopped herbs.

Serving Ideas: Baby vegetables look very attractive lightly steamed and served as a unique side dish to a main course. Serve baby lettuces as the basis for a conversation-piece salad. Use baby carrots, turnips, beets, cauliflower, kohlrabi, broccoli or corn to garnish a roast or seafood platter; or cook and chill to accent salads or a cold vegetable side dish. Serve steamed baby potatoes, eggplant or beans sauced just as you would the larger types, or serve with dips as an appetizer. Marinate vegetables for a cold salad or add vegetables to soup or stew.

Yield: 1/4 to 1/3 lb. baby vegetables = 1 serving.

Nutrition Facts: Specifics on baby varieties are not known; assume the same benefits as those found in the adult versions.

Varieties:

Baby Artichokes: (see Artichokes, page 80).

Baby Beans: Green snap, yellow wax and purple-podded beans come in miniatures.

Baby Beets: Small tender beets in golden and red varieties that can be enjoyed raw.

Baby Broccoli: Small heads of broccoli with deep green leaves.

Baby Cauliflower: In purple and white varieties; leaves at stem.

Baby Corn: Complete with husk and white silks, this mini-corn tastes as sweet as the big guys.

Baby Eggplant: *Baby Japanese Eggplant,* a miniature purple variety, is cultivated along with *Casper,* a round white baby eggplant, and *Easter Egg,* an egg-shaped variety with white skin and meat. *Thai Eggplant* is purple-skinned or green and white, with a round shape. All have a slightly spicier flavor than purple eggplant.

Baby French or Finger Carrots: Slender carrots about 3 to 5 inches long with fluffy green tops.

Baby Kohlrabi: In green and purple varieties, this baby looks and cooks just like its parents.

Baby Lettuce: Miniature baby green lettuce, bibb lettuce, red-leafed radicchio and bok choy are all available.

Baby Potatoes: Small Texas Finger and red rose potatoes all come baby-sized.

Baby Round or Planet Carrots: Small round carrots about the size of a small red radish with green tops.

Baby Turnips: In both white, purple-topped and rose-colored varieties, baby turnips have tender green leaves and roots, all edible raw or cooked.

Baby Vegetables with Spinach Dip

If you're weary of the same old vegetable appetizer platter, this is a beautiful change.

Lettuce leaves
2 lbs. assorted baby vegetables, trimmed, steamed, chilled

Spinach Dip:
2 cups packed fresh spinach leaves, chopped
1 cup mayonnaise or salad dressing
1/2 cup dairy sour cream
1 tablespoon chopped fresh basil or 1 teaspoon dried leaf basil
1 tablespoon chopped fresh dill or 1 teaspoon dill weed
1 teaspoon Dijon-style mustard
1/4 teaspoon Worcestershire sauce

Prepare Spinach Dip. Spoon dip into a small dish. Arrange lettuce leaves on a serving platter; place dip in center. Arrange baby vegetables on platter and serve. Makes 6 to 8 appetizer servings.

Spinach Dip:
In a medium saucepan, steam spinach over simmering water 2 minutes. Drain well, place on paper towels. Squeeze out all excess moisture. In a blender or food processor fitted with a metal blade, process mayonnaise, sour cream, spinach, herbs, mustard and Worcestershire sauce until smooth. If preparing in advance, cover and refrigerate up to 2 days. Makes 1-3/4 cups.

Preparation time: 15 minutes

Tip:
Vegetable shells make colorful containers for dips and spreads. Try a red or yellow bell pepper, acorn squash half, large whole mushroom caps, red cabbage leaf cups or a large red tomato with a scalloped edge. Save vegetable tops if it's appropriate, such as the top and stem of a bell pepper, for a whimsical "cover" for the dip.

Baby Vegetables. See diagram, page 156.

BEANS

Whether a bean is a snap bean, pod bean, shell bean or a dried bean is determined by its stage of development. Green beans and yellow wax beans are harvested at a very early stage and are actually the undeveloped pods of the bean. Shell beans, like kidney, long beans and cranberry beans, are the mature fresh seed; dried beans are the seeds which have dried in the pod.

Buying Tips: Look for good color, plumpness, and a fresh-looking, velvety coat on green or yellow snap beans. Pods should be free of wrinkles, rust (brown streaks or spots) and dryness. Heavy pods with very well-defined beans are likely to be old and tough. Select shelled beans that are plump, fresh-looking and devoid of brown spots.

Storage: Store fresh beans (snap beans or shelled) tightly wrapped in plastic bags in your refrigerator crisper (exception: sea beans should be wrapped loosely in moist paper towelling; plastic breaks down the texture of these beans). Use within a few days, particularly shelled beans. Field-ripened beans such as black-eyed peas and garbanzos can be stored in the refrigerator for up to 2 weeks before cooking.

Basic Preparation: Shelled fava beans must be peeled after cooking; slit the skin on one side of each bean and slip off peel. Chinese long beans, haricot verts and purple wax beans need only have their stems snapped off; cook whole or cut into 1-inch lengths. Cook sea beans as they are; prepare field-ripened black-eyed peas and garbanzos according to package directions. Steam, blanch or sauté snap beans or shelled beans. Cook with boiling water or sauté in oil or butter until nearly tender, about 2 to 4 minutes for thin varieties like haricot verts and Chinese long and 5 to 7 minutes for snap beans and shelled beans.

Serving Ideas: Try filling an omelet with cut Chinese long beans. Add them to a stir-fry or sauté them with red bell peppers and onions. Add cold cooked beans to a roast beef or smoked turkey salad, or use as a dipper on a cold vegetable platter. Sauce beans with a light cheese sauce, an herbed vinaigrette or a creamy salad dressing.

Yield: 1 lb. green snap, yellow snap, purple wax or haricots verts = 4 servings or about 4 cups cut up.
1 11-oz. package field-ripened black-eyed peas and garbanzos = 2 to 3 servings.
1/4 lb. shelled or 3/4 to 1 lb. unshelled beans (cranberry beans, fava beans and winged beans) = 1 serving.
2 lbs. beans in the shell = about 2 cups shelled beans.

Nutrition Facts: Black-eyed peas, garbanzos and winged beans contain lots of protein. Snap beans average 35 calories per 1 cup serving and are generous in minerals and A and B vitamins. High-protein beans average 200 calories per 1 cup serving.

Unusual Varieties:

Black-Eyed Peas: Normally found dried, black-eyed peas are now available in bags as a field-ripened product. The beans do not have to be soaked; they are ready to cook. Black-eyed peas are more like beans than peas, high in protein and a favorite in southern cooking. Can be served as a main dish.

Chinese Long Beans: Also called "yard long" beans or "asparagus" beans, these slender beans are normally about 1-1/2 feet long. These tender green beans from the Orient cook up very quickly, have a mild green bean taste and are good served hot or chilled.

Cranberry Beans: Pretty cranberry and white-streaked beans, also called "coco beans" in France, are shelling beans. These beans are not related to the cranberry. The thick pods house beans with a nut-like flavor that turn white when cooked. Considered the best bean for succotash by New England cooks.

Fava Beans: An Italian import, Fava beans are housed in a very large, pale green pod, lined with a soft, white interior that cushions the large round beans. If very fresh, both the pod and the beans can be eaten, but the beans themselves must be peeled to eat. Also called "broad beans," the pods are about 7 to 8 inches long; each pod holds 5 to 6 large beans. Taste is reminiscent of limas.

Garbanzo Beans: Like black-eyed peas, these are normally sold dried or canned. But field-ripened garbanzos, packaged in bags and ready to cook, can now be purchased in produce markets. These round, light brown beans are another good protein source, with a distinctive nutty flavor.

Haricot Verts (Ah-REE-co-VER): Half as thin as a pencil, these aristocratic beans of the green bean set are very delicate in texture and flavor. Harvested very early, these "filet beans" have stem ends that are easily snapped off.

Mung Beans: (See Sprouts, page 144).

Purple Wax Beans: Like small, slender yellow wax beans, these beans are a deep purple color that turns green when the beans are cooked. Tender beans with a green bean taste.

Sea Beans: An interesting, very delicate vegetable that looks like a fern and is actually a succulent. The plant grows close to the ocean and so absorbs the salt as it grows. Sea beans, also called "glassworts," have a pleasantly salty, mild taste, and taste great raw or lightly steamed. The "beans" are gold or rust-colored later in the season.

Winged Beans: Fascinating beans originally from Southeast Asia, these four-sided beans have "wings" that extend out from the center of a 4- to 5-inch long stalk. The taste will remind you of peas and beans together, and the texture is crisp. Every bit of a winged bean plant can be eaten: the leaves can be steamed like spinach, the succulent tendrils enjoyed like asparagus, and both the mushroom-like flowers and the roots are edible. Because of its delicious versatility, the winged bean has been dubbed "the supermarket on a stalk."

Soufflé-Topped Sausage & Vegetables

You can vary the vegetables to taste for this hearty main dish.

1-1/2 cups fresh beans (yellow or purple wax, Haricot verts, sea beans, green or Chinese long beans), cut in 1-inch pieces
1 lb. hot or sweet Italian sausage, broken up
1-1/2 cups thinly sliced zucchini
1 red bell pepper, seeded, cut in 1/2-inch chunks
1 garlic clove, finely chopped
1 cup ricotta cheese (8 oz.)
1 cup shredded Swiss, Monterey Jack or Cheddar cheese (4 oz.)
1/2 cup mayonnaise or salad dressing
1/3 cup milk
2 eggs
2 tablespoons grated Parmesan cheese

Preheat oven to 450F (230C). In a large saucepan, cover beans with 1 inch water. Cook, covered, 4 to 7 minutes or until crisp-tender. Drain and set aside. Meanwhile, in a large skillet, cook sausage 10 minutes. Drain, reserving drippings in skillet. In same skillet, sauté zucchini, bell pepper and garlic 3 minutes; drain. Stir in sausage and drained cooked beans. Turn mixture into a lightly oiled 2-quart soufflé dish or straight-sided casserole. In a blender or food processor fitted with a metal blade, process ricotta cheese, shredded cheese, mayonnaise, milk and eggs until blended. Pour mixture over vegetables in casserole. Sprinkle with Parmesan cheese. Bake 10 minutes. Reduce heat to 375F (190C); bake 25 to 30 minutes more or until puffed and golden. Serve at once. Makes 5 to 6 servings.

Preparation time: 25 minutes

Mid-Eastern Rice & Vegetable Salad

Serve this sophisticated salad at room temperature or chilled.

2 cups fresh beans (green, purple or yellow wax, haricots verts, Chinese long or Italian green beans), cut in 1-inch pieces
2 cups cooked brown or white rice
2 small tomatoes, chopped
2/3 cup sliced green onion

Herbed Vinaigrette Dressing:
3 tablespoons olive oil or vegetable oil
2 tablespoons red wine vinegar
2 tablespoons chopped parsley
1 garlic clove, finely chopped
2 teaspoons chopped fresh thyme or 1/2 teaspoon dried leaf thyme
2 teaspoons chopped fresh marjoram or 1/2 teaspoon dried leaf marjoram
1/2 teaspoon salt

Prepare Herbed Vinaigrette Dressing. In a medium saucepan, cover beans with 1 inch water. Bring to a boil; reduce heat. Simmer, covered, 4 to 7 minutes or until crisp-tender. Drain; rinse in cold water. In a large bowl, toss beans with rice, tomatoes and onions. Pour dressing over salad and toss. If preparing ahead, cover and refrigerate salad up to 48 hours. Makes 6 servings.

Herbed Vinaigrette Dressing:
In a shaker jar, combine olive oil, vinegar, parsley, garlic, thyme, marjoram and salt. Cover and shake well to mix. Makes 1/3 cup.

Preparation time: 15 minutes

BELL PEPPERS

The most common sweet bell pepper varieties, the green and red, have recently been joined by a number of colorful hybrids developed in the U.S. and in Europe. All are mild-tasting peppers with thick "walls" or sides and squared-off shapes.

Bell peppers are extremely versatile vegetables that can be enjoyed lightly cooked or raw, plain or stuffed. They are an economical buy at most times of the year, and take on the flavors of meats and other vegetables well. Roasting peppers, an Italian cooking technique, is an easy way to enjoy the smoky, intensely rich flavor character of sweet peppers, and is an easy peeling method as well. For hot peppers, see Chiles section, page 96.

Buying Tips: Look for plump, brilliantly-colored, well-shaped peppers with healthy-looking green stems. Avoid those with soft spots, cracks, or soft stems. Peppers should look crisp and be firm.

Storage: Refrigerate bell peppers up to several days in the crisper. Sweeter red, purple and yellow bell peppers will not keep as long as green peppers do because of their high sugar content. To freeze peppers, remove seeds and stems but do not blanch. Store in airtight freezer containers up to 6 months. Frozen peppers will lose their crisp texture but will be fine for recipes, main dishes, soups and stews.

Basic Preparation: Halve bell peppers from the stem to the base; remove seedy core, stems and white pith along ribs, if desired. Peppers can be sautéed, steamed, roasted or baked in recipes. To enjoy bell peppers alone, either sauté, stir-fry or roast. Sauté or stir-fry peppers in a small amount of oil for about 3 minutes or until tender-crisp. To roast peppers, see recipes for Roasted Bell Pepper Salad or Roasted Bell Pepper Soup, page 90. To micro-cook peppers, follow instructions in your recipe.

Serving Ideas: Use as dippers for low-cal dips or spreads as an appetizer. Use chopped cooked bell peppers to stuff other vegetables, such as squash or eggplant. Sauté bell peppers with olive slices, green beans, corn or squash; season with garlic, basil or rosemary. Purée bell peppers for soups, stews or savory sauces; sliver peppers to add to salads or oriental dishes. Stuff peppers with chopped cooked meats, cheeses or vegetables. Use roasted pepper strips in omelets, other egg dishes or sandwiches.

Yield: 1 lb. peppers = about 3 large peppers.
1 lb. peppers = 3 to 4 cups sliced or chopped peppers.
1 lb. roasted, peeled peppers = about 1-1/2 cups sliced.
1 bell pepper = 1 serving.

Nutrition Facts: One average bell pepper has only 8 calories! Bell peppers are high in fiber and vitamin C. Red and yellow varieties contain large amounts of vitamin A.

Unusual Varieties:

Chocolate: This is a brown bell pepper, sweet and green inside; pepper turns green when cooked.

Orange: A brilliant orange-colored pepper with a bright green stem. Retains most of its orangy color inside and out when cooked.

Pimiento: Still a rare find when fresh, these spicy-sweet red peppers are usually found in jars. They have a more elongated shape than the square bells.

Purple: Also called "Violetta," this beautiful deep purple pepper is the color of eggplant with bright green stems. The flesh inside is green and sweet; the outer skin turns green when cooked.

Red: Actually a green pepper left to ripen on the vine, red bell has more sugar in it, so it is sweeter tasting and slightly more tender.

Rouge Royale: A large red pepper hybrid with a spicier taste than regular red pepper and brilliant color. It retains its vibrant color when cooked.

Yellow: This dazzling golden yellow pepper has a green stem and yellow interior; color stays golden when cooked. Flavor is very sweet and mild.

White: Actually more of a creamy ivory color, white bell has an elongated shape and a very mild flavor.

Fajitas or Mexican Stir-Fry

Fajitas, pronounced fuh-HEE-tahs, is not an authentic Mexican dish, but a Southwestern American invention.

3 to 4 tablespoons vegetable oil
1-1/2 lbs. julienne-cut strips chicken breast or beef sirloin or 1-inch firm fish fillet chunks
3 red, yellow, orange or green bell peppers, seeded, slivered
1-1/2 cups thinly sliced red onion
1 cup sliced ripe olives, if desired
8 large flour tortillas, warmed

Accompaniments:
1/2 recipe Homemade Salsa, page 97
Shredded Monterey Jack or Cheddar cheese
Guacamole, page 20
Dairy sour cream
Sliced fresh chiles, as desired

In a large wok or skillet, heat 2 tablespoons oil. Stir-fry meat or fish about 3 minutes over high heat or until meat is cooked to desired doneness or fish is opaque. Remove from wok. Add more oil if necessary; stir-fry bell peppers, onion and olives, if desired, about 3 to 4 minutes or until they begin to brown. Add meat back to mixture; stir-fry 1 minute more to heat through. Spoon mixture onto warm tortillas. Roll up with desired accompaniments inside or on top. Makes 4 servings.

Preparation time: 30 minutes

Tip:
To warm tortillas, remove from package and wrap in aluminum foil. Heat in a 350F (175C) oven about 15 minutes for 8 tortillas.

Bell Pepper & Cheese Appetizers

Here's an easy snack to prepare.

4 bell peppers, cut in wedges
Olive oil or vegetable oil
2 to 3 oz. shredded or crumbled cheese (Cheddar, mozzarella or Swiss)
Toppings: Snipped chives, chopped nuts or green chiles, or sliced green onion

Preheat broiler. Place peppers, skin side up, on a baking sheet. Brush with oil. Broil about 4 inches from heat until blistered. Turn peppers over; broil until edges begin to brown. Sprinkle with cheese and toppings. Broil until cheese is melted and bubbly. Serve hot. Makes 24 pieces.

Preparation time: 10 minutes

Bell Peppers. See diagram, page 156.

Roasted Bell Pepper Soup

The sweeter peppers fare best in this full-flavored bisque.

4 yellow, red or orange bell
    peppers
3 tablespoons butter or margarine
3 tablespoons all-purpose flour
2 cups half and half (1 pint)
2 cups chicken broth
1/2 teaspoon salt
1/4 teaspoon white pepper
Dash hot-pepper sauce

Preheat broiler. Place bell peppers on broiler pan. Roast peppers 4 inches from heat, turning frequently with tongs, until charred on all sides. Remove; place peppers in a brown paper bag and close bag. Let stand 15 minutes to steam off skins. Pull off skins from peppers; remove stems and seeds. Chop peppers. In a blender or food processor fitted with a metal blade, process peppers to a purée. Set aside. In a large saucepan or Dutch oven, melt butter; stir in flour. Add half and half and chicken broth all at once. Cook and stir until mixture thickens and bubbles. Stir in bell pepper purée, salt, pepper and hot-pepper sauce; taste for seasoning. Cook and stir 2 minutes more or until heated through. Makes 5-1/2 cups or about 5 servings.

Preparation time: 25 minutes

Roasted Bell Pepper Salad

Roasting bell peppers brings out their rich smoky flavor.

5 bell peppers
Lettuce leaves
1/3 cup sliced ripe olives
Grated Parmesan cheese or
    crumbled blue cheese, if
    desired

Bell Pepper Vinaigrette:
1 reserved roasted bell pepper
1/2 cup olive oil or vegetable oil
1/3 cup white wine vinegar
1/3 cup chopped red onion
1 tablespoon chopped fresh basil
    or 1 teaspoon crushed dried
    leaf basil
1 clove garlic, minced
1/2 teaspoon salt
1/4 teaspoon pepper

Preheat broiler. Place bell peppers on broiler pan. Roast peppers, 4 inches from heat, turning frequently with tongs, until charred on all sides. Remove; place peppers in a brown paper bag; close bag. Let stand 15 minutes to steam off skins. Reserve 1 bell pepper for Bell Pepper Vinaigrette. Pull off skin from remaining peppers; remove stems and seeds. Julienne-slice peppers. Prepare Bell Pepper Vinaigrette. Arrange lettuce leaves on four salad plates; top with pepper slices and olives. Spoon vinaigrette over salads. Sprinkle on cheese if desired. Makes 4 salads.

Bell Pepper Vinaigrette:
Peel, seed and slice reserved pepper. In a blender or food processor fitted with a metal blade, process olive oil, vinegar, onion, basil, garlic, salt and pepper with sliced reserved pepper until nearly smooth. Makes 1-1/2 cups.

Preparation time: 25 minutes

Red Bell Pepper Pesto

This colorful sauce is sweeter than traditional basil pesto. Use on pasta, in salad dressings, over eggs, or on grilled meats, poultry or fish.

1 red, rouge royale, purple, yel-
    low or orange bell pepper,
    seeded, chopped
1/2 cup packed fresh basil leaves
2 tablespoons chopped fresh
    herbs, such as rosemary, orega-
    no, dill, marjoram, savory, sage
    or thyme
1 garlic clove, finely chopped
1/3 cup olive oil or vegetable oil
1 tablespoon lemon juice
1/3 cup chopped walnuts or
    almonds
1/4 cup grated Parmesan cheese

In a blender or food processor fitted with a metal blade, process bell pepper pieces, basil, desired chopped herbs, garlic, olive oil or vegetable oil and lemon juice until well blended. Add nuts and Parmesan cheese; process again until finely ground. Store in a covered container in refrigerator for up to 1 month. Makes 3/4 cup.

Preparation time: 10 minutes

Unusual Varieties:

Napa (Chinese): An elongated, pale green head, with large ribbed leaves and crinkly texture. Has a slightly sweeter taste and can be eaten raw, steamed or stir-fried.

Red: A deep purplish-red cabbage variety with a strong cabbage flavor. Red cabbage is often cooked or pickled, but is also good in slaws and as a holder for dips.

Savoy: A deeper, bright green colored round head cabbage, with pretty, crinkled leaves surrounding the core like a rose. Shred cabbage, use leaves as a garnish, or steam or boil.

Salad Savoy: In white and purple varieties, this attractive cabbage is actually an ornamental kale. Use the leaves to line a salad bowl, or cook as for kale (see Greens, page 106.)

Tip:
It's simple to reduce the strong odor that results from cooking cabbage; just drop a whole walnut into the cooking liquid.

CABBAGE

Green cabbage was highly regarded by the ancient Egyptians and Greeks. Thought the perfect hangover remedy, it was common practice to eat cabbage before imbibing at banquets. Red cabbage appeared on the scene around the Middle Ages. The French, Germans, and English traveled to America with cabbage seeds; both the settlers and the Indians began planting and eating this vegetable. They boiled fresh cabbage with corned beef and onions, which evolved into a New England specialty.

Surprisingly, cauliflower, broccoli, kale and turnips also belong to the botanical cabbage family. Intriguing varieties of green cabbage make it an even more versatile vegetable.

Buying Tips: Cabbages should be heavy for their size, with crisp, fresh-looking leaves and no brown streaks or spots. Try to buy green cabbages with the deep green leaves still attached, if possible. Red cabbage should have no black edges.

Storage: Wrap tightly in plastic bags; store cabbage in your refrigerator crisper from 4 to 7 days.

Basic Preparation: Cut or shred cabbage just before using. Discard old or wilted outer leaves, then halve and core head cabbages, or remove one inch from stem ends of Napa cabbage or salad savoy types. Steam or boil cabbage wedges, covered, for 5 to 8 minutes or until tender. Leaves will cook tender in about 2 minutes. To retain the bright red color of red cabbage, add lemon juice or wine to the cooking water.

To microwave cabbage wedges, cook in a shallow dish with a few tablespoons water on High (100%) power for 6 to 8 minutes.

Serving Ideas: Shred Napa or other cabbage to use in Chinese or Thai stir-fry dishes, or in eggroll or wonton fillings. Substitute savoy or red cabbage in slaw recipes to add color, or use the steamed leaves to wrap ground meat fillings, and top with a cheese sauce. Shred Napa cabbage and red cabbage for Chinese chicken salad, or for a pita sandwich filling. Use salad savoy leaves to attractively line a plate of raw vegetable appetizers.

Yield: 1 Napa cabbage = about 6 cups shredded.
1 2-lb. head green, savoy, or red cabbage = about 10 cups sliced, about 6 cups cooked.
1/2 lb. raw cabbage = 1 serving.

Nutrition Facts: Cabbage has few calories, averaging 18 calories per cup. Considered an aid to digestion and the intestinal system, cabbage is also rich in vitamin C and several minerals.

Thai Beef Salad

A warm sesame seed dressing spiked with a dash of hot sauce lends Far Eastern flair to roast beef salad.

1-1/4 lbs. top sirloin steak
Salt and pepper to taste
6 cups shredded Chinese (Napa) cabbage, savoy cabbage, bok choy leaves or salad savoy
1-1/2 cups julienne-cut cucumber
1 red bell pepper, seeded, slivered

Hoisin Dressing:
2 tablespoons vegetable oil
4 green onions, sliced
1 tablespoon sesame seed
1/2 cup red wine vinegar
3 tablespoons hoisin sauce
1 teaspoon sugar
1/4 teaspoon hot-pepper sauce

Prepare Hoisin Dressing. Preheat broiler. Lightly oil a broiler pan. Place steak on oiled broiler pan. Broil 4 inches from heat 10 to 12 minutes, turning once, for medium doneness. Season to taste with salt and pepper. Slice thinly in bite-sized strips. In a large bowl, toss together meat pieces, cabbage, cucumber and red pepper. Pour dressing over salad. Toss well to coat with dressing; serve at once. Makes 4 to 5 servings.

Hoisin Dressing:
In a large skillet, heat oil. Sauté green onions and sesame seed 3 minutes. Stir in vinegar, hoisin sauce, sugar and hot-pepper sauce. Cook 2 minutes more to heat through. Makes 2/3 cup.

Preparation time: 25 minutes

Tip:
Hoisin sauce is a condiment that can only be described as an oriental catsup. It has a pleasantly spicy flavor that can add zip to stir-frys, sautéed vegetables, barbecued meat or fish, and to sauces and dressings. Look for it in the oriental food section of your supermarket.

Creamed Cabbage with Apples & Walnuts

Cooked cabbage was never so elegant!

2 tablespoons butter or margarine
1 large Red Delicious apple, cored, thinly sliced
1/2 cup thinly sliced onion
1 garlic clove, finely chopped
1 lb. Chinese (Napa), Savoy or green cabbage, cut in 2-inch squares
2 tablespoons cornstarch
3/4 cup milk
1/4 teaspoon ground nutmeg
1/8 teaspoon pepper
1/4 cup grated Parmesan cheese
1/2 cup finely chopped walnuts
Chopped chives or parsley

In a large skillet, melt butter. Sauté apple slices, onions and garlic 2 minutes over medium-high heat. Add cabbage; cook 5 minutes more or until limp. Stir cornstarch into milk; add to skillet. Cook and stir until thickened and bubbly. Stir in nutmeg, pepper, Parmesan cheese and walnuts. Cook 2 minutes more. Sprinkle with chives or parsley to serve. Makes 4 to 5 servings.

Preparation time: 15 minutes

Two-Cheese Cabbage Slaw

Perfect for potlucks and picnics.

1/2 lb. finely chopped Chinese (Napa), Savoy, red or green cabbage
1 cup shredded carrot
1/4 cup finely shredded mozzarella or Swiss cheese (2 oz.)
1/4 cup finely shredded Cheddar cheese (2 oz.)

Slaw Dressing:
1/3 cup mayonnaise or salad dressing
2 tablespoons cider vinegar
2 tablespoons chopped fresh basil or 2 teaspoons dried leaf basil
1 garlic clove, finely chopped
1/4 teaspoon pepper

Prepare Slaw Dressing. In a large bowl, toss together shredded cabbage, carrot, shredded mozzarella or Swiss cheese and Cheddar cheese until well mixed. Pour dressing over salad and toss to coat well. Chill at least 1 hour before serving. If preparing in advance, cover and refrigerate up to 24 hours before serving. Makes 8 servings.

Slaw Dressing:
In a blender or food processor fitted with a metal blade, process mayonnaise, vinegar, basil, garlic and pepper until blended. Makes 1/2 cup.

Preparation time: 15 minutes

Quiche Mexicana

Tortillas form the simple crust for this easy main course dish.

1 tablespoon vegetable oil
2 cactus pads, thorns removed, julienned in 1/4-inch-wide strips
1 Anaheim chile, seeded, finely chopped
1/3 cup chopped green onions
6 (8-inch) flour or corn tortillas
1 cup shredded Cheddar or Monterey Jack cheese (4 oz.)
1/2 cup sliced ripe olives
6 eggs
3/4 cup milk
3/4 cup Homemade Salsa, page 97, or bottled salsa
1/4 teaspoon salt
Toppings: Guacamole, page 23, sliced ripe olives, sour cream, chopped green onions, fresh cilantro sprigs

Preheat oven to 350F (175C). In a large skillet, heat oil. Sauté cactus strips, chile and green onion 3 minutes. Remove from heat. Lightly grease a 12" x 8" casserole dish. Arrange tortillas, overlapping, in bottom and up sides of dish. Sprinkle cheese and olives in dish. In a large bowl, with a wire whisk, beat together eggs, milk, salsa and salt until blended. Stir in sautéed vegetables. Pour mixture evenly over ingredients in crust. Bake 35 to 40 minutes or until set. Let stand 5 minutes; cut in squares. Sprinkle on desired toppings. Makes 6 servings.

Preparation time: 15 minutes

CACTUS LEAVES/NOPALES

(no-PAHL-ees) Called "cactus pads" and "nopalitos," the leaves or pads of the nopal cactus were first used by the Aztecs as a source of food. The prickly pear cactus, which also bears fruit, (see Prickly Pears, page 71) grows in the southwestern U.S., Mexico and Central America.

Don't be put off by cactus leaves' thorny exterior. Once the tiny prickles are removed (most sold in markets have been de-spined), cactus leaves are simple to cook and taste like green bell peppers or snap beans. Popular in southwestern and Mexican cuisine, cactus leaves are as versatile as bell peppers, and take well to spicy condiments. This vegetable is often sold canned or pickled, but there's no comparison to fresh cactus leaves. Look for them in produce and ethnic markets all during the year.

Buying Tips: Look for fresh-looking green leaves, with a minimum of browning at the edges. Avoid bruised or moldy leaves; they should be neither soggy nor dry.

Storage: Refrigerate cactus leaves, out of the reach of children, for up to several weeks in the crisper.

Basic Preparation: With a sharp paring knife, trim off the "eyes" of each cactus pad, which houses the tiny thorns. Even if you can't see thorns, some are invisible so trim off all eyes. Then trim off all edges of the cactus pad; rinse in water and chop, cut in strips or dice. Steam or boil pieces for 5 to 8 minutes or until nearly tender, testing for doneness as you would for bell peppers. Serve cactus leaves hot, sprinkled with lemon juice and chili powder or grated Parmesan cheese, or rinse in cool water to add to a salad.

To micro-cook cactus leaves, slice in bite-sized strips and place in a shallow dish in 1/4 cup water. Cover loosely and cook on High (100%) for 3 to 4 minutes, turning dish once.

Serving Ideas: Add cooked cactus leaf pieces to scrambled eggs, browned ground meat, chicken salad or corn soup. Combine chilled cooked cactus with citrus fruit and a vinaigrette dressing for a refreshing salad, or add to sliced tomatoes. Add the strips to chili, stews or vegetable sautés. Sauté cactus with garlic, herbs and onions for a spicy side dish or condiment.

Yield: 1 lb. cactus leaves, trimmed and sliced = 4 to 5 servings.

Nutrition Facts: A 1/2 cup serving of cactus leaves contains about 29 calories. Cactus is high in fiber and contains iron and some protein.

CARDOON

(car-DUHN) Also called "cardoni" or "cadi," this celery look-alike is actually related to artichokes, because it belongs to the thistle family. Cardoon is an Italian favorite that was highly prized during the height of the Roman empire. It is also a staple in the households of southern France during the winter holidays.

The Mediterraneans brought cardoon to America, and it is now grown in northern California. Found in markets from October through May, cardoon tastes best cooked, like a cross between celery and artichokes. The pale green outer stalks of cardoon have soft prickles on them, and the stalks are topped with dainty leaves. Cardoon can be substituted for celery in recipes.

Buying Tips: Look for pale, fresh-looking cardoon with deep green leaves. Stalks should not be bruised or brown.

Storage: Store cardoon, wrapped tightly in plastic, in the refrigerator crisper section, for up to 1 week.

Basic Preparation: The outermost stalks must be removed and discarded, since they are very tough and cooking will not tenderize them. Trim ends of cardoon, then pare off the prickles and strings from the inner stalks and leaves. Halve the stalks crosswise, or slice to cook. Boil or steam pieces for 10 to 15 minutes or until tender. Add a teaspoon of vinegar or lemon juice to the cooking water to prevent discoloration. To cook in the microwave, place stalks in 1/4 cup water mixed with 1 teaspoon lemon juice in a shallow dish; cover loosely. Micro-cook on High (100%) power for 6 to 9 minutes, turning dish once.

Serving Ideas: Italians sauce cardoon with garlic, olive oil and tomatoes. The French serve the vegetable boiled and topped with a Gruyère cheese sauce. Serve cardoon cold, sliced over lettuce or tomatoes, with a vinaigrette dressing. A traditional Italian dressing consists of butter, olive oil, garlic and anchovies, a flavorful accent for cooked cardoon. Or use cardoon in any dish in which you would use celery.

Yield: 2 lbs. cardoon = about 1-1/2 lbs. cooked.
2 lbs. cardoon = 4 to 6 servings.

Nutrition Facts: Extremely low in calories, a 3-1/2-ounce serving of cooked cardoon has only 10. It's a fair source of potassium and other minerals, and a good source of fiber.

Cardoon & Artichoke Heart Salad

If you can't buy cardoon in your area, you can substitute one bunch of celery.

1 bunch cardoon
1/4 cup cider vinegar
1 large tomato, chopped
1 (14-oz.) jar marinated artichoke hearts
Lettuce leaves

Discard outer stems of cardoon. With a sharp paring knife, trim off prickles on inner stalks. Cut in 1/2-inch pieces. In a medium saucepan, place cardoon pieces with water to cover and 2 tablespoons of vinegar. Bring to a boil; reduce heat and simmer 6 to 8 minutes or until tender. Drain and rinse in cold water. In a large non-metal bowl, place cardoon and tomatoes. Drain artichoke hearts, reserving marinade; add hearts to cardoon mixture. In a shaker jar, place reserved marinade and remaining 2 tablespoons of vinegar; shake until mixed. Pour vegetables over vegetables; toss well. Cover and refrigerate 2 to 24 hours to allow flavors to blend. To serve, arrange lettuce leaves on a platter. Drain vegetables; spoon vegetables over lettuce. Reserve marinade for another salad. Makes 4 servings.

Preparation time: 15 minutes

Celery Root-Carrot Slaw

Serve this as a side dish for Grilled Flank Steak with Mangoes, page 52.

1-1/2 cups shredded celery root
2 tablespoons lemon juice
2 cups shredded green or red
  cabbage
1-1/2 cups shredded carrot
1/2 cup chopped walnuts or
  pecans
Cabbage leaves

Celery Seed Dressing:
1/4 cup mayonnaise or salad
  dressing
1/4 cup plain yogurt
1/4 teaspoon celery seed
2 teaspoons sugar
1/4 teaspoon pepper

Prepare Celery Seed Dressing. In a medium bowl, place celery root and lemon juice and cover with water. Let stand 5 minutes; drain well. In a large bowl, toss together shredded cabbage, celery root, carrots and walnuts. Toss dressing with salad ingredients to coat. If preparing ahead, cover and refrigerate up to 24 hours. Serve salad in a serving bowl lined with cabbage leaves. Makes 6 servings.

Celery Seed Dressing:
In a small bowl, stir together mayonnaise, yogurt, celery seed, sugar and pepper until blended. Makes about 1/2 cup.

Preparation time: 15 minutes

CELERY ROOT

Celery and celery root, like Beauty and the Beast, are alike in character but not in appearance. Celery root, an unattractive knobby brown root closely related to celery, has until recently gone unappreciated in America. But European cooks have savored celeriac, or celery root, for centuries, particularly during the fall and winter months.

This vegetable is cultivated for its tasty root, rather than its top. Celery root looks like a large misshapen turnip with a brown, hairy skin. But its appearance belies its pleasing taste. Peel off the skin to eat celery root raw or lightly cooked. The white meat tastes like a nutty water chestnut, but is more sophisticated and sweeter-tasting. Celery root is available most of the year.

Buying Tips: Opt for small or medium-sized celery roots, since larger roots may have a hollow or pithy center. Irregularity in shape and strong aroma are common, as are side roots or dirt on outer skin. If the root has leaves, they should be fresh and green. Avoid wet, bruised or dry-looking roots.

Storage: Celery root stores well in the refrigerator crisper like turnips or rutabagas, for up to 1 week.

Basic Preparation: Scrub root; cut off side roots and ends; trim off brown peel. The root discolors as soon as it's cut; dip slices or pieces in lemon juice and water until used. Slice, chop or cut into julienne sticks; steam, boil or sauté the root for 5 to 8 minutes or until tender. Or micro-cook half of a medium celery root, sliced: place in a dish with 1/2 cup water mixed with 1 tablespoon lemon juice; cover loosely. Micro-cook on High (100%) power for 6 to 8 minutes or until nearly tender. Let stand 3 minutes to finish cooking.

Serving Ideas: Serve cooked celery root drizzled with melted butter, topped with a cheese sauce or sprinkled with salt, pepper and grated Parmesan cheese. Serve raw celery root shredded for a salad or slaw, cut into sticks for a vegetable platter or as a natural snack food. Very tender cooked celery root can be mashed and served like potatoes. Or slice and sauté celery root with bacon and chopped red bell pepper for a tasty side dish.

Yield: 1 medium celery root = 3/4 to 1 lb.
1 medium celery root = about 4 servings.

Nutrition Facts: A 1/2-cup serving of celery root has about 20 calories. It's high in phosphorous and contains some B vitamins and iron.

CHILIES

Chilies have been a hot prospect for American cooks since the South Americans and Mexicans brought their spicy harvest across the border. The ancient Peruvian Indians called them "aji" (ah-hee), a term, when translated into Spanish became "chili." The hotness of a fresh chili can vary considerably with soil conditions and climate. Fresh chilies may be as short as 1 inch to as long as 7 inches, with degrees of hotness ranging from very mild to hair-raising.

Buying Tips: Look for brightly colored, fresh-looking chilies without signs of wrinkling or blisters. Bright green stems indicate just-picked freshness. Pale color is a sign of immaturity.

Storage: Store chili peppers, wrapped in plastic bags, in the refrigerator crisper no longer than 5 days. You can freeze chopped or sliced fresh chilies up to 6 months in airtight containers; however, they will lose some of their pungency and crisp texture.

SPECIAL NOTE: Chili peppers, no matter how mild, contain the oil capsaicin, which can cause a painful burning sensation on your skin, hands, lips and eyes. Wash hands thoroughly with soap and water immediately after handling chilies and wear gloves if chopping or slicing large amounts of the vegetable. Keep hands away from lips and eyes while handling chilies; if not wearing gloves, work with chilies under cold running water.

Basic preparation: True chili lovers can eat some varieties out-of-hand, as an accompaniment to Mexican dishes or eggs. To chop or slice chilies for recipes, slit peppers lengthwise and trim off stem end. Much of the spiciness of the chilies is contained in the veins and seeds; trim them off if less spiciness is desired. You can also soak hot chilies in salted ice water or milk for an hour before using to tone down the flavor. Use chilies whole, chopped or sliced in recipes or sprinkled over foods as a garnish. For peeled or roasted chilies, follow instructions for peeling bell peppers. (See Bell Peppers, page 88.)

Serving Ideas: Fresh chilies are used in oriental dishes, such as stir-frys, steamed dishes, soups and stews. Indians combine them with curries, such as lamb dishes and chicken stews. Chilies are compatible with Mexican and Latin American dishes, puréed for sauces, chopped into salsa or stuffed with meats and cheeses. Mild chili varieties are good deep-fried or folded into omelets. Use chopped chilies to add spunk to sautéed vegetables, broiled meats or fish or cheese sauce.

Yield: 1/2 lb. chilies = about 20 (3-inch) chilies.

Nutrition Facts: Chilies are very high in vitamin C; red varieties have large amounts of vitamin A. All varieties contain few calories.

Fresh Chili Varieties:

Anaheim: An elongated green pepper with a very mild flavor; mildest of all chilies. Tastes like a spicy green bell pepper; used in making chili rellenos. The red variety is available less often.

Fresno: A small, slender green chili that can be greenish-red in hue. This chili is fiery-hot.

Hungarian: A fatter, large chartreuse-colored chili pepper; usually mild and sweet in flavor.

Jalapeño: Considered one of the hottest chilies, jalapeños are deep green to reddish-green in color. Their shape is short and fat, with a rounded tip. Use sparingly.

Mexi-Bell: A hybrid between green bell peppers and chili peppers, this variety looks like a green bell pepper, sometimes with tinges of red. Mildly spicy flavor, less spicy if the seedy core and yellow interior "blisters" are removed.

Pasilla: Also called "ancho," pasillas look like a squared-off, elongated version of a deep green bell pepper. Pasilla chilies turn to vermillion red as they dry. Usually fairly mild in flavor.

Serrano: Treat this variety with the utmost respect—it's just about the hottest around! These are tiny, skinny green to bright red chilies used in small quantities.

Yellow: Also called "Caloro," "Caribe" and "Floral Gem," yellow peppers look much like jalapeños with pale golden skins. Flavor varies from hot to extremely hot.

Homemade Salsa

"Salsa" means sauce in Spanish. Enjoy!

3 cups finely chopped tomatoes
1 cup finely chopped red onion
1/2 cup finely chopped carrot
1 fresh Anaheim or pasilla chili, seeded, finely chopped
1 or 2 hot chilies, minced
3 tablespoons minced cilantro
1/2 teaspoon salt
1/4 teaspoon pepper
3 tablespoons tomato paste

In a large non-metal bowl, combine tomatoes, onion, carrot, chilies, cilantro, salt, pepper, and tomato paste. Cover and chill at least 30 minutes to blend flavors. If preparing ahead, cover and refrigerate up to 1 week. Makes 4-3/4 cups salsa.

Preparation time: 10 minutes

Sante Fe Cornbread

Hearty and spicy, this Southwestern bread goes well with soups, salads or with just a pat of butter.

1 cup yellow cornmeal
1 cup all-purpose flour
3 tablespoons sugar
4 teaspoons baking powder
1/2 teaspoon salt
1 fresh mild green Anaheim chili, seeded, diced
1/2 cup diced red bell pepper or pimiento
1/4 cup minced green onion
1 or 2 minced fresh hot chilies, such as jalapeños, serranos, Fresno or yellow, if desired
1 cup milk
1 egg
3 tablespoons vegetable oil

Preheat oven to 425F (220C). Grease bottom and sides of an 8" x 5" loaf pan. In a large bowl, stir together cornmeal, flour, sugar, baking powder and salt. Stir in diced Anaheim chili, red pepper, onion and hot chilies, if desired. In a small bowl, whisk together milk, egg and oil. Stir into dry ingredients about 1 minute or until nearly smooth. Pour batter into pan, spreading evenly. Bake 35 to 45 minutes or until a wooden pick inserted in center comes out clean. Cool 5 minutes; turn out onto wire rack. Invert loaf; slice to serve warm. Makes 1 loaf.

Preparation time: 10 minutes

Southwestern vegetables. See diagram, page 156.

CUCUMBERS

One of the oldest vegetables known to man, cucumbers came originally from southern Asia. The ancient Romans also treasured cucumbers, and their enthusiasm for the vegetable spread throughout Europe. Cucumbers require a humid environment, so they are coated with a thin wax to preserve the moisture content and enhance appearance. Unusual varieties are now appearing. One is a burpless cuke, developed in Europe and enjoyed there for centuries; another is a lemon cuke that looks more like a tennis ball than a vegetable. Cultivated the world over, cucumbers are available all year.

Buying Tips: Buy fresh-looking cukes that are crisp, not soft or mushy. Avoid those with any moldy or soft spots or ends. Avoid cucumbers with yellow spots; purchase ones that are small for their size, because they are likely to have fewer seeds.

Storage: Cukes need high humidity, so they tend to lose their freshness fast. Buy cucumbers that you intend to use or pickle shortly. Keep them in a cool, humid spot, or in your refrigerator crisper for up to 3 days. After that, cukes will become soft.

Basic Preparation: Peel waxed cucumbers; other varieties can be peeled if desired. Slice or chop cukes for use in recipes or to enjoy as a cool vegetable snack. To seed cukes for chopping, halve cucumbers lengthwise. With a grapefruit knife or the tip of a teaspoon, spoon out the seedy centers, then slice or chop as desired. Cucumbers can also be sautéed, stir-fried, or lightly steamed for up to 3 minutes so they retain their crispness. For pickling cucumbers, follow your recipe.

Serving Ideas: Cucumbers can be marinated easily in Italian vinegar and oil or soy sauce and ginger-type salad dressings, particularly with other vegetables. Serve sliced cucumbers with sliced tomatoes, olives and crumbled feta cheese for a Greek-style salad, or chop and sauté with corn and bell peppers for an innovative side dish. Cukes also pair well with citrus fruits, grapes, apples and pears for fruit salads. Chopped cucumber is a popular condiment and relish for Indian and Thai foods, especially spicy ones. Cukes are great steamed and tossed with butter and fresh herbs, or topped with sour cream. Use thick cucumber slices as hors d'oeuvre bases for a bit of salmon salad, caviar or shrimp. Or stuff seeded cucumber halves as you would zucchini and bake until filling is hot.

Yield: 1 lb. cucumbers = 2 medium regular cukes.
1/2 lb. cucumber = about 2 cups sliced.
1/2 medium cucumber = 1 serving.

Nutrition Facts: Cucumbers are a boon for dieters; five thick slices cost only about 5 calories. They are also a good source of calcium, phosphorous, and potassium.

Unusual Varieties:

Armenian: Slender, curved cukes with pale green, ribbed skin and a very mild, almost sweet flavor.

Hothouse/European/English: A seedless, burpless cucumber. It has a very long slender shape. Very delicate flavor.

Japanese: Very skinny, deep green-skinned cucumbers with somewhat bumpy skin. Mild taste.

Lemon: Unusual round cukes, with a pale yellow skin and seedy meat. Serve raw, most delicate flavor.

Pickling: Short, chubby, blunt-ended cucumbers with pale greenish-yellow skins.

SFran: Larger than pickling cucumbers, but have a chubby appearance and deep green, smooth skins. From Persia.

Stir-Fried Cukes & Peppers

A delicious accompaniment to any meal!

3 to 4 tablespoons vegetable oil
2 cups peeled thinly sliced cucumber
4 green onions, sliced
1 red or green bell pepper, seeded, slivered
2 small tomatoes, cut in thin wedges
1 tablespoon sesame seed
2 tablespoons chopped fresh mint
Salt and pepper to taste

In a large wok or skillet, heat 1 tablespoon of oil. Stir-fry cucumbers about 2 minutes; remove from wok. Add more oil if necessary; stir-fry green onions and bell pepper 3 minutes. Remove from wok. Add more oil; stir-fry tomatoes 1 minute. Add cucumbers and bell pepper mixture to wok. Sprinkle in sesame seed, mint, salt and pepper; mix well. Cover and cook 1 minute. Makes 5 to 6 servings.

Preparation time: 15 minutes

Unusual Varieties:

Casper: Slender, white-skinned eggplant about 6 inches long, with a green cap. Less bitter than purple-skinned eggplant.

Chinese White: Very slender variety, with a curled end, white skin, and shaped like a banana.

Easter Egg: Small, round, white-skinned eggplant about the size of a tennis ball. May also be smaller.

French: These look like the Easter Egg variety, except the skin is deep purple. Petite size varies.

Italian: This variety looks almost like a miniature American eggplant, with an oval, bulbous shape. However, the skin is streaked with purple and white.

Japanese: Like a miniature American eggplant, with a slender shape, about 5 to 7 inches long. Deep purple skin, sweeter, milder flavor than regular eggplant.

Puerto Rican: A chubby eggplant, 4 to 6 inches long, with purple- and white-streaked skin.

Thai: One of the most fascinating varieties; includes those with white, purple, green, and green-streaked skin. Rounded shapes may be as small as acorns or as large as an orange.

EGGPLANT

Enjoyed by Asians and Indians for thousands of years, eggplant really came into its own when Middle Easterners, Latins, and Europeans discovered it. The Italians didn't taste eggplant until the 15th century. In the 1600's, the English were introduced to a vegetable that was round and white like a goose egg, and the name stuck.

The familiar purple eggplant doesn't come close to looking like an egg, but many varieties of the vegetable have been cultivated since ancient times. Mediterraneans, quickly making up for lost time, have shown us delightful ways to use this versatile, mild-tasting vegetable. And varieties from the Thais, Japanese and Chinese allow us to try eggplant the oriental way.

Unusual varieties of eggplant are found in larger supermarkets, as well as Italian, Asian and Middle Eastern markets. Most varieties are widely grown and available nearly year-round.

Buying Tips: Eggplant is very perishable, so buy only what you intend to use in a few days. Look for plump eggplants with very shiny skins that are firm to the touch. A bright green cap also indicates freshness and good color. Eggplants should feel heavy for their size.

Storage: Store eggplant in a cool place, or wrap in plastic to store in refrigerator for up to 2 days. Freezing is not recommended, except in recipes.

Basic Preparation: Eggplant should be cooked until tender to eat. Trim off cap; peel eggplant if desired. Slice, chop or cut into bite-sized sticks. Sauté in a small amount of oil and chicken broth (using too much oil will cause eggplant to soak it up), boil in broth, grill or microwave until tender. Eggplant pieces take 20 to 30 minutes to cook tender. To microwave, place chopped or sliced eggplant in 1/4 cup water in a loosely covered dish. Micro-cook on High (100%) for 3 to 5 minutes or until tender.

Serving Ideas: Eggplant is a bland vegetable that takes on other flavors well. Garlic, herbs such as rosemary, oregano and basil, as well as tomato sauce and white sauces are appropriate flavor-enhancers. Use cooked eggplant in relishes, steamed vegetable mixtures, stir-frys or stuffed vegetable dishes. Eggplants themselves are delicious stuffed with meats, vegetables and cheeses. Grill eggplant slices and top with cheese, then allow cheese to melt and sprinkle on fresh chopped basil. Or bread eggplant and deep-fry to serve with a marinara sauce.

Yield: 1-1/2 lbs. any variety = about 4 servings.
1/2 lb. peeled, chopped or cubed = 2 cups.
1 lb. raw eggplant = 1/2 lb. cooked.

Nutrition Facts: Eggplants average about 40 calories per 1-cup serving. High in fiber, low in sodium and offers some potassium.

Turkey & Eggplant Provençale

Boned fresh turkey, in cuts labeled tender-loins, breast slices and boneless breast, is readily available. No thawing is needed.

1 (3/4-lb.) eggplant
1-1/4 lb. turkey tenderloins
　(about 2)
2 tablespoons vegetable oil
1 large onion, diced
2 garlic cloves, finely chopped
3 medium tomatoes, chopped
1/4 cup chopped fresh parsley
1 tablespoon chopped fresh basil
　or rosemary or 1 teaspoon dried
　mixed herbs
1 bay leaf
1/2 teaspoon salt
1 teaspoon cornstarch
3/4 cup dry red wine
Hot cooked rice or noodles

Trim ends from eggplant; peel if desired. Chop in 1/2-inch chunks; set aside. Slice turkey pieces horizontally to make 4 thin slices. Halve slices crosswise to make 8 pieces. In a large skillet or Dutch oven, heat oil. Brown turkey pieces on all sides. Remove from pan, reserving drippings in pan. Sauté chopped eggplant with onion and garlic 5 minutes. Pour off excess fat. Add turkey pieces, tomatoes, parsley, basil or rosemary, bay leaf and salt. In a glass measure, stir cornstarch into wine; pour into skillet. Bring to a boil; reduce heat. Simmer, covered, 20 minutes. Uncover; cook 5 minutes more. Serve over rice or noodles. Makes 4 servings.

Preparation time: 20 minutes

Eggplant Fans With Peppers & Cheese

Try this easy fanning technique with summer squash or potatoes.

3 (1/2-lb.) eggplants
2 red bell peppers
4 oz. mozzarella or Monterey Jack
　cheese slices
1 tablespoon vegetable oil
1/2 cup chopped green onion
1 garlic clove, finely chopped
2/3 cup marinara or spaghetti
　sauce
1 tablespoon chopped fresh basil
　or 1 teaspoon dried basil
1 tablespoon chopped fresh
　oregano or 1 teaspoon dried
　leaf oregano
1 tablespoon chopped fresh rose-
　mary, marjoram or thyme or 1
　teaspoon mixed dried herbs

Preheat oven to 375F (190C). Trim eggplants at both ends; do not peel. Halve lengthwise; place cut side down on board. For fans, make 1/2-inch-wide lengthwise slits in eggplant halves to within 1/2 inch of stem end (do not cut through stem). Place fans skin side up in a shallow baking dish. Seed bell peppers; slice in 1/4-inch-wide strips. Slice cheese slices in 1/4-inch-wide strips. Insert strips of bell peppers and cheese into slits in eggplant. In a medium skillet, heat oil. Sauté onions and garlic 2 minutes. Stir in marinara sauce, basil, oregano and desired herbs; heat through. Drizzle over eggplant fans. Bake, uncovered, 35 to 45 minutes or until tender. With a wide spatula, carefully transfer fans to platter; spoon on sauce. Makes 6 servings.

Preparation time: 20 minutes

Curried Eggplant Spread

Similar to a caponata, or marinated egg-plant relish, this spread has a spunkier curry flavor. Serve it spread on French bread, crackers, or toasted party bread rounds.

1 (1-lb.) eggplant
Lemon juice
2 tablespoons vegetable oil
1 small onion, chopped
1 cup grated carrot
1/4 cup drained sliced pimiento
1 garlic clove, finely chopped
1/4 cup tomato sauce
2 tablespoons red wine vinegar
2 tablespoons curry powder
1 tablespoon chopped cilantro
1/2 teaspoon salt
Lettuce leaves

Lay eggplant on its side. With a small sharp knife, cut a lengthwise slice off top third of eggplant. Use a grapefruit knife or small knife to trim out pulp from remaining 2/3 of eggplant, leaving a shell about 1/2-inch thick. Chop finely. Peel slice cut from eggplant; chop finely. Sprinkle shell with lemon juice; wrap and refrigerate until needed. In a large skillet, heat oil. Sauté chopped eggplant with onion, carrot, pimiento and garlic over high heat about 5 minutes or until tender. Reduce heat. Stir in tomato sauce, vinegar, curry powder, cilantro and salt. Simmer, uncovered, 20 minutes, stirring occasionally. In a blender or food processor fitted with a metal blade, process vegetables until coarsely chopped. If preparing ahead, cover and refrigerate mixture up to 48 hours in advance. To serve, line eggplant shell with lettuce leaves. Turn mixture into eggplant shell. Makes 1 cup.

Preparation time: 25 minutes

Fennel & Carrot Salad

The feathery leaves make an attractive garnish.

2 fennel bulbs
2 cups shredded lettuce leaves
1 cup julienne cut carrot

Spicy Mayonnaise:
1/2 cup mayonnaise or salad
   dressing
1 tablespoon milk
1 garlic clove, finely chopped
1 teaspoon Dijon-style mustard

Prepare Spicy Mayonnaise. Trim fennel, reserving leaves. Quarter fennel; cut in julienne sticks. Chop reserved leaves to make 1/4 cup. In a large bowl, toss together fennel sticks, fennel leaves, lettuce leaves and carrot. Spoon mayonnaise over salad. Toss to coat well with dressing. Makes 4 servings.

Spicy Mayonnaise:
In a small bowl, stir together mayonnaise or salad dressing, milk, garlic and mustard. Makes 1/2 cup.

Preparation time: 15 minutes

FENNEL/SWEET ANISE

For the past thousand years, fennel has been cultivated in Europe and Asia. The Romans grew it for the fragrant, herblike green leaves that they used for a seasoning. Fennel is known for its tasty bulb, aromatic leaves, and for the seeds harvested from mature plants.

If you're confused about the label "sweet anise" often given fennel the vegetable, know that true anise is grown solely for the seeds it produces. Anise seed is used to flavor candy, breads and sweet pastries. But every part of the fennel plant has a mild anise or licorice flavor, though not a sweet one.

Fennel bulbs look similar to celery, with a white bulbous base that extends into celery-like stems. Fernlike green leaves grow from the top. Fennels' very mild anise flavor is more delicate when cooked, although you can enjoy this vegetable raw also. Fennel is an elegant vegetable that only needs a light sauce or melted butter and herbs to dress it.

Buying Tips: Purchase from about August through May. Look for clean bright-white bulbs with crisp stalks. Leaves should be bright green and fresh-looking. Look for a bulb that is compact, since a spreading bulb may be woody and overly mature. Avoid dry-looking bulbs, or those with brown spots.

Storage: Fennel should be used as soon as possible. Refrigerate, wrapped tightly in plastic, in refrigerator crisper for 1 to 2 days.

Basic Preparation: Wash and scrape any blemishes from the bulb; trim off woody stalks to within 1 inch of the head. Reserve the leaves for a garnish. Slice the head vertically, chop or cut into 1-inch chunks. Enjoy it raw as a vegetable snack or dipper, or boil or steam fennel to cook, in a small amount of boiling water for 10 to 15 minutes until fork-tender. To microwave fennel: place 2 trimmed bulbs in 1/4 cup water in a shallow, loosely covered dish. Micro-cook on High (100%) power for 7 to 9 minutes or until nearly tender. Let stand 3 minutes to finish cooking to the tender stage.

Serving Ideas: Chop fennel raw to add to chicken salad, pita bread sandwich fillings or chopped salads. Cube fennel for dipping raw, or to deep-fry in batter. Slice fennel to cook and serve with a light cheese sauce, or to chill for a marinated Italian dressing salad. Layer chilled cooked fennel slices with tomatoes and thinly sliced mild cheese; marinate in garlic dressing. Or grill fennel bulbs, brushed generously with olive oil and sprinkled with herbs.

Yield: 1 lb. fennel = 1 large bulb.
1 serving = 1/2 large bulb.

Nutrition Facts: One serving of fennel has only about 30 calories. This vegetable also contains vitamins A and C in good quantity.

Fennel in Nutmeg Sauce

Nutmeg complements the mild anise flavor of fennel. The sauce also pairs well with steamed baby carrots, kohlrabi and potatoes.

1 lb. (2 medium heads) fennel
2 cups water or chicken broth
**3 tablespoons chopped fennel
    leaves**

Nutmeg Sauce:
2 tablespoons butter or margarine
2 tablespoons flour
1 cup half and half
**Reserved 1/2 cup liquid from
    fennel or chicken broth**
1/2 teaspoon salt
1/4 teaspoon ground nutmeg

Prepare Nutmeg Sauce. Trim fennel, discarding woody stems and reserving leaves. Slice fennel. In a medium saucepan, bring water or broth to a boil. Add fennel slices; reduce heat. Simmer, covered, about 30 minutes or until tender. Drain, reserving 1/2 cup of cooking liquid for sauce. Place on a warm platter; cover and keep warm. Pour sauce over fennel. Sprinkle with chopped fennel leaves. Makes 4 servings.

Nutmeg Sauce:
In a small saucepan, melt butter. Stir in flour. Add half and half and reserved liquid all at once. Stir in salt and nutmeg. Cook and stir until mixture thickens and bubbles; cook 2 minutes more. Makes 1-3/4 cups.

Preparation time: 10 minutes

Cardoon, Celery Root, Fennel & Kohlrabi. See diagram, page 156.

Unusual Varieties:

Braided Garlic: In keeping with ancient traditions of stringing garlic bulbs together, you can buy braids of 15 to 25 garlic bulbs. Hang for decorative use and to have garlic on hand for cooking.

Elephant Garlic: Looks like a giant version of common garlic. About the size of an apple, elephant garlic has the typical papery husk that encloses large cloves arranged around a central stalk. This variety is much milder and less pungent than regular garlic. Sizewise, 1 clove of elephant garlic is equivalent to 10 cloves of regular garlic; 1 clove is equivalent to 1 onion in recipes.

Roasted Garlic

Roasting makes garlic sweet and spreadable, without any of the bitterness.

1 whole bulb garlic or elephant garlic
1/4 cup olive oil or vegetable oil
1 tablespoon chopped fresh marjoram or rosemary or 1 teaspoon crushed dried mixed herbs
Salt and pepper to taste

Preheat oven to 350F (175C). Remove outer paper covering from garlic bulb, leaving bulb whole. Slice off top of garlic bulb to expose cloves. Pour olive oil or vegetable oil into a shallow baking dish; brush garlic with oil. Sprinkle with herbs, salt and pepper. Cover and roast in oven 30 to 40 minutes for regular garlic, 1 hour for elephant garlic, or until cloves are soft. Remove soft garlic from cloves while warm. Serve warm. Makes 4 servings for regular garlic and 6 servings for elephant garlic.

Preparation time: 5 minutes

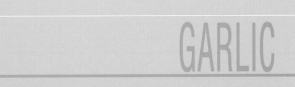

Once called the "stinking rose," garlic holds much greater culinary status now than it did in ancient Roman times. Then, the patricians gave it to their laborers to keep up their strength; the wealthy citizens considered garlic too pungent for their own taste. Throughout 5000 years of flavorful history, it seems that garlic has been used mainly as a cure-all for everything from depression to deadly epidemics. Culinarily, the least understood fact about garlic is that the longer you cook it, the milder and sweeter it becomes. So if you like the sharper, more pungent qualities of garlic, use it raw. Otherwise, try long, slow cooking. You will be surprised at what a benevolent herb garlic can be.

Buying Tips: For all varieties, look for firm, fresh-looking bulbs with papery white to purplish-white husks.

Storage: Never refrigerate garlic bulbs; garlic requires a cool, dry place with good ventilation. Or store garlic bulbs and cloves in a garlic jar, a ceramic container with holes that permit good air circulation. Hang garlic braids out of bright sunlight, in a cool spot away from strong lighting. Garlic will keep this way for up to 2 months.

Basic Preparation: Peel back the papery husk from a bulb of regular or elephant garlic to expose the cloves. Remove one clove at a time; peel and use whole, or peel, chop, mince or press garlic to mash for recipes. To peel a large number of garlic cloves, drop cloves in boiling water; drain after 30 seconds; cool.

Serving Ideas: Chop or mince garlic to flavor sauces, salad dressings, to sauté with vegetables or meats, or to mix into soft butter for a spunky spread. Rub whole cloves over toasted French bread, then spread with soft butter for traditional garlic bread. Use soft roasted cloves of garlic as a flavorful condiment for meats, fish, roasted vegetables or grilled chicken or spread on French bread.

Yield: 1 small clove garlic = about 1/8 teaspoon minced.
1 clove elephant garlic = about 2 teaspoons minced.
1 clove elephant garlic = 8 to 10 cloves regular garlic.

Nutrition Facts: Some experts say that garlic may help to reduce harmful cholesterol and promote a healthy cardiovascular system. Garlic is low in calories, about 4 per clove, with traces of many vitamins and minerals.

Garlic-Studded Pork Roast

The garlic slivers become mild and soft, flavoring the pork throughout as it roasts.

1 (2-1/2 to 3-lb.) pork loin roast, rolled, tied
5 to 6 cloves garlic or 1 clove elephant garlic, thinly sliced
2 tablespoons paprika
1 tablespoon fresh chopped oregano or 1 teaspoon crushed dried leaf oregano
1 tablespoon fresh chopped thyme or 1 teaspoon crushed dried leaf thyme
2 teaspoons chili powder
1/2 teaspoon white pepper
1/2 teaspoon cumin
1/2 teaspoon salt
1/4 teaspoon pepper
About 2 tablespoons vegetable oil

Preheat oven to 325F (165C). Place pork roast on a rack in a shallow roasting pan. With a small sharp knife, cut thin slits along top, sides and ends of roast about 1/2 inch deep. Insert garlic slices in slits. In a small bowl, stir together paprika, oregano, thyme, chili powder, white pepper, cumin, salt and pepper until well mixed. Rub outside of roast with oil. Sprinkle on seasoning mixture, rubbing it well into meat. Roast meat, uncovered, 2 to 2-3/4 hours or until meat thermometer inserted in thickest part of roast registers 170F (75C). Let roast stand, covered, 5 minutes. Remove strings from roast; slice thinly. Makes 6 to 8 servings.

Preparation time: 15 minutes

Roasted Garlic Spread

Present this aromatic hors d'oeuvre in a small round loaf of dark bread that has been hollowed out and lined with lettuce. Cube the scooped-out bread to serve with the spread.

10 large cloves garlic or 2 cloves elephant garlic, peeled
1/4 cup vegetable oil
1 (8-oz.) pkg. cream cheese, room temperature
1/2 cup dairy sour cream
1 teaspoon Worcestershire sauce
1-1/2 teaspoons chopped fresh thyme or 1/2 teaspoon dried leaf thyme
1/4 teaspoon dry mustard
1/4 teaspoon salt
1/4 teaspoon pepper
2 tablespoons sliced green onion
2 tablespoons chopped fresh parsley
Crackers, French bread slices or vegetable sticks

Preheat oven to 350F (175C). Place garlic cloves and oil in a small baking pan; brush garlic with oil. Bake, covered, in oven about 30 minutes or until tender. Remove from oven; cool 15 minutes. Spoon soft garlic from cloves into a blender or food processor fitted with a metal blade. spoon soft garlic from cloves. Add oil; process until smooth. Scrape down sides of container with rubber spatula if necessary. Add cream cheese, sour cream, Worcestershire sauce, thyme, mustard, salt and pepper; process until blended. Stir in onion and parsley. Serve warm. If preparing ahead, cover and refrigerate up to 2 days; let stand at room temperature 30 minutes before serving. Serve spread with crackers, bread or vegetable sticks. Makes 1-2/3 cups.

Preparation time: 15 minutes

Thai Ginger-Peanut Chicken

Serve any leftover mixture chilled over lettuce the next day for an intriguing salad.

2 tablespoons water
2 tablespoons dry sherry
2 tablespoons soy sauce
1 tablespoon dark-brown sugar
1/8 teaspoon cayenne pepper
1/4 cup sesame oil or vegetable oil
6 green onions, sliced
2 tablespoons minced fresh gingerroot
3 cloves garlic, minced
4 boned, skinned chicken breasts, cut in julienne strips
1 red, yellow, orange or green bell pepper, slivered
3/4 cup peanut halves
Hot cooked rice or steamed shredded cabbage

To prepare sauce, in a small bowl, stir together water, sherry, soy sauce, brown sugar and cayenne. Set aside. In a wok or large skillet, heat 1 tablespoon of oil. Stir-fry onions, ginger and garlic 2 minutes (do not allow garlic to brown). Remove from pan. Add more oil to pan; stir-fry chicken pieces about 3 minutes. Remove from pan. Add more oil if necessary; stir-fry bell peppers 2 minutes. Add onion mixture, chicken and peanut halves to pan; stir in sauce mixture. Stir well to coat with sauce. Cover and cook 1 minute more to heat through. Serve immediately over cooked rice or steamed cabbage. Makes 3 or 4 servings.

Preparation time: 20 minutes

Mom's Molasses Ginger Cookies

Preserved ginger or candied ginger for these oversized cookies can be found with dried spices at large supermarkets and gourmet shops.

2 cups all-purpose flour
3 tablespoons finely chopped preserved ginger
1 tablespoon minced fresh gingerroot
2 teaspoons baking soda
1 teaspoon ground cinnamon
1/4 teaspoon ground cloves
3/4 cup vegetable shortening
About 1-1/3 cups granulated sugar
1 cup packed brown sugar
1 egg
1/4 cup dark molasses

Preheat oven to 350F (175C). In a medium bowl, stir together flour, preserved ginger, gingerroot, soda, cinnamon and cloves. Set aside. In a large bowl, beat together shortening, 1 cup of sugar and brown sugar until fluffy. Beat in egg and molasses until blended. Stir dry ingredients into molasses mixture until well mixed. For each cookie, shape dough in 1-1/2-inch balls; roll in remaining 1/3 cup of sugar to coat. Place cookie balls 3 inches apart on ungreased baking sheets. Flatten balls with bottom of glass dipped into sugar. Bake 12 to 14 minutes or until golden brown and almost set in centers. Let cookies stand on baking sheet 1 minute; place on wire racks to cool. Makes 24.

Preparation time: 15 minutes

GINGERROOT

Truly a gift from the Orient, gingerroot is an ancient favorite of Southeastern Asians, who passed it on to Europe. Today gingerroot is used widely in Thai, Indian, Malaysian and oriental dishes. If you're a fan of ground ginger, you'll find gingerroot a zestier, much more gingery flavormaker than the best powder. It will add flavor punch to everything from soup to nuts.

Fresh ginger is actually a rhizome, or stem, not a root; however, it looks like a gangly knobby root that branches off in several directions. The skin is pinkish-brown and shiny. Inside, the pale yellow, juicy meat has the powerful aroma and spicy flavor of ginger. The roots are called "hands" in the trade, and you can purchase a small 3-inch piece or a foot-long root. Hawaii, Puerto Rico, Fiji and South America bring gingerroot to our markets all year.

Buying Tips: Look for plump, very firm gingerroot with shiny, pinkish-brown skins. Bumps on the root are characteristic of fresh ginger. Avoid shriveled or wrinkled ginger. If desired, have your produce manager cut a short piece for your initial try.

Storage: Store ginger as you would garlic, in a cool, dry place for up to 1 month. Once peeled and cut, ginger should be tightly wrapped and refrigerated; store this way for up to several weeks. You can also store peeled, sliced ginger covered with dry sherry in a tightly sealed container in your refrigerator for up to 1 year.

Basic Preparation: Gingerroot can be used raw or cooked in recipes. Use sparingly at first to become acquainted with the strong flavor. Trim off ends and tiny knobs with a small sharp knife; strip off brown skin. Grate, mince or finely chop the yellow portion for recipes, or to flavor ethnic dishes. Use slices or chunks to flavor cooking liquid for soups, stews, vegetables or fruits; then retrieve and discard when the dish is served.

Serving Ideas: Ginger adds fresh flavor to soups, salad dressings, roasts, poultry, fish, vegetables, fruits and quick breads. Use minced ginger to spice up poached pears, baked apples or fruit compote. Rub ginger over fish or chicken; add it to the marinade. Ginger is particularly flavorful when combined with onions, garlic and spicy peppers. Spice up lemonade or iced tea by steeping it with gingerroot slices; or stir minced ginger into muffins or nut bread. Fresh ginger can be substituted for ground ginger in dessert recipes; use discretion.

Yield: 1 tablespoon grated fresh gingerroot = about 1/4 teaspoon ground ginger.

Nutrition Facts: Ginger used in recipes yields such a small amount per individual serving that the calories are negligible.

GREENS

"Greens" is a term used for leafy greens that have strong, bitey flavors; they're used cooked as often as raw. Collards, mustard greens, kale and turnip greens fall into this category. All of these spicy leaves have their pasts in ancient history; they were an important food for the wandering tribes in India, China, the Mediterranean and Asia.

In the southern states, greens were particularly well accepted, and became an important part of their regional cuisine. With current concerns about health and diet, greens have been recognized for their nutritional punch. Available year-round, greens are at their peak between November and June. For information on milder varieties, see Lettuces, page 118.

Buying Tips: Look for fresh, young, tender greens with good color for the variety and no limpness in the leaves. Avoid yellowing leaves, coarse, dry-looking stems and dirty leaves and stems. Mustard greens may have a bronze tinge or several shades of green; these are normal characteristics. Coarse leaves are probably tough.

Storage: Discard bruised or flabby leaves; wrap greens in damp paper towels and place in plastic bags in the crisper section of the refrigerator. Use greens within 3 to 5 days for optimum flavor.

Basic Preparation: Rinse leaves in cool water to remove sand and dirt; trim off stems and strip the leaves from thick midribs in such varieties as kale and Swiss chard. Taste greens; if they are tender and fairly mild, they can be used raw. Otherwise, cook greens before eating by steaming, boiling or microwaving. Tear, chop or shred greens; steam or boil, covered, with 1/2 inch of water for 7 to 10 minutes for mustard greens; 8 to 15 minutes for beet or turnip greens; 10 to 15 minutes for collards, dandelion greens, fiddleheads and kale; and 1 to 2 minutes for Swiss chard.

To microwave greens, place 1/2 pound of torn greens with water that clings to them in a loosely covered shallow dish. Micro-cook on High (100%) power for 4 to 7 minutes, depending on variety.

Serving Ideas: The most common method of cooking greens is by sautéing in oil or bacon drippings, steaming and covering with a cream sauce, or by boiling in a flavorful broth, such as from a cooked hambone. Add torn greens to soups and stews; mix several greens to take advantages of the different flavors. (Blanch bitter ones before adding to the pot.) Toss hot steamed greens with vinaigrette or Italian dressing.

Yield: 1/2 lb. greens, untrimmed = 1 serving, or 1/2 cup cooked. 1 lb. most greens = 1 to 1-1/2 cups cooked.

Nutrition Facts: Just 1 serving of greens will provide more than a day's requirement for vitamins C and A, large amounts of iron and calcium, plus fiber and minerals. Greens vary slightly in calorie count, ranging from 20 to 35 calories per serving.

Varieties:

Beet greens: As important as the flavorful root, beet greens can have a tender bite and mild flavor when used in salads or lightly steamed.

Collards: Considered one of the mildest greens, collards are medium-green in color with torn-looking edges on the leaves. Full-flavored, collards are actually a type of kale.

Dandelion greens: A different plant than common dandelions, these long-stemmed, delicate leaves have a pleasantly bitter flavor. The pale green leaves are available most often during the summer and early fall months.

Fiddlehead Greens: Found growing wild in the spring in Canada and Oregon, fiddleheads are not commercially produced. Their whimsical name comes from the curled, fernlike shape, which resembles the scrolled head of a violin. The delicate taste and texture are very similar to asparagus.

Kale: Actually a member of the cabbage family, kale has heavy-texture, elongated, musty-green leaves with tightly curled edges. Cabbage-like flavor.

Mustard Greens: Known for their spunky, bitey flavor, mustard greens have large medium-green leaves with frilly edges. Young or freshly harvested greens can be enjoyed raw, but older greens are too bitter and must be cooked to temper the flavor. You'll also find oriental mustard greens; they are typically milder.

Ornamental Kale: Also called "salad savoy"; see Cabbage, page 91.

Swiss Chard: In varieties with purple and white stalks and deep green leaves with purple or white veins, chard is a type of beet that does not develop a tuberous root. The leaves have a mild flavor of spinach and beets; the stems taste like celery.

Turnip Greens: Like mustard greens, turnip greens also have a lively, pleasantly bitter flavor and are best enjoyed cooked. The leaves are long, slender and deeply indented in shape; they may or may not be attached to turnip roots.

Steamed Greens with Bacon

Try this as a side dish for eggs, roast pork, or broiled meats.

6 slices bacon
1 lb. kale, mustard, collard, Swiss chard, beet or turnip greens, or spinach, stems removed, chopped (6 cups)
1/4 cup water
1 tablespoon chopped fresh basil, or 1 teaspoon dried leaf basil
Salt and pepper to taste

Cook bacon till crisp. Drain, leaving 2 tablespoons drippings in pan. Add chopped greens, water and basil. Cover and cook over medium heat 10 to 15 minutes for kale or collards; 5 to 7 minutes for beet, mustard or turnip greens or 2 minutes for spinach or Swiss chard. Crumble bacon; toss into greens. Season to taste with salt and pepper. Makes 4 servings.

Preparation time: 15 minutes

Tomato, Greens & Cheese Pizza, page 108.

Stuffed Eggplant

Choose hot or sweet sausage to taste.

2 (1-lb.) eggplants
1 lb. Italian sausage
1 tablespoon vegetable oil
2 bell peppers, seeded, cut in 1/2-inch chunks
1 cup half-slices red onion
1 clove garlic, minced
1 tomato, chopped
1 cup chopped collard or dandelion greens
2 tablespoons chopped fresh parsley
1 tablespoon chopped fresh rosemary or 1 teaspoon crushed dried rosemary
1 tablespoon chopped fresh oregano or 1 teaspoon crushed dried oregano
1/2 teaspoon salt
1/4 teaspoon pepper
2 oz. sliced mozzarella cheese, cut in 1/2-inch strips

Preheat oven to 400F (205C). Halve eggplant lengthwise; place cut side up on a greased baking sheet. Brush with oil. Bake uncovered 20 minutes. Scoop out pulp from eggplant, leaving a 1/4-inch shell on bottom and sides. Chop pulp. In a large skillet, brown sausage 10 minutes; drain and reserve 2 tablespoons drippings in skillet. In same pan, sauté bell peppers, onion and garlic 2 minutes. Stir in chopped eggplant pulp, tomato, greens, parsley, rosemary, oregano, salt and pepper; cook 10 minutes more. Add sausage back to skillet. Spoon sausage mixture into eggplant halves on baking sheet. Cover; bake 15 minutes or until filling is heated through. Uncover; top with cheese strips. Return to oven about 5 minutes or until cheese melts. Makes 4 servings.

Preparation time: 25 minutes

Tomato, Greens & Cheese Pizza

Packaged hot roll mix makes the time-saving crust.

1 (16-oz.) pkg. hot roll mix
1-1/4 cups warm water (125F/50C)
3 tablespoons vegetable oil
4 large tomatoes, chopped, or 6 cups cherry or pear tomatoes, halved
1 cup chopped onion
1 garlic clove, finely chopped
2 tablespoons chopped fresh basil
1/4 teaspoon pepper
2 cups fresh collard or mustard greens torn into bit-sized pieces
2 cups shredded mozzarella cheese (8 oz.)
6 slices bacon, cooked, crumbled
2 tablespoon chopped fresh parsley

Preheat oven to 425F (220C). In a large bowl, place flour mixture from hot roll mix. Stir in yeast from packet. Stir in water and 2 tablespoons oil until flour is moistened. Turn dough onto a floured surface; shape into ball. Knead 5 minutes. Pat dough into a greased 10" x 15" x 1" jelly-roll pan. Prick dough all over with fork. Cover; let rise 15 minutes. Meanwhile, Blanch greens in 1/2 inch of boiling salted water 3 minutes; drain well. In a large skillet, heat remaining oil. Sauté tomatoes, onions, garlic, basil and pepper 3 minutes; drain. Spoon tomato mixture over dough to within 1 inch of edges. Arrange spinach leaves over tomato sauce; sprinkle on cheese, bacon and parsley. Bake for 15 to 20 minutes or until crust is golden. Cut into squares. Makes 9 servings.

Preparation time: 30 minutes

Tortellini-Sausage Soup

This dump-in-the-pot-soup couldn't be easier! Serve with warm crusty bread.

1 lb. sweet or hot Italian sausage, cut in 1/2-inch pieces
1 lb. beet, kale, collard, turnip, dandelion or mustard greens or spinach, stemmed, torn in bite-sized pieces
4 cups beef broth
4 cups water
1 (9-oz.) pkg. cheese-filled tortellini or other stuffed pasta
1 large zucchini or yellow squash, diced
1 cup broccoli florets
1 cup whole corn
1 tablespoon chopped fresh basil or 1 teaspoon dried leaf basil
1 tablespoon chopped fresh oregano or 1 teaspoon dried leaf oregano
Salt and pepper to taste
Shredded mozzarella cheese

In a medium skillet, cook sausage 10 minutes; drain well. If using mustard greens, cook in boiling water 2 minutes; drain well. In a 4-quart Dutch oven or stockpot, stir together sausage, greens, broth, water, tortellini, zucchini or yellow squash, broccoli, corn, basil and oregano. Bring to a boil; reduce heat. Simmer, partially covered, 15 to 20 minutes or until tortellini and vegetables are nearly tender. Season to taste with salt and pepper. Ladle soup into bowls; sprinkle mozzarella cheese on top as desired. Makes 2-1/2 quarts.

Preparation time: 15 minutes

Tip:
Recipe can be halved.

Tip:
While barbecuing meats like beef, pork and lamb, try tossing some sprigs of pungent herbs like thyme, rosemary and oregano on the coals, then wrap roasts in herb sprigs and tie with kitchen string. The herbs will impart a subtle flavor to the meat, and your barbecue will have a superb aroma.

Kohlrabi & Potatoes in Dill Butter

Try this as a side dish for Herb-Stuffed Roast Lamb, page 110.

**1 lb. (2 bulbs) purple or green
  kohlrabi**
1 lb. red potatoes
1/4 cup butter or margarine
**1 tablespoon chopped fresh dill
  or 1 teaspoon dillweed**
1/8 teaspoon pepper

Cut off and discard the root end of kohlrabi. Remove all stems and leaves from kohlrabi bulbs. Reserve for another use. Wash and peel bulbs. Halve bulbs; slice 1/4-inch thick. Wash potatoes; halve and slice 1/4-inch thick. In separate 2-quart saucepans, place kohlrabi and potatoes in water to cover. Bring to boiling; reduce heat. Simmer, uncovered, for 25 to 30 minutes or until vegetables are tender. Drain well; arrange slices on a serving platter. In one of the pans, melt butter or margarine; stir in dill and pepper. Drizzle mixture over vegetables; serve. Makes 6 servings.

Preparation time: 15 minutes

HERBS

Fresh herbs' irresistable fragrances and intriguing folklore have permeated nearly 5000 years of history. From savory to sweet, ambrosial to pungent, herbs have had their culinary uses as well as medicinial ones. Through the centuries, herbs have been used as a love potion, protection against baldness, to ward off vitamin deficiencies, planted for decorative foliage, and used as symbols of wealth and good will toward the gods.

During the Middle Ages, herbs became important culinarily, and were used extensively in sauces, conserves, pastries, puddings, teas and wines. Today, supplies of fresh herbs in markets are proliferating, and their culinary possibilities are endless. With myriad fresh fruits and vegetables available now, seasoning with fresh herbs seems very apropos. Once you've sampled the zesty, distinctive flavors of fresh herbs, you won't be satisfied with the dried versions. For information on garlic, see page 103 and for sweet anise, see Fennel, page 101.

Buying Tips: Purchase herbs that have fresh-looking leaves and stems with no yellowing or brown spots. Purchase herbs only when you need them, in small quantities.

Storage: Refrigerate herbs with the stems in water and the leaves wrapped loosely in plastic; keep for up to 1 week. Or place stems of herbs in 2 inches of water in a tall glass jar; screw top on tightly. Change water daily; herbs will stay fresh up to 10 days. Basil and sage leaves can be layered in glass jars and covered with oil; refrigerate up to several months. Herbs generally freeze well; store in plastic freezer bags with air blown into them. Discard stems from basil, mint, oregano, parsley and sage before freezing. Some discoloration may result.

Basic Preparation: Wash herbs; gently pat dry on paper towels. Discard woody or tough stems. Tear, chop, mince or finely chop herbs in food processor or blender for use in recipes or to sprinkle over foods. In general, use fresh herbs sparingly to become acquainted with their distinctive flavors. Use whole sprigs to garnish foods like roasts or vegetable dishes. Use kitchen shears to quickly snip a bunch of herbs. To use several herbs in a soup or stew, make a Bouquet Garni: enclose sprigs of parsley, bay leaves, sage, thyme, rosemary and oregano as desired with a peeled garlic clove in cheesecloth; retrieve the spicy bundle just before serving.

Serving Ideas: See Chart, page 110.

Yield: 1 tablespoon chopped fresh herbs = 1 teaspoon crushed dried herbs.

Herb-Stuffed Roast Lamb

It's not necessary to have the lamb butter-flied; the herb mixture is spooned into the cavity created by boning the roast.

1/4 cup minced fresh parsley
3 tablespoons chopped fresh herbs, such as sage, oregano, marjoram, rosemary, thyme or basil
2 tablespoons chopped chives
2 garlic cloves, finely chopped
2 tablespoons vegetable oil
1/2 teaspoon salt
1/4 teaspoon pepper
1 (3- to 3-1/2-lb.) boned leg of lamb roast
1 cup beef broth
1/3 cup red wine
1 tablespoon cornstarch

Preheat oven to 325F (165C). In a small bowl, stir together parsley, desired herbs, chives and garlic. Mix in oil to form a paste. Trim fell and excess fat from lamb. Spread herb mixture evenly over opening formed from boning. Fasten roast together with skewers; tie securely with kitchen string. Place lamb fat side up on a rack in a shallow roasting pan. Sprinkle roast with salt and pepper. Roast about 2 hours for medium or until a meat thermometer inserted in thickest part (not touching skewers) registers 160F (70C). Transfer to a warm platter and cover. Skim fat from pan drippings, scraping to loosen crusty bits. Add broth to pan drippings; strain into a small saucepan. In a glass measure, stir together wine and cornstarch and stir into saucepan. Bring to a boil; reduce heat and simmer 2 minutes. Slice lamb; serve with gravy. Makes 8 to 10 servings.

Preparation time: 20 minutes

Twisted Herb Bread

Serve this quick, fragrant bread with salads, soups or a special barbecue. Frozen bread dough eliminates the kneading and first rising steps required with traditional yeast dough.

1 loaf frozen bread dough, thawed
1/4 cup melted butter or margarine
1/2 cup fresh chopped basil
2 tablespoons chopped fresh desired herbs such as savory, chives, chervil, rosemary, marjoram, oregano, thyme or dill
2 tablespoons chopped drained pimiento
1 garlic clove, finely chopped
1 tablespoon grated Parmesan cheese

On a lightly floured surface, roll bread dough to a 14" x 10" rectangle. Cut dough in half lengthwise to

make 2 (14" x 5") rectangles. In a small bowl, stir together melted butter or margarine, basil, desired herbs, pimiento and garlic. Spread mixture generously on both pieces of dough to within 1 inch of edges. Starting from the long side, roll up, pinching all edges together to make two cylinders. Lay dough cylinders side by side; twist 2 rolls together, sealing at both ends, to make 1 loaf. Place on a greased baking sheet. Cover; let rise in a warm place about 30 minutes or until double. Meanwhile, preheat oven to 375F (175C). Brush loaf lightly with remaining butter mixture or vegetable oil. Sprinkle with Parmesan cheese. Bake 25 to 35 minutes or until deep golden brown and loaf sounds hollow when lightly tapped. Cool on rack. Serve warm. Makes 1 loaf.

Preparation time: 20 minutes

1.Italian parsley. 2.Spicy globe basil. 3.Italian basil. 4.Baby dill. 5.Sweet basil. 6.Cinnamon basil. 7.Cilantro. 8.Lemon basil. 9.Opal Basil. 10.Garlic chives. 11.Chervil. 12.Thyme. 13.Sage. 14.Marjoram. 15.French tarragon. 16.Oregano. 17.Regular thyme. 18.Gingerroot. 19.Peppermint. 20.Lemon thyme. 21.Regular mint. 22.Orange mint. 23.Trailing rosemary. 24.Spearmint. 25.Marjoram.

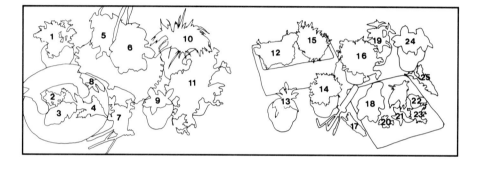

Fresh Herbs. See diagram, above.

FRESH HERB GUIDE

Herb	Flavor	Uses
Basil (Red, Green, Cinnamon, & Opal)	Rich, robust, peppery.	In pesto, tomato dishes, with spinach, mild cheeses, on pizza, all vegetables, eggs.
Bay Leaves	Subtle, with balsam & honey overtones.	Soups, stews, marinades, pickling, salad dressing, with corned beef.
Chervil	Mild, oniony, parsley-sweet.	In salad dressings, light sauces, with vegetables, chicken, fish, steamed vegetables, eggs for garni.
Chives	Mild, oniony.	Over baked potatoes, fish, chicken, white sauce, cheese dishes, egg dishes, pot roasts, cheese spreads, soups.
Cilantro or Coriander	Musty parsley flavor.	In Mexican, Thai and oriental dishes, with chicken and fish, in tomato sauce, with pork and sausage, in curry dishes.
Dill (Crown, Baby)	Fragrant, savory.	Crown used in pickling, Baby with eggs, salmon or other fish, in chicken salad, with tomatoes, green beans, cauliflower, zucchini.
Epazote	Pungent, savory.	Said to prevent flatulence, used widely in Mexican cookery. Add to bean dishes, chili, robust soups, stews.
Italian Parsley	Zesty parsley flavor.	Use wherever parsley would be used; in soups, stews, for a garnish, with eggs, potatoes, any cooked vegetable, in butter, bouquet garni.
Lemon Balm	Zesty lemon.	Flavor iced tea, fruit drinks, salads, soups, fruit compotes, carrots, peas, fish.
Lemon Grass	Delicate lemon.	Peel off outer layer; chop tender center to use in Thai dishes, salads, hot tea, marinades, with chicken, fish, fruit.
Lemon Verbena	Definite lemon.	Use mainly in jellies, desserts, puddings, tea, ice cream.
Marjoram	Like a mild oregano.	Use in Italian and Greek dishes, in spaghetti sauce, on pizza, pork, lamb, beef, in salad dressing, with eggplant, Jerusalem artichokes, Swiss chard, and mushrooms.
Mint (Orange, Spearmint, Peppermint)	Sweet peppermint or spearmint flavor.	With fresh fruit, lamb, carrots, potatoes, peas, tomatoes, salads, in iced tea, tropical or fruit drinks.
Oregano	Spicy, pungent.	Use in Italian dishes, pizza, tomato sauce, in sausage, with pork, lamb, beef, in meat marinades, with tomatoes, cabbage.
Parsley	Mild, sweet.	Breath-freshner, easy garnish. Add to soups, stews, salad dressings, chop into vegetables, poultry stuffings, sauces.
Rosemary	Pungent, spicy.	Superb with lamb, pork, on barbecued meats, with tomatoes, eggplant, in marinades, salad dressings.
Sage, Pineapple Sage	Musty, pungent.	Good with duck, beef, pork, in tomato-based dishes, in hearty soups, stews, turkey stuffing, with organ meats.
Savory (Summer, Winter)	May be sweet to pleasantly bitter.	Perfect for all cooked vegetables, red meats, egg dishes, tomato-based dishes, sauces, salad dressings.
Tarragon	Delicate licorice flavor.	In lightly seasoned chicken and fish dishes, with mild cheese and creamy dips, in salad dressing, with cooked summer squash, peas, mushrooms, artichokes, beans.
Thyme (Lemon, Caraway, English)	Spicy, savory but zesty.	Perfect for roasts, chicken, salad dressings, marinades, cheese dishes, stuffings, soups, stews.

Horseradish Mustard Dip

Great with raw vegetables, or as a spread for a roast beef sandwich.

1 cup mayonnaise or salad
  dressing
1/2 cup Dijon-style mustard
2 to 3 tablespoons grated
  horseradish
2 tablespoons white wine
1 tablespoon snipped chives
1 teaspoon brown sugar
1/4 teaspoon paprika

In a medium bowl, stir together mayonnaise or salad dressing, mustard, horseradish to taste, wine, chives, brown sugar and paprika. Cover and chill at least 1 hour to allow flavors to blend. Makes 1-2/3 cups.

Preparation time: 5 minutes

Fresh Horseradish Sauce

Serve with roast beef or lamb.

1/3 cup cubed horseradish
2 tablespoons lemon juice
1 cup dairy sour cream
1/4 teaspoon salt
1 tablespoon minced chives or 1
  clove minced garlic
Salt and pepper to taste

In a blender or food processor fitted with a metal blade, process horseradish and lemon juice until horseradish is finely minced. Add sour cream, salt and chives or garlic; process again just until mixed. Season to taste with salt and pepper. Makes 1-1/2 cups sauce.

Variation:
Horseradish Mayonnaise: Substitute 1 cup mayonnaise for sour cream.

Preparation time: 10 minutes

HORSERADISH

Perhaps the zestiest, most eye-opening herb around, horseradish adds a spunky quality to everything that goes with it. This pungent flavor-maker is nothing new; its use is ancient history to the Asians, Romans and Greeks.

Horseradish is a slender, brown-skinned root that has the unmistakable, strong-smelling aroma of the familiar condiment. A pungent oil in the root gives horseradish its trademark hot flavor. A distant relative of mustard, horseradish grows wild in many parts of the world, including the eastern U.S. Horseradish is available in markets practically all year.

Buying Tips: Check that the roots are very firm, with the aroma of horseradish at the ends. Avoid shriveled roots that have a bitter scent.

Storage: Refrigerate the horseradish root, tightly wrapped, in your refrigerator crisper for up to several months. Refrigerate or freeze grated horseradish in airtight containers for several months.

Basic Preparation: Scrub root thoroughly; peel off brown skin. Finely grate by hand or in a food processor or blender as needed. Use as a condiment on red meat sandwiches, add to cream sauces, or mix into seafood cocktail sauces. Note: grated horseradish can bring tears from the cook more easily than onions can.

Serving Ideas: Used mainly as described above and in recipes in this section.

Yield: 1 condiment serving = 1/2 to 1 teaspoon grated.

Nutrition Facts: Calories in fresh horseradish are negligible; but the root is rich in phosphorous, potassium and calcium.

Spicy Beef Bagelwiches

Enjoy these for a Sunday night supper.

1 lb. sliced cooked roast beef,
  turkey breast or ham
4 lettuce leaves
4 bagels, split horizontally, and
  toasted, if desired
1 cup sprouts (kaiware, etc.)
4 slices red onion

Horseradish Dressing:
1/4 cup mayonnaise or salad
  dressing
2 tablespoons plain yogurt
1-1/2 teaspoons prepared
  horseradish
1 teaspoon Dijon-style mustard
1 teaspoon chopped chives

Prepare Horseradish Dressing. Cut meat slices into julienne strips; place in a medium bowl. Toss meat with Horseradish Dressing. Arrange lettuce leaves on bottom halves of bagels. Top with meat salad. Arrange a slice of onion and sprouts on top. Top with second bagel slice. Makes 4 sandwiches.

Horseradish Dressing:
In a small bowl, stir together mayonnaise or salad dressing, yogurt, horseradish, mustard and chives until well blended. Makes 1/2 cup.

Preparation time: 15 minutes

JICAMA

(HIC-ah-muh) Also called a Mexican potato, jicama hails from Central America and Mexico, where it is a staple. It was first introduced to the U.S. in Mexican and Southwestern dishes, but jicama is so versatile that it's now popular in our American reportoire as well.

Like potatoes, jicama grows underground as a tuber. Its globular shape can be as small as an apple or as large as a squash. Jicama is covered with a thick brown skin, with a short root attached. Inside, you'll find pristine white flesh that looks like an apple or raw potato. Raw, jicama is sweet, juicy and crisp, perfect as a snack vegetable. Cooked lightly, it becomes milder, but retains its crispness, like a water chestnut. Best of all, jicama is inexpensive, low in calories and proliferates in produce markets all during the year.

Buying Tips: Size is not an indication of flavor or ripeness. Look for firm, dry roots with clean brown skins. Avoid mushy, bruised or dirty jicama.

Storage: Jicama stores well in a cool dry place for up to several weeks. Do not refrigerate or freeze.

Basic Preparation: Trim off attached root; with a sharp paring knife, strip off the thick brown peel. The white meat can be chopped, sliced, shredded, or cut into julienne sticks to enjoy as a vegetable snack or to use in recipes. Enjoy raw as is or dip in salsa, sour cream dips or guacamole. Traditionally, Mexicans dip sticks in lime juice, then roll in chili powder for a snack. Steam or stir-fry jicama for 1 to 2 minutes, or microwave in a shallow, loosely covered dish with 2 tablespoons water at High (100%) power for the same amount of time. Season with herbs or salt and pepper and melted butter.

Serving Ideas: Jicama is great pickled with onions, peppers and herbs. Stir-fry jicama with Chinese vegetables; season with soy sauce, ginger, and garlic. It takes on other flavors readily, as potatoes do. Use jicama wherever you would use water chestnuts or sunchokes (Jerusalem artichokes). Add shredded jicama to fresh fruit salads, especially citrus; add to a pita sandwich. Sprinkle over a sliced tomato salad or add to vegetable relishes. Perfect for a vegetable dipper platter or as an after-school snack for kids. Add to soups and stews near the end of cooking or toss into marinated vegetable mixtures.

Yield: 1 lb. jicama = 4 to 6 servings.
1 lb. jicama = about 3 cups chopped or shredded.

Nutrition Facts: A 3-1/2-ounce serving of jicama is just 45 calories. It's a good source of vitamin C, and contributes some calcium and iron.

Deep-Fried Jicama Sticks

These make an easy hot appetizer. Make your own salsa or buy it ready-made at the heat level you desire.

1/2 lb. jicama, peeled, or 1 lb. sunchokes, cut in 1-1/2- x 1/4-inch sticks
1-1/2 cups Italian seasoned bread crumbs
1/3 cup grated Parmesan cheese
2 tablespoons minced fresh parsley
1 teaspoon chili powder
1/4 teaspoon salt
4 eggs
Oil for deep-frying
1-1/2 cups Homemade Salsa, page 97, or bottled salsa

In a medium saucepan, steam jicama over boiling water 2 minutes. Rinse in cool water; drain well. In a shallow bowl, stir together bread crumbs, cheese, parsley, chili powder and salt. In another shallow bowl, beat eggs until frothy. Line a baking sheet or tray with wax paper. Dip jicama sticks into egg mixture, then in bread crumb mixture to coat all sides. Repeat dipping in egg, then in bread crumbs to coat well. Place crumb-coated pieces on paper-lined tray. Pour oil into a deep skillet or wok to a depth of 2 inches. Heat to 365F (185C). Fry jicama, a few pieces at a time, about 1 minute or until golden brown. Drain on paper towels. Serve warm with salsa for dipping. Makes about 24.

Preparation time: 15 minutes

Kohlrabi with Cheddar Sauce

Here, kohlrabi tastes like mild cauliflower. Try the sauce on beans, asparagus, turnips, broccoli and potatoes, too.

4 bulbs purple or green kohlrabi
Water
Salt and pepper to taste

Cheddar Sauce:
2 tablespoons butter or margarine
1 tablespoon flour
3/4 cup milk
1/2 cup shredded sharp Cheddar cheese
1/4 teaspoon salt
Dash bottled hot pepper sauce

Cut off and discard the root end and all stems and leaves from kohlrabi bulbs. Wash and peel bulbs. Cut into 1/2-inch cubes. In a 3-quart saucepan, place kohlrabi pieces with water to cover. Bring to boiling; reduce heat. Simmer, uncovered, 20 to 25 minutes or until tender. Prepare Cheddar Sauce. Drain kohlrabi; season with salt and pepper to taste. Arrange kohlrabi on a platter and pour sauce over. Makes 4 servings.

Cheddar Sauce:
In a small saucepan, melt butter or margarine; stir in flour. Add milk all at once; cook and stir until mixture thickens and bubbles. Stir in cheese, salt and hot pepper sauce until cheese melts. Cover and keep warm over very low heat till needed. Makes 1 cup.

Preparation time: 20 minutes

KOHLRABI

(Coal-ROB-ee) Taken directly from the German, kohlrabi translates to "cabbage turnip." The result of cross-breeding between cabbage and turnips, this intriguing vegetable is a favorite of Eastern Europeans, Germans and Asians. It's not a root, but actually a swollen stem that is globe-shaped, with green stems and leaves that jut out on all sides. Kohlrabi may be green or red; the latter is the color of beets with red-veined leaves.

Kohlrabi has a mild, turnip-like flavor, in keeping with its name, and is as easy to prepare as potatoes. The leaves, like spinach, can be cooked with the vegetable, along with the delicately-flavored stems. You can stuff the bulb as you would squash or bell peppers or cook kohlrabi as a vegetable side dish. Or serve kohlrabi raw with other fresh vegetables for a waist-watching snack.

Buying Tips: Look for kohlrabi from May through November. Smaller kohlrabi bulbs will be sweetest. The bulbs should be clean and firm, with unblemished skins and healthy-looking leaves.

Storage: Refrigerate kohlrabi, tightly wrapped in plastic, in the crisper section. Store up to 1 week. Do not freeze.

Basic Preparation: Strip off stems and leaves; stems can be chopped or sliced julienne-style and leaves torn for use in recipes. It's not necessary to peel small kohlrabi; if larger than an apple, peel off thick skin with a sharp paring knife. Quarter the bulb, or slice, chop or cut into julienne sticks. Or hollow out the bulb with a grapefruit knife to use the bulb for stuffing. Serve kohlrabi raw as a snacking vegetable, or boil, steam or sauté until tender. Kohlrabi chunks take 20 to 25 minutes to steam or boil tender. To microwave chunks or slices of kohlrabi, place in a shallow dish with 1/4 cup water; cover loosely. Micro-cook on High (100%) power for 3-1/2 to 5 minutes. Let stand 3 minutes until nearly tender.

Serving Ideas: Stuff whole kohlrabi with ground meat or turkey and chopped vegetables; top with cheese. Add kohlrabi chunks or slices to potato casseroles, or steam with pieces of green or yellow summer squash to add color. Shred kohlrabi into carrot-raisin salad, add to sandwich fillings, or sprinkle into tossed salads. Add sticks of kohlrabi to coleslaw or stir-fries. Roast kohlrabi to serve with beef or pork and meat juices. Cook kohlrabi till tender and mash to mix with mashed rutabagas or potatoes.

Yield: 1 lb. kohlrabi, with stems = 4 medium bulbs.
2 lbs. kohlrabi, trimmed and cooked = about 4 servings.
1 kohlrabi bulb = 1 serving.

Nutrition Facts: One serving of kohlrabi is about 25 calories. It contains moderate amounts of calcium, vitamin C and vitamin A and potassium.

LEEKS

A leek looks like an overgrown green onion, with a fat white tip, wide green leaves, and the same hairy protrusion at the bulb end. But what sets leeks apart from onions is their subtle flavor. Take your cue from the Europeans, who know and appreciate leeks as a sweet, delicate cousin of the onion, far more sophisticated and delectable.

Because leeks have such a sweet, unassuming flavor, they make an elegant side dish in themselves. Leeks are the subtle ingredient in vichyssoise or cold potato soup. Sliced raw, leeks add elegance to salads or appetizers. Look for them all year, to use like onions in almost any savory dish.

Buying Tips: Leeks may be 1/2 to 2 inches thick at the white base; size does not affect flavor, but smaller leeks are sometimes more tender. Look for crisp, white bulbs with healthy green leaves and no soft spots or browning. Avoid leeks with dry-looking leaves.

Storage: Wrap leeks tightly in plastic and refrigerate in the crisper section. Leeks will store for up to 2 weeks, if kept dry. Do not freeze; the leeks will become bitter.

Basic Preparation: The most important aspect of preparing leeks is cleaning them, since dirt and grit collects among the long green leaves. Remove withered outer leaves; trim off the hairy base from white portion. Trim off green leaves to within 2 inches above the white part. Split the leaves down to the white; wash under cold running water until all grit and sand rinse away. Slice crosswise, quarter lengthwise, or chop trimmed leek to use in recipes, raw or cooked. Or braise leeks whole in broth for 10 to 20 minutes, depending on the thickness of the leeks. To microwave leeks, place whole or sliced in a shallow dish with 1/4 cup chicken broth or water; cover loosely. Micro-cook on High (100%) power for 7 to 9 minutes for whole leeks, or 3 to 5 minutes for 1/4-inch slices.

Serving Ideas: Leeks are delicious incorporated into quiches, scalloped potatoes, vegetable casseroles, and omelets. Slice leeks raw to toss into green salads, on a roast beef sandwich, or with marinated vegetables. Sauté leeks with bacon and sunchokes for a side dish, or add chunks to a pot roast or stew. Purée cooked leeks for soups, pâtés or flavored cheese spread. Substitute leeks for green onions in oriental dishes. Leeks are famous in Cock-a-Leekie soup, an English-style chicken soup with vegetables.

Yield: 2 lbs. leeks = about 4 servings.
1 lb. leeks, trimmed = 2 cups chopped raw, 1 cup cooked.

Nutrition Facts: One serving of leeks has about 55 calories. Leeks contain calcium, potassium, phosphorous and some vitamin C.

Leek Skillet Bread

This leek-topped bread is at its best fresh and warm. Serve hearty wedges with a soup or salad.

3 tablespoons butter or margarine
6 leeks, white part only, washed and thinly sliced
6 green onions, finely chopped
1 garlic clove, finely chopped
2 tablespoons finely chopped pimiento
1/2 teaspoon salt
1/4 teaspoon pepper
1-1/2 cups milk
1 egg
1-1/2 cups buttermilk baking mix
1/2 cup shredded Swiss or Monterey Jack cheese (2 oz.)

Preheat oven to 400F (205C). In a 9- or 10-inch oven-proof skillet, melt butter or margarine; sauté leeks, green onions and garlic about 3 minutes or till leeks are tender. Stir in pimiento, salt and pepper. Cook about 3 minutes more or until leeks begin to brown, stirring frequently. Remove pan from heat. In a medium bowl, whisk together milk and egg. Stir in baking mix and Swiss or Monterey Jack cheese. Pour batter over leek mixture in skillet. Bake about 30 to 40 minutes or until golden brown. Invert a round platter over pan; turn bread out onto platter. Transfer any leeks that remain in skillet onto top of bread. Cut into wedges; serve warm. Makes about 8 servings.

Preparation time: 10 minutes

Baked Leeks with Shallots & Almonds

This makes a nice accompaniment to Roast Chicken with Apricot-Pecan Stuffing, page 20.

8 whole leeks, 3/4 inch thick
1/4 cup butter or margarine
3 shallots, peeled, finely chopped
1/3 cup fresh bread crumbs
1/2 cup slivered almonds
2 tablespoons chopped parsley
1/4 teaspoon paprika

Preheat oven to 375F (190C). Clean leeks; trim off hairy ends. Cut crosswise into 1-inch pieces. Place in a large saucepan with water to cover. Bring to boiling; reduce heat. Simmer 8 to 10 minutes or just until tender. Drain. Arrange leeks in a 12" x 8" x 2" baking dish. In a small skillet, melt butter or margarine. Sauté shallots 2 minutes. Stir in bread crumbs, almonds, parsley and paprika. Spoon mixture over leeks. Bake 15 minutes. Remove from oven. Preheat broiler. Broil leeks for a few seconds or just until crumbs are golden. Makes 4 servings.

Preparation time: 15 minutes

Leeks & Salsify In Cream Sauce

Here's a heartwarming side dish for a Sunday roast.

1 lb. salsify or scorzonera
3 tablespoons lemon juice
2 tablespoons butter or margarine
2 to 3 leeks, white part only, sliced
1 tablespoon flour
3/4 cup half and half
1 tablespoon minced fresh parsley, chives, or chervil or 1 teaspoon dried herb
1/2 teaspoon Italian herbs
1/2 teaspoon salt
1/4 teaspoon pepper

Trim and peel salsify or scorzonera; slit lengthwise and cut into 1-inch pieces. Drop immediately into lemon juice mixed with water to cover. Drain; place pieces in lightly salted water to cover; bring to boiling. Reduce heat; simmer 10 to 12 minutes or until tender; drain. In a large skillet, melt butter or margarine; sauté leek slices 2 to 3 minutes or until limp. Stir in flour; add half-and-half all at once. Cook and stir until mixture begins to boil; reduce heat and stir in parsley, chives or chervil, Italian herbs, salt and pepper. Stir in cooked salsify; cook, covered, 1 minute more to heat through. Makes 4 servings.

Preparation time: 20 minutes

Leeks, Parsnip & Carrot Soufflé

Serve as a meatless main dish or as an accompaniment to poultry.

1-1/2 cups finely shredded parsnips
1-1/2 cups finely shredded carrots
2 tablespoons butter or margarine
1/2 cup chopped leeks
2 tablespoons flour
1 cup chicken broth
1 tablespoon snipped chives
1/2 teaspoon ground nutmeg
1/4 teaspoon salt
1/8 teaspoon pepper
4 eggs, separated

Preheat oven to 400F (205C). Lightly butter a 1-1/2-quart soufflé dish or straight-sided casserole. In a steamer over simmering water, cook parsnips and carrots 6 to 8 minutes or until nearly tender. Drain. In same pan, melt butter or margarine; sauté leeks until limp. Stir in flour; add broth all at once, cooking and stirring until mixture thickens and bubbles. Remove from heat. Stir in chives, nutmeg, salt and pepper. Whisk in egg yolks, 1 at a time. Stir in parsnips and carrots. Beat egg whites until stiff; fold into vegetable mixture. Turn into prepared soufflé dish. Bake 25 to 35 minutes or until puffed and golden. Serve at once. Makes 4 main-dish or 6 to 8 side-dish servings.

Preparation time: 20 minutes

LETTUCES

There's a galaxy of beautiful salad greens in markets today, colored green to purple and red, in flavors mild to piquant. The resurgence of salads in American diets has brought on a "green renaissance" at the supermarket. So many salad green varieties abound, that head lettuce, once a salad staple, is now just the tip of the iceberg, as lettuces go.

Lettuce grew wild since early Roman times, but it wasn't until the advent of refrigerated train cars that lettuce could be commercially grown and made available year-round. Now it's possible to make a conversation-piece salad with nothing but a variety of lettuces and a homemade vinaigrette dressing. But don't restrict these delectable leaves to just salad-making; their culinary advantages make them useful for cooked dishes, too.

Buying Tips: Look for fresh-looking leaves, bright color for the variety, and firm heads. Avoid lettuces and greens with brown-tinged leaves. Lettuces should be heavy for their size.

Storage: Do not separate leaves from the head until ready to prepare lettuce for serving. Store, loosely wrapped in plastic, in the refrigerator crisper section for up to 1 week. Do not store lettuce adjacent to apples, melons or pears; these fruits give off ethylene gases which can cause browning of lettuce.

Basic Preparation: For leaf lettuces, tear leaves from core; for sorrel, watercress and mache, cut off brown stems. For Belgian endive, trim off bottom 1/4 inch to separate leaves. Wash leaves thoroughly; dry on paper towels or use a lettuce dryer. Tear, never cut lettuce for salads, since knives cause browning on cut edges. Or use torn leaves in recipes.

Serving Ideas: Combine leaves of different colors, textures and flavors in salads with fruits, vegetables, cheeses and meats. Use cheeses such as brie, camembert, blue, feta and sharp Cheddar in combination with radicchio, Belgian endive, watercress and chicory. Add torn lettuces to creamy vegetable soups; purée to thicken. Steam romaine or sorrel leaves to wrap around meat fillings as for stuffed cabbage. Use pretty leaves to line a roast platter, to chop into stuffings, or to add to sautéed or stir-fried vegetables at the last minute of cooking. Use lettuce leaves to hold sandwich fillings instead of using bread. Fill Belgian endive leaves with pâté or salmon salad as an hors d'oeuvre.

Yield: 1 lb. torn lettuce = 5 (2-cup) servings.
1 lb. lettuce = (average) 10 cups torn.

Nutrition Facts: All salad greens are extremely low in calories, about 7 to 10 calories per cup. Varieties contain vitamins A and C, iron, and calcium in varying amounts. All are generous in fiber content.

Unusual Varieties:

Arrugula (ah-ROOG-ah-la): Like miniature dandelion greens, arrugula leaves are deep green, slender and undulating in shape. Also called "rocket," arrugula has a sprightly peppery flavor that mixes well with milder greens.

Belgian Endive (AHN-deev): Originally from Belgium, this vegetable comes in tightly packed, cone-shaped heads. The leaves are silvery-white with pale yellow-green tips, about 3 to 4 inches long and 1 inch wide. Somewhat bitter flavor. Can be served raw or braised whole as a vegetable.

Bibb or Boston Lettuce: Bibb lettuce is a small head lettuce with delicate rounded leaves that are bright green at the edges and yellow at the base. Flavor is delicate and fresh. "Limestone" is a name given to this type of lettuce when greenhouse-grown.

Chicory: A type of frilly endive, chicory has elongated, curly-edge leaves attached to a stem. This green has a pleasantly bitter flavor and makes a pretty garnish.

Escarole: A hardy variety of leaf lettuce with graceful elongated leaves that are somewhat irregular. Flavor is robust with a pleasant bite.

Green Leaf Lettuce: This is the frilly-edged, green leafy variety that is commonly used by restaurants in place of iceberg lettuce. Very mild, fresh flavor, multipurpose lettuce.

Mache (mosh): Also called "corn salad" or "lamb's lettuce." A gourmet variety with long stems ending in delicate, teardrop-shaped green leaves. Flavor is mild and nutty.

Cabbages, Greens, Lettuces & Sprouts. See diagram, page 157.

Radicchio (rad-DEEK-ee-oh): An Italian import, radicchio comes in small, tightly packed round heads. The leaves are a beautiful red-violet to purple color, with a white-streaked base. Radicchio has a pungent, spicy flavor.

Red Leaf Lettuce: A red-tinged variety of green leaf lettuce; a mild-flavored lettuce that's as versatile as the green.

Romaine: A foot-long head of deep green, oval leaves with paler leaves in the center. Romaine is sweet and mild-tasting.

Sorrel (soar-RELL): Lemony-tasting, with long-stemmed leaves like spinach, sorrel has a more pronounced flavor than spinach. Steam and use like spinach when more flavor is desired.

Spinach: It has deep green, pointed leaves with stems attached. Mildly robust flavor; excellent raw or lightly steamed.

Watercress: It has stems like parsley, with tiny rounded leaves attached from base to tips. The taste is spicy and slightly peppery; used often in cooking as well as fresh.

Four-Greens Salad

Sometimes the most interesting salads are composed of nothing more than a variety of flavorful lettuces.

2 cups torn romaine lettuce
1-1/2 cups torn radiccio or red leaf lettuce
1 cup torn escarole, sorrel, bibb or chicory
1 cup watercress sprigs or 1 head of Belgian endive, trimmed, and leaves separated
Lime-Mustard Dressing, page 56, or Walnut Dressing, page 57 or Vinaigrette Dressing, page 154

In a large salad bowl, toss together all lettuces. Prepare desired salad dressing; pour over salad. Toss well and serve. Makes 4 to 5 servings.

Preparation time: 10 minutes

Romaine & Zucchini Soup

Be sure to use fresh herbs for this light, creamy soup; dried herbs will not provide the same character.

1 tablespoon vegetable oil
1 cup chopped onion
1 garlic clove, finely chopped
3 cups chicken broth
3 cups chopped romaine lettuce, sorrel, spinach, Swiss chard leaves or fiddlehead greens
2 medium zucchini, chopped (1-3/4 cups)
1/2 cup half and half
2 tablespoons chopped fresh herbs, such as basil, dill, chervil, chives or tarragon
1/2 teaspoon salt
1/8 teaspoon pepper

In a Dutch oven or large saucepan, heat oil. Sauté onion and garlic until onion is tender. Stir in broth, romaine lettuce and zucchini pieces. Bring to boiling; reduce heat. Simmer, uncovered, 10 minutes. In a blender or food processor fitted with a metal blade, process soup in 2 batches to a purée. Return to pan. Slowly stir in cream. Season soup with herbs, salt and pepper. Heat through but do not boil. Makes 4 servings (4-1/2 cups).

Preparation time: 20 minutes

Stir-Fried Sorrel with Mushrooms

Briefly frying the sorrel retains its brilliant color.

3 to 4 tablespoons peanut oil or cooking oil
1-1/2 cups sliced fresh mushrooms, such as shiitake, oyster, chanterelle or brown
1/2 cup sliced red onion
1 bunch (1 lb.) fresh sorrel or spinach, washed, stems removed
1/4 teaspoon salt
1/8 teaspoon crushed red pepper

In a wok or large skillet, heat 2 tablespoons oil over high heat. Stir-fry mushrooms and red onion until vegetables are limp. Remove from pan. Add more oil; stir-fry sauce 1 minute or just until it begins to wilt. Add mushrooms and onion back to pan; sprinkle with salt and red pepper. Stir-fry 1 minute more. Serve immediately. Makes 4 servings.

Preparation time: 15 minutes

Cheese-Stuffed Belgian Endive

Next time, try filling the dainty, elongated leaves of Belgian endive with liver pâté, or salmon or tuna salad.

2 heads Belgian endive
1 (4-oz.) pkg. herbed cheese spread, softened
About 24 walnut or pecan halves
1/2 lb. red or green seedless grapes

Trim off bottom 1/4 inch of Belgian endive; separate leaves. Spread about 1 rounded teaspoon cheese spread in bottom third of each endive leaf cavity. Place filling side up on a platter; garnish each with a walnut or pecan half. With kitchen shears, cut grapes into small clusters; arrange around filled endive pieces. Makes about 2 dozen appetizers.

Preparation time: 10 minutes

Unusual Varieties:
Note: All varieties except Enoki must be cooked; never eat raw.

Cepes (seps): Also called "porcini," cepes have an Italian heritage, and a rich flavor that's a reminder of hazelnuts. Usually only available dried, cepes have an earthy flavor and delicate texture.

Chanterelles (shan-TRELLS): Also called "trumpets," these resemble beautiful golden or yellow-orange trumpets. These large mushrooms range from delicately nutty to almost meaty in flavor. Purchase fresh or dried.

Enoki (ee-KNOCK-ee): Popular in Oriental cookery, these long-stemmed white mushrooms have puffy little caps and a very soft texture. Very bland in flavor.

Hedgehog: Has a beigy-orange cap with large uneven round caps. A small one is about silver dollar size. Rich, hearty mushroom flavor. Buy fresh or dried.

Japanese Honey Mushroom: Also called "hon shimeji," these have thicker stems and larger caps than enoki. Medium brown color; hearty mushroom flavor.

Morels (mohr-ELLS): Convoluted like raisins, morels are very dark brown in color with a spongy texture. Flavor is considered the best among mushrooms; it's rich and hearty, almost meaty. These must be cooked to eat. Available fresh or dried.

Oyster: An oriental mushroom that looks like pretty white or gray calla lilies with very large caps, short stems. Another oyster mushroom, "pink coral," has a peachy-pink color; its shape is like a small trumpet with curled edges. Has a mild oyster flavor. Purchase fresh or dried.

MUSHROOMS

Fungus, though an unappetizing botanical term, actually describes what a mushroom is—a plant that has no stems, seeds or flowers, but propogates through its spores. Mushrooms generally need dark, moist areas to grow, so they are often cultivated in darkness, or in caves. They are still harvested growing wild as often as they are cultivated by commercial growers.

Button mushrooms, or the familiar brown mushrooms found in stores, have recently been overshadowed by nearly a dozen new varieties. Several of the most intriguing types of mushrooms were brought to us from the Far East, and are now widely available, both fresh and dried, in the U.S. Prices tend to be steep for some of the new mushrooms, but expanded cultivation should bring costs more in line with brown mushrooms. Once you've tried the newcomers, your mushroom burger will never be the same.

Buying Tips: Look for mushrooms with firm, plump, spongy caps. Avoid mushrooms with slimy or yellowish undersides. Buy only the amount you will use within 2 days.

Storage: For best storage, remove fresh mushrooms from the package and spread them out in 2 layers at most on a paper towel-lined tray. Cover loosely with a lightly dampened paper towel. For dried mushrooms, store in a cool dry place for up to 6 months. Freezing fresh mushrooms is not recommended.

Basic Preparation: For enoki and Japanese honey mushrooms, cut off 1/2 to 1 inch of the base and withered stems. Separate mushrooms; rinse lightly and dry with paper towels. For other mushrooms, trim off bottom 1/4 inch of stems, chop or slice mushrooms as needed. (Exception: trim off entire stem of shiitake variety; they're tough.) Serve mushrooms sliced or chopped for recipes or to eat with vegetable dips. Sauté, stir-fry, steam or simmer mushrooms by themselves or in recipes. Microwaving is not recommended.

Serving Ideas: Sauté mushrooms in butter with chopped chives, leeks or mild onions. Spoon sautéed mushrooms over steaks, grilled chicken or omelets. Slice mushrooms for tossed salads, stir-frys, soups or stews. Marinate mushrooms in a spicy vinaigrette, with bell peppers and olives. Use delicate varieties in quiche, rolled in crepes with a creamy sauce, over eggs Benedict, or stuffed into Cornish game hens.

Yield: 1 lb. fresh mushrooms = 4 to 6 servings, cooked.
8 oz. fresh mushrooms = about 3 cups sliced.

Nutrition Facts: Mushrooms contain about 18 calories per cup raw. Some mushrooms contain a small amount of protein and a healthy dose of fiber. They are a fair source of B vitamins, calcium, phosphorous and other minerals.

Pom Pom: Whimsical, dwarf-like mushrooms with small caps, delicate texture. White in color, nutty flavor.

Shiitake (sheet-AH-kee): A delicious, earthy-textured mushroom, with long, woody stems and large, floppy dark brown caps. Stems are too tough to eat; use caps only. Flavor is rich and meaty; delicate texture. Buy fresh or dried.

Wood Ear: Almost like brown elephant ears, these lobster-rich mushrooms have no stems. They have a pleasantly chewy texture.

Wild Rice Shiitake

Shiitake mushrooms lend their rich, buttery flavor to this elegant rice dish.

1 cup uncooked wild rice
3 cups beef broth
1/2 cup long grain white rice
1 tablespoon fresh chopped
  chervil or chives, or 1 teaspoon
  dried herb
4 oz. fresh shiitake mushrooms
1/4 cup butter or margarine
4 green onions, chopped
1 garlic clove, finely chopped
1/2 cup toasted pecans
2 tablespoons snipped parsley
Salt and pepper to taste

Soak wild rice, if necessary, according to package directions; drain. In a 2-quart saucepan, combine rice and beef broth. Bring to boiling; reduce heat. Simmer, covered, 20 minutes. Stir in white rice and chervil or chives. Cover and simmer 20 minutes more or until rices are done and liquid is absorbed. Meanwhile, remove stems from shiitake mushrooms and discard. Slice tops thinly (cut large tops in half first). In a medium skillet, melt butter or margarine. Sauté mushrooms with onions and garlic for 3 minutes or vegetables are tender. Stir into cooked rice with pecans and parsley. Season to taste with salt and pepper. Makes 6 servings.

Preparation time: 15 minutes

Two-Mushroom Salad

Easily prepared ahead, this exotic marinated mushroom salad is perfect for a first course.

1 (3.5-oz.) pkg. enoki mushrooms
2 cups sliced sautéed shiitake,
  chanterelle or brown mushrooms
1-1/2 cups sliced yellow squash or
  zucchini
Bibb or other lettuce leaves
1 cup watercress or parsley sprigs

Two-Herb Dressing:
2/3 cup olive oil or salad oil
1/2 cup red or white wine vinegar
2 teaspoons fresh chopped thyme,
  or 1/2 teaspoon dried leaf
  thyme
2 teaspoons fresh chopped
  rosemary, or 1/2 teaspoon dried
  rosemary

Prepare Two-Herb Dressing. Set aside. Trim 1 to 2 inches off lower stems of enoki mushrooms; separate mushrooms. In a shallow glass dish, place mushrooms with sliced mushrooms and squash or zucchini. Shake dressing; pour over vegetables. Stir to distribute dressing. Cover and refrigerate 1 hour to allow flavors to blend. If preparing ahead, refrigerate up to 24 hours. For salads, drain dressing from mushrooms, reserving for another salad. On a medium platter or 4 salad plates, arrange lettuce leaves. Spoon mushroom mixture on lettuce. Garnish with watercress. Makes 4 servings.

Two-Herb Dressing:
In a shaker jar, combine olive oil or vegetable oil, red or white wine vinegar, thyme and rosemary. Cover and shake well to mix. Makes about 1 cup.

Preparation time: 15 minutes

Mushrooms & Shallots Zinfandel

This heavenly mushroom and onion combination makes a great topping for eggs, steaks, seafood or grilled favorites.

2 tablespoons butter or olive oil
1/2 lb. fresh mushrooms, sliced
4 shallots, peeled and thinly
  sliced
1/2 cup dry red wine, such as
  zinfandel or burgundy
2 teaspoons fresh chopped
  tarragon or 1/2 teaspoon dried
  tarragon

In a large skillet, heat butter or oil. Sauté mushrooms and shallots for 2 to 3 minutes, stirring frequently. Stir in wine and tarragon; cook and stir about 3 minutes or until almost all the liquid has evaporated. Serve at once. Makes 3 or 4 servings.

Preparation time: 10 minutes

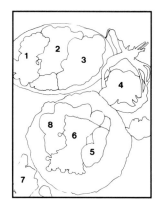

1.Hon shimeji (Japanese honey mushrooms). 2.Wood ear. 3.Shiitake. 4.Oyster. 5.Big brown mushrooms. 6.Enoki. 7.Dried porcini. 8.Pom pom.

Mushrooms. See diagram, opposite page.

OKRA

(OAK-rah) Okra has been part of the cuisine of Egypt, Africa, and Arabia along with the Mediterranean countries for hundreds of years. It was brought to America both by the French settlers and the slaves, who settled in the southern United States, particularly Louisianna. Today okra is very much a part of the colorful creole, Cajun and southwestern styles of cooking.

Gumbo is probably the most popular dish in which okra is found. Both names are African. But okra can add its mild flavor to many other dishes as well. Okra has a unique characteristic; when it's cooked for a long time, it develops a sticky, gelatinous texture that works to thicken soups or stews. Cooked briefly, okra has a slightly crisp texture and delicate asparagus flavor.

Buying Tips: Look for tender pods, with a bright green color and no blemishes or brown spots. If pods are pale-colored with stiff tips, they are likely to be tough; shriveled pods are old.

Storage: Keep okra crisp and fresh wrapped tightly in plastic and stored in the refrigerator crisper. Use within 3 days.

Basic Preparation: To cook okra for sautés or side dishes, trim off the stems from pods without puncturing the pods. Do not cook okra in brass, iron, or copper utensils, which will discolor the pods (although this will not affect their quality). Sauté or stir-fry pods for 2 to 3 minutes; boil or steam them for 5 to 8 minutes or until crisp-tender. Toss with butter and seasonings or lemon juice. To add okra for slow-cooked dishes such as stews or soups, trim and slice the pods; add okra as directed in recipe. To micro-cook okra, arrange pods in a shallow dish with 1/4 cup water; cover loosely. Microwave on High (100%) power for 4 to 6 minutes. Let stand 3 minutes.

Serving Ideas: Okra takes on flavors of tomato-based dishes very well, and is also compatible with vegetables like bell peppers, eggplant, zucchini, corn and potatoes. Add okra to vegetable mixtures, quiche, stuffed peppers and Mexican dishes. Chill lightly cooked okra to toss into main dish salads or relishes. Okra can be deep-fried in batter, scalloped like potatoes and pickled. Add a dash of ground red pepper, garlic and onion to serve sautéed okra southern-style. Try cooked sliced okra cold with tomatoes and cheese for an easy salad.

Yield 1 lb. = 4 servings.
1 lb. = 3-1/2 cups sliced.

Nutrition Facts: At 35 calories per serving, with twice the daily requirement of vitamin C, okra is a nutritional bargain. Add to that lots of vitamin A, calcium, iron and B vitamins.

Cajun Vegetable Medley

Serve this colorful medley in steamed bell pepper shells.

- 1/2 lb. okra
- 2 tablespoons vegetable oil
- 1 cup sliced onion
- 1 cup niblet corn or cut purple wax, green or Chinese long beans
- 1 green, red, orange, purple or yellow bell pepper, seeded, chopped
- 3 large tomatoes, diced
- 2 teaspoons fresh chopped thyme, or 1/2 teaspoon crushed dried thyme
- 2 teaspoons fresh chopped oregano or 1/2 teaspoon dried leaf oregano
- 1/2 teaspoon paprika
- 1/2 teaspoon salt
- 1/8 to 1/4 teaspoon cayenne pepper

Wash okra; pat dry with paper towels. Trim off stems and caps; slice 1/4-inch thick. In a large skillet, heat oil. Sauté okra with onion, corn and bell pepper about 5 minutes. Stir in tomatoes, thyme, oregano, paprika, salt and cayenne pepper. Cook and stir 3 to 5 minutes or until vegetables are tender. Makes 4 to 5 servings.

Preparation time: 15 minutes

Southern-Style Frittata

Try serving this open-faced omelet in wedges right from the skillet.

2 tablespoons vegetable oil
1 cup thinly sliced okra
1 green onion, chopped
6 eggs
1 tablespoon water
1/2 teaspoon salt
1/2 cup diced cooked chicken
1 small tomato, finely chopped
1 tablespoon chopped fresh basil
   or 1 teaspoon dried basil
2 teaspoons chopped fresh thyme
   or 1/2 teaspoon crushed dried
   thyme
1/8 teaspoon bottled hot-pepper
   sauce
1/2 cup shredded Swiss or
   Monterey Jack cheese (2 oz.)

In a large oven-proof skillet, heat oil. Sauté okra and green onion 5 minutes. In a medium bowl, with wire whisk, beat together eggs, water and salt until blended. Stir in chicken, tomato, basil, thyme and hot-pepper sauce. Pour mixture over vegetables in skillet. Cook over medium-high heat 3 to 5 minutes or until eggs begin to set. Meanwhile, preheat broiler. Sprinkle Swiss or Monterey Jack cheese over frittata; place skillet under broiler until cheese melts and top is light golden brown. Cut into wedges. Makes 5 to 6 servings.

Preparation time: 15 minutes

Tip:

Some cooks add a little baking soda to the cooking water for green vegetables, such as asparagus and snap beans, because it enhances their brilliant green colors. In truth, baking soda actually acts to destroy the vitamins in these vegetables. So the best way to preserve the color is to cook these vegetables as briefly as possible, draining them immediately to stop the cooking.

Santa Fe Cornbread, page 97; Cajun Vegetable Medley, opposite page.

ONIONS

It would be difficult to flavor many savory dishes without adding onions. Chives, garlic, shallots, green onions and leeks, with their varying degrees of pungent flavor, are all related, and have been around almost since the beginning of time. The brown onion, with its layer-upon-layer construction, had almost mythical qualities for the early Egyptians, who felt it was a symbol of everlasting life.

Brown onions are fully mature onions, whereas green onions are onions harvested early with green stems still attached. Sweeter varieties like the Walla Walla, and petite onions such as the pearls, offer cooks a wide choice when it comes to adding an oniony flavor to recipes. As with garlic, onions will always be more pungent raw than cooked; slow cooking brings out their delicate sweetness.

Buying Tips: Look for firm, well-shaped onions with healthy-looking skins and no sprouting. Onions should be dry, without soft spots.

Storage: Onions require cool, dry storage with good air circulation. Do not refrigerate onions until cut; then wrap tightly in plastic to keep out odors and store in the crisper. Chopped or sliced onions can be frozen in airtight containers up to 1 year; use in cooked dishes.

Basic Preparation: To prepare the large onion varieties, slip off papery skins, trim off stem ends. Mince, chop or slice onions to enjoy raw in salads or on sandwiches, or to cook in recipes. To peel pearl onions easily, drop them in boiling water for 3 minutes. Trim off stem ends and slip off peels. Sauté, steam, deep-fry, bake whole, or stir-fry any onion variety as a side dish or in recipes. Onions, sliced or chopped, will sauté or stir-fry tender in about 3 minutes. Bake onions whole for about 45 minutes or until tender; pearl onions, about 30 minutes. Deep-fry in batter until golden brown, about 1-1/2 minutes. Microwave as directed in recipes.

Serving Ideas: Stuff whole large onions as you would bell peppers, with meat, bread crumbs and herbs, or vegetables and cheeses. Slice vidalia or Maui onions to serve over a mushroom pizza, or to stuff a lamb roast. Add the sweet or pearl varieties to soups, stews, pot roast, poultry stuffings, relishes and salsas. Impale peeled pearl onions on skewers with other vegetables; grill until tender. Add pearl onions to cooked pasta, salads, or layer on sandwiches. Use red onion slices with roast beef for pita sandwiches, or layer with tomatoes and mozzarella cheese for an impromptu salad. Sauté sweet onions with fruit like apples and pears for a sweet and savory side dish or condiment.

Yield: 1 lb. onions = 4 servings.
1/2 lb. onions = 2 cups sliced, 1 cup cooked.

Nutrition Facts: One serving of cooked onions has only about 30 calories, raw about 40. Onions are free of fat and cholesterol and are a good source of potassium.

Unusual Varieties:

Bermuda: These large onions have a flattened globular shape with brown skins. Very mild and crisp; use thick slices for sandwiches and burgers.

Maui: Grown on the Hawaiian island of Maui, these onions are globes with very light golden brown skins. Their taste is surprisingly sweet and mild.

Pearl Onions: In gold, red and white skins, these small round boiling onions are about 1/2-inch in diameter. They have a mildly pungent flavor. Use in stews and for barbecuing.

Red Onions: Large, spherical onions with flattened stem ends, these pretty onions have red-violet skins. They make attractive additions to sandwiches and sautés. Zesty onion flavor.

Vidalia: Another sweet onion. Grown in Georgia, Texas and Southern California, Vidalias have flattened round shapes. They have golden brown skins with white onion inside. As sweet and mild as the Maui onion.

Walla Walla: From, you guessed it, Washington state, Walla Wallas are the original sweet onion variety. These are large, flattened onions with golden brown skins.

Maui Onion & Cheese Pie

*To save time and effort, purchase re-
frigerated, pre-rolled pie pastry or a
frozen pastry crust.*

1 9-inch unbaked pastry shell
2 tablespoons butter or margarine
1-1/2 cups thinly sliced Maui,
  Vidalia or Walla Walla onions
1 cup shredded mozzarella or
  Swiss cheese (4 oz.)
3 eggs
1 cup milk
1/2 cup dairy sour cream
1 tablespoon all-purpose flour
1 tablespoon fresh chopped basil
  or 1 teaspoon dried basil
2 teaspoons fresh chopped thyme
  or 1/2 teaspoon leaf thyme
1/2 teaspoon salt
1/4 teaspoon pepper

Preheat oven to 450F (230C). Bake
pie shell 5 minutes. Remove from
oven; reduce oven temperature to
325F (165C). In a large skillet, melt
butter or margarine. Sauté onions
until limp and golden brown, stirring frequently. Remove from heat.
Spoon onions into bottom of pie
shell. Sprinkle cheese over onions. In
a medium bowl, whisk together eggs,
milk, sour cream, flour, basil, thyme,
salt and pepper until blended. Pour
mixture over onions and cheese.
Carefully transfer to oven; bake 40 to
50 minutes or until a knife inserted
halfway between center and edge
comes out clean. Let stand 5 minutes. Makes 6 servings.

Preparation time: 15 minutes

Apple-Glazed Pearl Onions

*The flavors of apples and onions marry
deliciously for this not-too-sweet, not-too-
tart side dish.*

1 (10-oz.) pkg. red, white or gold
  pearl onions
2 tablespoons vegetable oil
2 small Grannysmith or tart cooking apples, cored, halved, thinly
  sliced
1/3 cup raisins
2 tablespoons madeira or sweet
  wine
1 tablespoon cider vinegar
1-1/2 teaspoons honey
1 tablespoon chopped fresh chives
  or parsley

In medium saucepan, place unpeeled onions with water to cover.
Bring to boiling; reduce heat and
simmer 5 minutes Drain well; cool
slightly. Trim off stem ends of
onions; slip off skins. In a large skillet, heat oil. Sauté apple slices with
onions about 5 minutes. Stir in
raisins, wine, vinegar, honey and
chives or parsley. Cook over medium
heat, stirring frequently, about 5
minutes more or until onions are
tender. Makes 5 to 6 servings.

Preparation time: 20 minutes

Herb-Roasted Sweet Onions

*Roasted onions are as simple to make as
baked potatoes. If you already have a roast
in the oven at a higher or lower temperature, you can bake the onions alongside.
Adjust the time accordingly.*

4 Walla Walla, Vidalia, Bermuda
  or Maui Onions, unpeeled
2 tablespoons butter or margarine,
  melted
1 tablespoon fresh chopped basil
  or 1 teaspoon dried basil
2 teaspoons fresh chopped sage or
  1/2 teaspoon ground sage
2 teaspoons fresh chopped
  rosemary or 1/2 teaspoon dried
  rosemary

Preheat oven to 350F (175C). Place
onions in an oiled baking dish; prick
several times. Cover; bake 45 minutes. Remove from oven; allow to
cool slightly. Carefully remove skins.
With a vegetable peeler or small
sharp knife, scoop out a 1/2-inch section from the top of each onion. In a
small dish, stir together melted butter or margarine, basil, sage and
rosemary. Brush mixture generously over onions; spoon remaining
mixture into indentations in onions.
Return to oven. Bake, uncovered, 15
to 20 minutes more or until tender.
Makes 4 servings.

Preparation time: 10 minutes

ORIENTAL VEGETABLES

Part of the mystique surrounding oriental cooking involves the intriguing vegetables used. Many of the vegetables native to Japanese, Thai, and Chinese peoples come in unfamiliar shapes and flavors. But now that most of those mysterious ingredients have travelled successfully from East to West, American cooks have the opportunity to become acquainted with them and cook in Far-Eastern style.

Buying Tips: All oriental vegetables should be purchased when fresh-looking. Bitter melon should be firm, not soft and mushy. Bean sprouts should be crisp, without brown stains. Choose burdock, daikon and lotus root that are firm, not limp; roots should be clean and bruise-free. Black radish should be firm, with dull black skin and no blemishes or soft spots. Water chestnuts should be fresh-looking, with dark brown shells that are dry, and without bruises or mold.

Storage: Refrigerate all oriental vegetables, tightly wrapped, in your refrigerator crisper. Bean sprouts, water chestnuts, bitter melon and winter melon should be used within a couple of days. Bitter melon becomes soft when stored next to tomatoes, bananas, and avocados, from the gases given off; try to keep them separated. Bok choy, daikon, lotus root and black radish will keep for up to a week, tightly covered, in the refrigerator. Do not freeze these vegetables.

Basic Preparation: For bean sprouts, rinse thoroughly; pat dry.

To prepare Bitter Melon, halve lengthwise; remove seeds and discard. Slice or chop as desired; blanch for 1 to 2 minutes to remove the bitterness.

Peel skin from black radish; shred to use.

For bok choy, discard any wilted leaves; chop or tear leaves and chop or slice the stalks.

To prepare burdock, scrub the root and scrape off the skin just before using. Peel only as much of the root as you need.

Lotus root must be cooked before eating. Peel and trim ends; slice thinly; steam or boil until tender.

Winter melon also requires cooking until tender.

Serving Ideas: Enjoy shredded daikon on a smoked turkey sandwich. Try adding bits of cooked lotus root, winter melon or bitter melon to your favorite vegetable soup. Oriental vegetables can be used to jazz up scrambled eggs, chicken salad or poultry stuffings.

Nutrition Facts: All oriental vegetables are very low in calories, averaging about 20 calories per 1/2 cup serving. Daikon and bok choy are good sources of vitamin C and calcium; bok choy leaves also contain vitamin A. Black radishes are low in sodium and bean sprouts are a good source of protein and vitamins. Water chestnuts have large amounts of potassium; burdock is generous in vitamin B.

Oriental Vegetable Varieties:

Bean Sprouts: Also called mung bean sprouts, these are the seeds of legumes that have germinated and formed slender shoots. The sprouts themselves are tender, pale shoots, with a crisp texture and a mild, nutty flavor. Most often used raw or very lightly cooked.

Bitter Melon: Not a melon at all, but a cucumber-like vegetable, bitter melon must be cooked to remove some of the tart flavor. Skin is bumpy, bright green, and houses a cucumber texture with small, centrally located seeds. About six inches long, bitter melon has a refreshing squash-like flavor, with a pleasant touch of tartness.

Black Radish: A large, round black-skinned radish with a creamy white interior, black radish tastes more like rutabaga than the American red radish. This spicy vegetable can be used raw or cooked for a somewhat milder flavor.

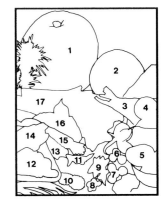

1.Winter melon. 2.Winter melon. 3.Burdock. 4.Black radish. 5.Lotus root. 6.Lychees. 7.Longans. 8.Jujubes. 9.Chinese pea pods. 10.Bittermelon. 11.Sugar snap peas. 12.Fresh waterchestnuts. 13.Lemon grass. 14.Baby bok choy. 15.Daikon. 16.Bitter melon. 17.Bok Choy.

Oriental Vegetables; see diagram, opposite page.

Bok Choy: Available in miniature and full-sized varieties, bok choy is like oriental celery. The snowy white stalks have large, deep green leaves that look like spinach. Both the stalks and leaves can be used, raw or cooked. It has a sweet, mild celery taste.

Burdock or Gobo Root: A long, slender Japanese root vegetable, used as a starch and prized for its mild, sweet flavor. Burdock has an earthy taste and chewy texture. Can be steamed and served on its own, or added to sukiyaki, stir-fries or sautéed vegetable mixtures. The skinny roots have thin brown skin and white meat; they may be 1 to 1-1/2 feet in length. Serve cooked.

Chinese Long Beans: See Beans, page 86.

Chinese (Napa) Cabbage: See Cabbage, page 91.

Chinese Pea Pods: See Pea Pods, page 134.

Daikon: Another radish, this one is very long (a foot or more), with tan-colored skin and pure white flesh. Like an oriental horseradish root, daikon adds a spiciness to dishes raw, as a condiment, or cooked.

Japanese Cucumber: See Cucumbers, page 98.

Japanese Eggplant: See Eggplant, page 99.

Lotus Root: This potato-like root looks very similar to daikon, with its brown skin and white flesh, but it has a very delicate, sweet flavor. Like Swiss cheese, lotus root is filled with holes that run the length of the root. When sliced crosswise, the slices look like doilies. Use raw or cooked.

Oriental Mushrooms: See Mushrooms, page 121.

Water chestnuts: Fresh water chestnuts have a wonderful nutty taste that is much more interesting and delicious than the canned variety. Water chestnuts are covered in a dark brown shell that can be easily peeled, leaving a flattened, round, ivory-white vegetable inside. Chop or shred; use raw or lightly cooked.

Winter Melon: This large, green melon is much like a squash; usually sold in pieces or slices. It's occasionally available as a small, tender melon. The green outer skin has a white waxy bloom, and the flesh is white, with a mild squashlike, slightly bitter taste. Cook until tender to use in soups or stir-fries.

Cactus, Orange & Water Chestnut Salad

Strips of cactus leaves resemble green bell pepper in this salad.

2 cactus pads, thorns removed, julienned
Lettuce leaves
2 oranges, peeled, thinly sliced
1/2 cup sliced water chestnuts
1/2 cup sliced red onion

Lime Dressing:
1/4 cup vegetable oil
3 tablespoons lime juice
1/8 teaspoon hot-pepper sauce
1/8 teaspoon salt

Prepare Lime Dressing. In a medium saucepan, place cactus strips with water to cover. Bring to a boil; reduce heat. Simmer 2 minutes. Rinse in cool water; drain. Line 4 salad plates with lettuce leaves. Arrange cactus pieces, orange slices, water chestnuts and onion over lettuce. Pour dressing over salads. Makes 4 salads.

Lime Dressing:
In a shaker jar, place oil, lime juice, hot-pepper sauce and salt. Cover and shake well to mix. Makes about 1/2 cup.

Preparation time: 15 minutes

Japanese Stir-Fried Vegetables

Burdock adds a mild, sweet flavor to this Far-Eastern combo.

1 burdock root (about 4 oz.) or 1 cup sliced turnips
1 tablespoon lemon juice
2 Japanese eggplants or 1/2 medium eggplant, peeled, cut into 1/2-inch chunks
1/2 cup chicken broth
1 tablespoon teriyaki sauce
1 tablespoon chopped fresh cilantro, if desired
2 teaspoons cornstarch
4 to 5 tablespoons vegetable oil
1 garlic clove, finely chopped
1 red bell pepper, seeded and slivered
4 green onions, cut into 1-inch pieces

Peel burdock, half at a time, then slice thinly. Immediately drop into a saucepan with lemon juice and water to cover. Bring to boiling; reduce heat and simmer 5 minutes. Add eggplant; simmer 5 minutes more or until vegetables are nearly tender. Drain. For sauce, stir together the broth, teriyaki sauce, cilantro, if desired, and cornstarch. Set aside. In a wok or large skillet, heat 2 tablespoons oil. Stir-fry drained burdock pieces 2 minutes; remove from wok. Add more oil if necessary; stir-fry eggplant and garlic 2 minutes. Remove from wok. Add more oil; stir-fry bell pepper and onions 3 minutes. Stir sauce mixture; pour into center of wok. Cook and stir until mixture thickens and bubbles. Return all vegetables to wok; stir to coat with sauce. Cover; cook 1 to 2 minutes until hot. Makes 4 servings.

Preparation time: 20 minutes

Chinese Vegetable Salad With Toasted Sesame Dressing

Line the salad bowl with red cabbage leaves for an eye-catching presentation.

2 cups shredded Chinese (Napa) cabbage
2 cups sliced bok choy leaves and stalks
1 cup fresh bean sprouts
1 cup julienne-sliced cucumber
1 cup julienne-sliced Daikon

Toasted Sesame Dressing:
2 tablespoons vegetable oil
1/2 cup sliced almonds
4 green onions, sliced
2 tablespoons sesame seeds
1/3 cup vegetable oil
3 tablespoons rice vinegar or white wine vinegar
2 tablespoons sugar
1/2 teaspoon pepper
1/2 teaspoon salt

Prepare Toasted Sesame Dressing; set aside. In a large salad bowl, toss together Chinese cabbage, bok choy, sprouts, cucumber and daikon. Stir sesame dressing mixture; pour over salad. Toss well to coat. Serve at once. Makes 6 servings.

Toasted Sesame Dressing:
In a small skillet, heat 2 tablespoons oil. Add almonds, onions and sesame seed. Sauté, stirring frequently, over medium-high heat until almonds begin to brown. Remove from heat. Stir in 1/3 cup oil, vinegar, sugar, salt and pepper. Makes 1 cup.

Preparation time: 20 minutes

Western-Style Spring Rolls

Both egg roll skins and spring roll skins are used by Orientals to wrap up fillings. Look for them in the dairy or freezer case.

2 tablespoons vegetable oil
2 small chicken breasts, skinned, boned, chopped, or 8 oz. peeled shrimp, chopped
1-1/2 cups finely chopped wood ear, shiitake or fresh brown mushrooms
1/2 cup sliced green onion
1 garlic clove, finely chopped
1-1/2 cups finely chopped bok choy leaves
8 fresh water chestnuts, peeled, finely chopped
1 cup fresh bean sprouts
2 tablespoons grated black radish, if desired
2 tablespoons soy sauce
1 tablespoon hoisin sauce
1 tablespoon dry sherry
1 beaten egg
10 spring roll or egg roll wrappers, thawed if frozen
Vegetable oil for shallow-fat frying
Soy sauce for dipping

In a large skillet, heat 2 tablespoons oil; sauté chicken or shrimp with mushrooms, onion and garlic for 3 minutes or until chicken is cooked. Stir in bok choy, water chestnuts, sprouts and black radish if desired; remove from heat. In a small bowl, stir together soy sauce, hoisin sauce and sherry; whisk in egg until blended. Pour mixture over chicken filling; toss well to mix. Place 1 egg roll skin with 1 point facing you. Spoon about 1/4 cup of filling on center half of skin. Fold bottom point of skin over filling, tucking point under filling. Fold side points over filling, then roll up skin toward remaining top corner. Moisten top point with a little water; fold over and press lightly to seal. Repeat with remaining spring roll skins and filling. In a wok or deep skillet, pour oil to a depth of 2 inches. Heat to 365F (185C). Fry spring rolls, a few at a time, in oil for 2 to 3 minutes or until golden brown. Drain on paper towels. Serve spring rolls hot with soy sauce for dipping. Makes 10 spring rolls.

Preparation time: 30 minutes

Chinese Fried Rice

Fried rice is an ingenious oriental method of using up leftover rice, meat and vegetables. It's worth making extra rice for the previous night's dinner just to have this dish.

2 tablespoons vegetable oil
2 eggs, lightly beaten
3 green onions, sliced
2 cups cold cooked rice
1 cup finely chopped cooked beef, pork, chicken, turkey, fish or shrimp
1 cup chopped bok choy or daikon
1/2 cup chopped bean sprouts or water chestnuts
1 tablespoon soy sauce
1 tablespoon dry sherry
1 tablespoon shredded black radish, if desired

In a large skillet, heat 1 tablespoon oil. Scramble eggs until firm. Remove eggs from pan; cut into shreds. Add eggs back to pan with remaining oil and onions. Sauté 2 minutes. Stir in rice, cooked meat, fish or shrimp, bok choy or daikon, bean sprouts or water chestnuts, soy sauce, sherry and black radish, if desired. Cook and stir 3 minutes more or until mixture is heated. Makes 4 servings.

Preparation time: 15 minutes

PARSNIPS

Beloved in France and Europe, the parsnip deserves more popularity among produce in this country. One of the sweetest, most delectable vegetables around, parsnips are easy to prepare, inexpensive and extremely versatile.

Parsnips are cousins to carrots, celery, parsley and fennel, and their flavor holds much of the characteristic sweetness. Some people think that freshly harvested parsnips are nearly as sweet as candy. It's said that parsnips are at their flavor best when dug up after the first spring thaw.

Resembling white carrots, parsnips can be enjoyed raw or cooked. Shop for them year-round; peak supplies can be found October through April.

Buying Tips: Look for firm white parsnips the size of carrots; gargantuan ones are likely to have pithy centers and less flavor. Avoid soft parsnips with many small rootlets.

Storage: Wrap tightly in plastic; store parsnips in your refrigerator crisper drawer. Store them for up to 10 days.

Basic Preparation: Trim off ends; peel with a vegetable peeler as you would carrots. Cook as for carrots or serve raw as a vegetable snack. Chop, shred, slice or cut into julienne sticks for recipes. Steam, boil, stir-fry, sauté or bake parsnips until tender. Very tender parsnips can be mashed like potatoes. Steam, boil or sauté parsnips for 7 to 9 minutes; bake chunks 30 minutes with a roast or other vegetables. Microwave parsnips by placing slices in a shallow loosely covered dish with 1/4 cup water. Micro-cook on High (100%) power for 2-1/2 to 4 minutes; let stand 3 minutes until tender.

Serving Ideas: Toss cooked parsnips with butter and brown sugar, herbs and cream or a cheese sauce. Purée parsnips to mix with potatoes and turnips for a side dish, or to thicken creamy soups. Add parsnips to beef stews, chicken noodle soup or pot pie. Stir-fry this vegetable with sweet onions and summer squash for a side dish, flavor with basil and dill. Scallop parsnips like potatoes; deep-fry slices for an appetizer or sauté with bacon and garlic. Add shredded raw parsnips to salads or sandwich fillings.

Yield: 1 lb. parsnips = 3 servings.
1 lb. parsnips = about 1-2/3 cups chopped or sliced.

Nutrition Facts: One serving of parsnips has about 90 calories. High in sodium and also vitamin A, potassium, iron and other minerals.

Chocolate Parsnip Cake

Like carrots in carrot cake, parsnips add moistness and tenderness to this rich, chocolatey cake. Top it with the powdered sugar topping or your favorite fudge frosting, if you like.

1 cup grated parsnips
1-3/4 cups all-purpose flour
1-1/4 cups packed brown sugar
1/2 cup unsweetened cocoa
   powder
1-1/2 teaspoons baking soda
1/2 teaspoon salt
1-1/4 cups buttermilk
1/2 cup shortening
3 eggs
1 teaspoon vanilla extract
1 cup raisins or chopped walnuts
2 tablespoons sifted powdered
   sugar
1 tablespoon unsweetened cocoa
   powder

Preheat oven to 350F (175C). Grease and lightly flour a 12-cup fluted tube or plain tube pan. In a steamer over simmering water, cook grated parsnips 5 minutes; drain well. Set aside. In a large bowl, measure flour, brown sugar, cocoa powder, baking soda, salt, buttermilk, shortening, eggs and vanilla. Beat 1/2 minute on low speed to moisten ingredients; beat 3 minutes on high speed, scraping bowl frequently. Stir in parsnips and raisins or walnuts. Pour into prepared pan. Bake 45 to 55 minutes or until a wooden pick inserted in center comes out clean. Cool in pan on wire rack 20 minutes; turn out onto rack to cool completely. When cake is cool, stir together powdered sugar and cocoa powder; sift over cake. Cut into wedges. Makes 1 (10-inch) cake.

Preparation time: 20 minutes

Cucumbers, Eggplants, Garlic, Leeks, Onions & Shallots. See diagram, page 157.

PEA PODS

Shell peas have been around for nearly twelve thousand years, but peas in edible pods were a much more recent development. Of the two varieties of edible-pod peas, the "sugar snap" pea was introduced just 10 years ago. Developed by Dr. Calvin Lamborn, a world-renowned plant breeder in Idaho, sugar snaps are a familiar vegetable in markets today.

"Chinese pea pods" or "snow peas" as they are often called, are another variety of edible-pod peas, brought to us from the Orient. The delicious advantages of the edible-pod peas versus shelled peas include a much sweeter flavor, ease of preparation (no shelling necessary) and a short cooking time (or none at all). The "snow peas" and sugar snaps are sweet and juicy when raw, used with dips or stuffed with cheese. The edible pods contain fewer smaller peas that are more tender than shell peas, and their calorie count is considerably lower. Look for pea pods year-round with peak supplies in spring and fall.

Buying Tips: Pods should be firm, crisp and bright green. Pale green spots on sugar snaps are typical; avoid pods with browning or a shriveled appearance.

Storage: Store tightly wrapped in plastic in the refrigerator crisper drawer for up to several days. Pea pods can be frozen in airtight containers; however, color and texture will suffer.

Basic Preparation: Unless using the stringless sugar snaps, remove strings by taking hold of the leafy stem and pulling it from end to end. If peas to be used in recipes are very long, halve pods crosswise, if desired. Enjoy peas raw as a vegetable snack or as a dipper or stuff for recipes. Or steam, sauté or stir-fry pea pods just until tender, about 2 minutes. Micro-cook snow peas by placing them in a shallow dish with 2 tablespoons water; cover loosely. Microwave on High (100%) power for 2 to 3 minutes or until crisp-tender.

Serving Ideas: Wrap sugar snap peas with string cheese for an easy appetizer or stuff pea pods with tiny shrimp or seasoned cream cheese. Skewer steamed snow peas wrapped around cooked mushrooms, scallops or large shrimp for an elegant hors d'oeuvre; dip into mustard mayonnaise. Add pea pods to cold salads, broth-based soups, oriental stir-fries or rice pilaf. Serve pea pods as a hot side dish with dill butter or flavor with lemon and garlic.

Yield: 1 lb. pea pods = 4 servings.

Nutrition Facts: A 4-ounce serving of pea pods contains about 60 calories. Pea pods are low in sodium, high in fiber, and contribute some A, B and C vitamins.

Varieties:

Chinese Pea Pods/Snow Peas: A flat pea pod, also edible, filled with a few tiny green peas. String attached; sweet flavor. The original oriental variety, never shelled.

Sugar Snaps: Plump, juicy green pods filled with small, tender green peas. A cross between a garden pea and a "snow pea"; found in both stringless and string-attached varieties. Both pod and peas are edible; do not shell peas.

Dill Cheese-Stuffed Pea Pods

Use the dill mixture to stuff the pea pods, or as a dip.

1/2 lb. uncooked sugar snap peas
    or Chinese pea pods, stringed
1 (8-oz.) pkg. cream cheese, room
    temperature
1/4 cup lemon-flavored yogurt
2 teaspoons Dijon-style mustard
1 tablespoon chopped fresh dill
    or 1 teaspoon dillweed
1 teaspoon lemon juice
1 (4-oz.) jar pimiento strips,
    drained

If stuffing peas, use a small paring knife to cut a slit along 1 side of each pea pod. In a blender or food processor fitted with a metal blade, process cream cheese, yogurt, mustard, dill and lemon juice until blended. If not stuffing peas, add pimiento; process until blended. If stuffing peas, spoon or pipe about 1 teaspoon cream cheese mixture into pea pods; garnish each with a strip of pimiento. If preparing dip or stuffed peas in advance, cover and refrigerate up to 24 hours. Thin dip, if necessary, with milk after chilling and serve with pea pods. Makes 4-1/2 dozen stuffed pea pods or 1-1/3 cups dip.

Preparation time: 15 to 30 minutes

Pea Pod Egg Drop Soup

Here's a great five minute soup to serve with a sandwich lunch.

4 cups chicken broth
4 green onions or 2 trimmed leeks, chopped
1/2 cup sliced bamboo shoots
1-1/2 cups sugar snaps or Chinese pea pods, stringed
2 eggs, lightly beaten

In a Dutch oven, pour chicken broth. Add green onions and bamboo shoots. Cover; bring to boiling. Add pea pods; boil 1 minute. Pour in beaten eggs in a thin stream; cook 1 minute more or until eggs cook. Stir soup to break up cooked egg. Makes 5 servings.

Preparation time: 5 minutes

Stir-Fried Pea Pods & Peppers

Sesame oil, found in oriental food sections of large supermarkets, is a flavorful oil to use in vegetable stir-fries.

2 tablespoons red wine vinegar
2 tablespoons soy sauce
1/2 teaspoon sugar
2 to 3 tablespoons sesame oil or vegetable oil
2 red bell peppers, seeded, slivered
1 garlic clove, finely chopped
2 cups fresh sugar snap or Chinese pea pods, stringed
1 cup sliced fresh or canned drained water chestnuts
1 tablespoon sesame seeds

In a small bowl, stir together vinegar, soy sauce and sugar. Set aside. In a wok or large skillet, heat 2 tablespoons oil. Over high heat, stir-fry bell peppers and garlic 3 minutes. Remove from wok; add more oil if necessary. Stir-fry snow peas and water chestnuts 1 minute. Add bell peppers back to wok. Add sesame seeds and vinegar mixture; toss to coat vegetables with sauce. Cook 1 minute more to heat through. Makes 4 servings.

Preparation time: 15 minutes

Stir-Fried Pea Pods & Peppers, above; Thai Ginger-Peanut Chicken, page 104.

PLANTAINS

(PLAN-tins) Plantains are cooking bananas, prized in tropical countries for their virtues as a vegetable, not a fruit. Mild-flavored and starchier than sweet yellow bananas, plantains are always cooked, which develops the flavor and softens the texture. They are usually served as a side dish, much like potatoes, although they are sometimes cooked with sugar or honey for a dessert.

Plantain varieties were cultivated first by the Southeast Asians; they are now grown extensively in India, Egypt, Africa, the Pacific islands and South America. They resemble large, greenish-yellow bananas with black spots and thick skins. Plantains can be used when green (unripe), yellow or black (fully ripe). Green plantains have an astringent, bitter taste, while black plantains are sweet and tender. Bake, fry or sauté plantains as a vegetable, or add to pot roast or stew for a new twist on potatoes. Available all year.

Buying Tips: Purchase plantains that are fully yellow in color, firm and heavy. Black spots are a normal characteristic. These bananas are usually purchased individually, rather than in bunches.

Storage: Store bananas in a cool dry place for up to 1 week.

Basic Preparation: Trim off ends of fruit with a small paring knife; strip off skin (it adheres more tightly to the fruit than sweet banana skins do). Slice, chop or quarter fruit for recipes. Or bake plantains in their skins in a 350F (175C) oven for about 40 minutes until tender. Sauté plantain chunks or slices in butter or oil for 6 to 8 minutes or until golden brown and tender. For mashed cooked plantains, boil in water to cover for 15 to 20 minutes until tender; mash like potatoes. Micro-cooking plantains is not recommended. Season cooked plantains with salt and pepper.

Serving Ideas: Philippinos wrap quartered plantains in egg roll skins, deep-fry them and sprinkle with sugar for a sweet snack. Or slit and stuff plantains with cheese; bake until tender. Especially good sautéed with sausage and herbs. Try baking plantains with a pork or beef roast, basting with meat juices until tender. Add plantain chunks to soups and stews during the last 30 minutes of cooking time. Scallop slices of plantains or prepare au gratin style, as for potatoes.

Yield: 1 plantain = 1 serving.
1 lb. plantain = 2 to 3 medium plantains.

Nutrition Facts: One plantain contains about 190 calories, cooked. Plantains are a superb source of potassium and also provide vitamin C and phosphorous.

Brazilian Plantains

A spicy tomato sauce adds spunk to chicken, plantains and spinach.

About 2 to 3 tablespoons butter or margarine
2 medium-ripe plantains, peeled, sliced 1/4-inch thick (2 cups)
4 boneless chicken breasts, pounded 1/4-inch thick
1 bunch mustard greens or spinach, washed, stems removed

Spiced Tomato Sauce:
2 tablespoons butter or margarine
1 cup chopped onion
2 cloves garlic, chopped
4 fresh tomatoes, chopped
1/4 cup chicken broth
1 teaspoon chili powder
1/2 teaspoon salt
1/4 teaspoon cumin
1/4 teaspoon pepper

Prepare Spiced Tomato Sauce; cover and keep warm. In a large skillet, melt butter or margarine over medium-high heat. Sauté plantain slices 5 minutes, turning once. Remove from skillet, reserving drippings in pan. Brown chicken breasts quickly on both sides, turning once. Add mustard greens and plantains to skillet, cover. Cook 3 to 5 minutes more or until wilted. Serve chicken and vegetables with Spiced Tomato Sauce. Makes 4 servings.

Spiced Tomato Sauce:
In a large skillet, melt butter; sauté onion and garlic until onion is limp. Add remaining ingredients. Bring to boiling; reduce heat. Simmer, covered, 10 minutes. In blender or food processor fitted with a metal blade, process mixture briefly until tomato is finely chopped. Return to skillet; cover and keep warm until needed. Makes 2-2/3 cups.

Preparation time: 25 minutes

POTATOES

Unusual Varieties:

Baby potatoes: Russets, white potatoes and red potatoes now come sized about 1 inch in diameter. Smaller than new potatoes, the babies have tender skins and a sweet, mild flavor.

Boniatos: A Cuban type of sweet potato with a creamy texture and pink, purple or red skin. Meat is white or yellow and it tastes like a drier, blander sweet potato.

Finnish Potatoes: Grown in Washington state, these golden-skinned potatoes have a creamy yellow interior and buttery flavor when cooked. It's said that adding butter isn't necessary.

New Potatoes: Young red potatoes, usually about 1-1/2 inches in width; ball-shaped. Mild flavor, tender skins.

Purple Potatoes: Medium-sized potatoes that look like russets, except that the skins are a dark purple to blackish-purple. Inside color is bright purple when cut; the color becomes lighter when potatoes are cooked. Flavor and texture are identical to russet potatoes. From Peru.

Round Red Potatoes: Globular red-skinned potatoes with mild, waxy meat and sweet flavor. Very tender and delicious.

Sweet Potatoes: Elongated shapes with coppery russet skins, sweet potatoes have light or dark orange meat. Their flavor is sweet and the texture is very similar to squash.

Texas Finger: Diminutive, thumb-sized potatoes with russet skins and russet potato characteristics. An interesting appetizer or snack-sized potato.

White Potatoes: In "round" and "long" varieties, with names that describe their shape, white potatoes have golden brown, thin and tender skins with tender, waxy meat. Mild flavor.

It would be hard to imagine dining in America for a week without eating potatoes. But you'll find more than the familiar brown russets in markets today. Tiny russet and red potatoes, buttery-tasting yellow potatoes, and brilliant purple (yes, purple!) potatoes have appeared on the scene. Now that potatoes have been vindicated from their fattening reputation (1 medium potato has the same calorie count as an apple), there's no reason not to enjoy the new spud spinoffs.

Buying Tips: All potatoes should be very firm with clean, fairly pristine skins and few eyes. Choose well-shaped potatoes free from wrinkling, green streaks or soft spots.

Storage: All potatoes require a cool, humid atmosphere for storage. Potatoes will keep well in the refrigerator crisper for up to several weeks. Potatoes stored over 50F will begin to sprout and shrivel. Never freeze potatoes, except in recipes.

Basic Preparation: Scrub all potatoes well. Peel skins if desired, but new varieties generally have tender skins with good flavor. Some varieties darken when cut; place cut pieces in water with some lemon juice added if cooking is delayed. Small potatoes can be steamed or boiled in 12 to 15 minutes or until tender. Larger varieties, cut into chunks or sliced, will boil or steam in 20 to 30 minutes. Bake larger varieties whole in a 350F (175C) oven for 45 to 60 minutes until tender. Microwave potatoes by placing small varieties, whole, or 1/4-inch thick slices of larger varieties in a shallow dish with 1/4 cup water; cover loosely. Micro-cook on High (100%) power for 4 to 5 minutes, turning once. Let stand 3 minutes. For medium to large varieties, puncture to micro-cook whole 5 minutes; let stand 5 minutes.

Serving Ideas: Steam or boil small potatoes until nearly tender, then sauté in butter and herbs to finish cooking. Or place partially steamed small potatoes on skewers with other vegetables and grill until done. Stuff yellow Finnish or Yukon potatoes with cheeses or chopped cooked vegetables for a main dish, or slice and sauté with bell peppers and squash for a colorful side dish. All varieties can be prepared as you would russets.

Yield: 1 lb. potatoes = 12 to 18 of the small variety, or 3 medium size potatoes.
2 lbs. potatoes = 6 servings.
1 lb. potatoes = 3 cups sliced, 2-1/4 cups diced, or 2 cups cooked and mashed.

Nutrition Facts: All potato varieties contain about the same calories, about 100 calories for a 5-ounce serving when boiled, steamed or baked. Potatoes are high in fiber, potassium and vitamin C, with some B vitamins. They're also a good source of minerals and iron.

Yams: Sweet potatoes are often mis-named yams. True yams are natives of the tropics, with pale-colored meat that is sweeter than sweet potatoes. Obtain in ethnic Asian and Hispanic markets.

Yellow Rose Potatoes: Reddish, thin skins, medium-sized potatoes with buttery-tasting meat like the Finnish variety.

Yukon Gold Potatoes: Regular-sized yellow-skinned potatoes with mild, slightly sweet flavor. Smooth, moist texture.

Sweet Potato Slaw

Shredded raw sweet potato makes a delicious crisp slaw.

3 cups finely shredded uncooked sweet potato
1/2 cup chopped pecans or walnuts
1/2 cup golden or dark raisins
1 tablespoon grated orange peel

Orange Salad Dressing:
1/4 cup mayonnaise or salad dressing
1/4 cup sour cream
2 tablespoons orange juice
1 teaspoon sugar
1/4 teaspoon salt
1/8 teaspoon pepper

In a large bowl, toss together shredded potato, pecans or walnuts, golden or dark raisins and orange peel. Prepare Orange Salad Dressing; toss with salad to coat well. If preparing ahead, cover and chill in refrigerator up to 24 hours before serving. Makes 5 or 6 servings.

Orange Salad Dressing:
In a small bowl, stir together mayonnaise or salad dressing, sour cream, orange juice, sugar, salt and pepper till blended. Makes about 2/3 cup.

Preparation time: 15 minutes

Mini Potato Hors d'oeuvres

Use your imagination to garnish these cream and herb-stuffed potatoes.

2 lbs. small new potatoes, baby potatoes or Texas fingers
1/4 cup dairy sour cream
1/4 cup mayonnaise or salad dressing
1 teaspoon lemon juice
1 tablespoon chopped fresh tarragon or 1 teaspoon dried tarragon
1 tablespoon chopped fresh basil or 1 teaspoon dried basil
1/4 teaspoon pepper
Toppings: Fresh herb sprigs, crumbled cooked bacon, minced chives, chopped walnuts, pimiento strips, olive slices, caviar

Place potatoes in a large saucepan in water to cover. Bring to boiling; reduce heat and simmer 10 to 12 minutes or until tender. Drain; cool. With a melon baller or tip of a vegetable peeler, scoop out a 1/2-inch cavity in top side of each potato. Reserve scooped-out potato for another use. In a small bowl, stir together sour cream, mayonnaise or salad dressing, lemon juice, tarragon, basil and pepper. Spoon or pipe mixture into cavity of each potato; garnish with desired Toppings. If preparing in advance, cover and refrigerate up to 6 hours ahead. Makes 32 to 40 appetizers.

Preparation time: 20 minutes

Garden Potato Salad

To create a hot side dish, omit lettuce. Cook vegetables until crisp-tender; toss with dressing and serve.

1-1/2 cups cooked, cubed potatoes
1 cup shredded carrot
1 cup thinly sliced yellow summer squash or zucchini
Lettuce leaves

Parmesan Dressing:
1/4 cup vegetable oil
1/4 cup white wine vinegar
1/4 cup grated Parmesan cheese
1/4 teaspoon pepper

In a large bowl, toss together cubed potatoes, shredded carrot and squash slices. Arrange lettuce on four salad plates; spoon vegetable mixture over lettuce. Prepare Parmesan Dressing; drizzle over salads. Makes 4 servings.

Parmesan Dressing:
In a shaker jar, combine oil, wine vinegar, Parmesan cheese and pepper. Cover and shake well to mix. Makes 3/4 cup.

Preparation time: 15 minutes

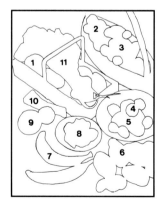

1. Rutabagas. 2. Baby red potatoes. 3. Yellow rose potatoes. 4. Baby purple potatoes. 5. Yellow Finnish potatoes. 6. Purple potatoes. 7. Plantains. 8. Sunchokes. 9. Turnips. 10. Horseradish root. 11. Beets with leaves.

Roots, Plaintains & Tubers. See diagram, opposite page.

Finnish Potato Rosti

Though this scrumptious potato side dish is Swiss in origin, this version gets its Scandinavian nickname from the Yellow Finnish potatoes used.

6 medium to large Yellow Finnish or Yellow Rose potatoes
1 cup shredded Swiss, Jarlsburg or Gruyère cheese (4 oz.)
2 tablespoons butter or margarine
1 cup finely chopped onion or leeks
1/2 teaspoon salt
1/4 teaspoon pepper

With a fork, pierce potatoes several times. In a Dutch oven, place potatoes and enough water to cover. Bring to boiling; reduce heat and simmer 30 to 40 minutes or until potatoes are nearly tender. Drain potatoes; rinse in cold water until cool enough to handle. Preheat oven to 350F (175C). Peel potatoes. In a medium bowl, coarsely grate potatoes; toss gently with 1/2 of cheese. In a Dutch oven or large saucepan, melt butter or margarine. Sauté onions until lightly browned. Toss with potato mixture. Add salt and pepper. Butter a 9-inch pie plate generously on bottom and sides. Using a spatula or back of a spoon, pack potato mixture firmly against bottom and sides of pie plate. Bake 20 to 30 minutes or until browned on top. Place a round heatproof serving platter over pie plate; invert. Sprinkle remaining 1/2 cup cheese over potatoes; return to oven for 3 to 5 minutes to melt cheese. Cut into wedges to serve. Makes 8 servings.

Preparation time: 30 minutes

Purple Potato Chips

Soaking the potato slices in ice water before frying makes the potatoes crisper and puffier when fried. You can also use the orange type of sweet potato.

4 to 5 purple potatoes, medium red rose potatoes, or 2 large yellow sweet potatoes, peeled
1 quart vegetable oil
Toppings: Salt, grated Parmesan cheese or crushed dried Italian herbs

Slice potatoes thinly; place in a bowl of ice water. Let stand 30 minutes. Drain potato slices; pat dry on paper towels. In a Dutch oven or large saucepan, heat oil to 365F (185C). Fry potatoes, several slices at a time, for about 2 minutes or until crisp. Drain well on paper towels. Sprinkle with desired toppings. Serve warm. Makes 6 to 8 servings.

Preparation time: 20 minutes

Baby Potatoes Polonaise

The butter-crumb topping is also delicious on steamed broccoli or asparagus.

1 lb. baby potatoes, trimmed
1/4 cup butter or margarine
2 tablespoons fresh bread crumbs
1 hard-cooked egg, chopped
1 tablespoon chopped fresh parsley

In a large saucepan, steam baby potatoes over simmering water 4 to 8 minutes or until nearly tender; drain. Arrange baby potatoes on a serving platter; cover and keep warm. In same pan, melt butter. Stir in bread crumbs; cook until golden. Drizzle mixture over potatoes. Sprinkle with chopped egg and parsley and serve. Makes 4 to 5 servings.

Preparation time: 15 minutes

Sweet Potato Purée

Try this delicious twist on mashed potatoes for your next fall or winter dinner. You can substitute white or red potatoes for the sweet potatoes, but omit the cinnamon.

1-1/2 pounds rutabagas, turnips or kohlrabi, trimmed, peeled, cut into 1/2-inch chunks
1-1/2 pounds sweet potatoes or yams, peeled, cut into 1/2-inch chunks
3 tablespoons butter or margarine
1/4 cup half and half or milk
1/2 teaspoon ground cinnamon
1/2 teaspoon salt
1/8 teaspoon pepper
2 tablespoons chopped parsley

In separate 2-quart saucepans, place rutabaga and potato chunks in water to cover. Bring to boiling; reduce heat. Simmer, uncovered, for 25 to 35 minutes or until vegetables are tender. Drain vegetables; place together in a large bowl. Add butter or margarine, half and half or milk, cinnamon, salt and pepper. Using potato masher or mixer, mash vegetable mixture. Or in blender or food processor fitted with a metal blade, process mixture until smooth. Transfer to serving bowl; sprinkle with parsley. Makes 6 servings.

Preparation time: 20 minutes

Garden Vegetable Sauté

Always peel turnips before cooking, since the skin is extremely bitter. Turnips taste almost glamorous in this flavor-filled dish.

2 tablespoons olive oil or vegetable oil
1 lb. turnips or kohlrabi, trimmed, peeled, julienne-cut
1 cup julienne-cut carrots
1 cup julienne-cut zucchini, yellow squash or jicama
1 garlic clove, finely chopped
1 teaspoon lemon juice
2 teaspoons fresh chopped thyme or 1/2 teaspoon dried leaf thyme
1/2 teaspoon salt
1/8 teaspoon pepper

In a large skillet, heat olive oil or vegetable oil. Add turnips, carrots, zucchini and garlic. Sauté over medium-high heat 3 to 5 minutes, stirring frequently, or until vegetables are crisp-tender. Stir in lemon juice, thyme, salt and pepper. Taste for seasonings. Makes 4 servings.

Preparation time: 15 minutes

RUTABAGAS/TURNIPS

The texture and flavor of turnips and rutabagas are somewhat similar when cooked, and they are often interchangeable in recipes. They are in peak supply from October through March, though you'll find them in some quantity all year.

Rutabagas are larger than turnips. They have no stems or green tops attached. Their flesh is yellow and more solid than turnips. Turnips are more perishable vegetables, with attractive purple-tinged white skins. Often the green leaves are attached and can also be cooked and served as a vegtable.

Buying Tips: Both vegetables should feel very firm, with no shriveling or softness. Buy rutabagas that are heavy for their size with clean skins. They are usually waxed to hold in moisture. Turnips, if young and sweet, will be tied in bunches with their greens still attached. Look for fresh-looking leaves and unblemished skin. Avoid very large turnips, since they will probably be bitter.

Storage: If turnips have leaves on them, twist off the leaves and store separately in plastic. Wrap turnips and refrigerate with the leaves in the refrigerator crisper for up to 1 week. Rutabagas, wrapped tightly, can be refrigerated up to 1 month. Do not freeze vegetables unless cooked and puréed.

Basic Preparation: Turnips should be peeled if medium- to large-size; rutabagas must always be peeled and trimmed. Young turnips are tasty raw as a vegetable snack; rutabagas and larger turnips should be cooked. Boil, sauté, bake or micro-cook these vegetables until tender. Boil chopped or sliced turnips in water to cover for 6 to 8 minutes; rutabagas for 25 to 30 minutes. Bake whole turnips in a 350F (175C) oven for 35 to 40 minutes; rutabagas, chunked, for about 1 hour or until tender. Microwave chopped rutabagas with 1/4 cup water in a shallow, loosely-covered dish; cook on High (100%) power for 9 to 11 minutes. Let stand 3 minutes. Micro-cook cubed turnips with 2 tablespoons water in a shallow dish, loosely covered, on High (100%) for 8 to 10 minutes. Let stand 3 minutes.

Serving Ideas: Both vegetables are popular mashed, seasoned and buttered, and mixed with mashed potatoes, carrots or parsnips. Add baby turnips to creamy vegetable soups and purée to thicken. Use smaller turnips on raw vegetable platters or cut up and marinated with other vegetables. Stir-fry partially cooked rutabagas or turnips with other vegetables, ginger and garlic.

Yield: 1 lb. rutabagas or turnips = 3 to 4 servings.
1 lb. rutabagas or turnips = 4 cups chopped or sliced raw; or 2 to 2-1/3 cups cooked, mashed.

Nutrition Facts: Both turnips and rutabagas have about 32 calories per serving. They're high in fiber. Rutabagas have more vitamin A and C than turnips, but turnips are richer in iron.

SALSIFY/SCORZONERA

Because this unusual root tastes mildly of fresh oysters, it is often called "oyster plant." Salsify looks much like a thin parsnip that is covered with grasslike sprouts. This long root has pale creamy white skin with leafy green shoots that sprout from its top. A native of Central and Southern Europe, salsify is harvested in the fall to enjoy through the winter as a cooked and seasoned vegetable. The leaves from the plant are often used in salads.

Today oyster plant is commercially cultivated, but also still found growing wild, especially in the Southern U.S. A black-skinned variety, called "scorzonera," is a close relative of salsify and can be prepared in exactly the same way. Look for these delicate, sweet-tasting roots in markets from October through May.

Buying Tips: Both salsify or oyster plant and scorzonera should have firm crisp roots. If they are limp or soft, they're old.

Storage: Tear off the leaves, if available, and refrigerate in a plastic bag in the crisper for up to 3 days. Store the roots separately, loosely wrapped, in the refrigerator for up to 4 or 5 days.

Basic Preparation: Trim root ends; scrape roots with a vegetable peeler to remove skins and shoots. Slice, chop or cut into 1/2-inch cubes; drop cut pieces in lemon juice and water to prevent discoloration. Boil or steam salsify or scorzonera or add to soups or stews as a vegetable. Cook pieces in boiling water to cover or steam for 10 to 20 minutes, depending on size of pieces, until tender. Microwave the chopped or sliced roots by placing pieces in 1/4 cup water with 1 tablespoon lemon juice in a loosely covered shallow dish. Micro-cook on High (100%) power for 6 to 8 minutes; let stand 3 minutes until tender.

Serving Ideas: Salsify or scorzonera taste best in recipes that are mildly seasoned. They can often be used in place of sunchokes or parsnips. Sauté the root with other vegetables such as carrots and turnips; season with a lemon-butter parsley sauce. Use salsify as the basis for a creamy soup; purée the root after cooking to thicken soup. Toss the cooked roots with mild sauces such as mozzarella cheese, cream sauce or a mild vinegar and garlic. Add scrozonera or salsify to chicken soup, veal stew or noodle casseroles.

Yield: 1 lb. scorzonera or salsify = about 3 servings.
1 lb. root = 2 to 2-1/4 cups cooked, sliced.

Nutrition Facts: Calorie counts vary, depending on how long the roots have been stored before sale. One serving of fresh salsify has about 15 calories; stored roots can have as much as 80 calories per serving. The roots are low in sodium.

Fried "Oyster" Cakes

This eastern treat is similar to crab cakes. Serve as a first course or appetizer.

1 lb. salsify or scorzonera
3 tablespoons lemon or lime juice
Water
1/4 cup minced onion
1/2 teaspoon salt
1/4 teaspoon pepper
2 tablespoons minced fresh parsley
1-1/2 tablespoons minced drained pimiento
1 beaten egg
1 tablespoon water
1-1/2 cups seasoned dry bread crumbs
3 tablespoons cooking oil
Mild salsa or sour cream

Trim and peel salsify or scorzonera; slit lengthwise and slice thinly. Immediately plunge into lemon or lime juice mixed with water to cover. Drain; place slices in a medium saucepan with lightly salted water to cover. Bring to boiling; reduce heat and simmer 6 to 8 minutes or until tender. Drain; transfer to a blender or food processor fitted with a metal blade. Add onion, salt and pepper. Process until mashed. Stir in parsley and pimiento. With lightly floured hands, shape mixture into 6 patties about 3/8-inch thick. Cover and chill for 30 minutes or up to 24 hours ahead. To cook patties, whisk beaten egg with 1 tablespoon water in a shallow bowl; place bread crumbs in another shallow bowl. Dip patties first in egg mixture to coat, then in bread crumbs to coat well. In a large skillet, heat oil; fry patties on both sides for 5 to 7 minutes or until golden. Serve with salsa or sour cream. Makes 6 servings.

Preparation time: 20 minutes

Varieties:

Golden/Brown: The familiar brown-skinned variety has a rich, mild flavor; yellow flesh. Dutch origin.

Red/Purple: With reddish- or purplish-hued skins and reddish interior. Somewhat stronger-flavored than brown shallots. French origin.

Toasted Baguette Niçoise

Here's a sophisticated French-style pizza for a spur-of-the-moment snack or hors d'oeuvre.

1 loaf baguette French bread
2 tablespoons olive oil or
** vegetable oil**
2 red, purple, orange, yellow or
** green bell peppers, seeded,**
** slivered**
5 shallots, peeled, sliced
2 garlic cloves, finely chopped
1/2 cup sliced ripe olives
1 (2-oz.) can anchovies, if desired,
** drained**
2/3 cup grated Parmesan cheese

Preheat broiler. Slice bread in half lengthwise; place on broiler pan. In a large skillet, heat olive oil or vegetable oil. Sauté bell peppers, shallots and garlic 3 minutes or until peppers and shallots are very tender but not brown. Spoon mixture onto cut sides of bread halves, spreading evenly over bread. Sprinkle on olives; arrange anchovies over topping, if desired. Sprinkle on cheese. Place under broiler about 2 minutes or until cheese melts and bread toasts. Cut bread diagonally into diamond-shaped pieces about 3 inches long. Serve hot. Makes 2-1/2 dozen pieces.

Preparation time: 15 minutes

SHALLOTS

(shel-LOTS) Aristocrats of the onion family, shallots have been a European favorite for hundreds of years. The flavor of shallots is much more sophisticated than that of onions, and their richness makes them highly touted by chefs for sauces and slow-cooked meat dishes.

Shallots look like miniature brown- or purple-skinned onions, but their rounded shape is usually flattened on one side. A peeled shallot separates into 2 or 3 cloves, like garlic. A few shallots go a long way, chopped or sliced. They can also be enjoyed whole and braised or slow-cooked to serve as a vegetable on their own. Once cultivated mainly by the French, shallots are now grown all over the U.S.

Buying Tips: Avoid shallots that have sprouted or ones that looked dry or shriveled; they are old. Shallots should be firm, with fresh-looking skins and good shape.

Storage: Shallots store like onions in a cool, dry place. Keep them for up to several weeks, but check from time to time. Shallots do not keep as long as onions do.

Basic Preparation: Trim ends of shallots and slip off paper skins. Chop or slice to use raw or cooked or cook shallots whole as a vegetable. Sauté or stir-fry cut-up shallots; use medium-low heat so that they do not become bitter. Note that shallots cook faster than onions do. Shallots sauté in about 2 to 3 minutes when chopped or sliced. Braise or bake whole shallots for 15 to 20 minutes or until tender. Use microwave to prepare shallots as directed in recipes.

Serving Ideas: Sautéed sliced or chopped shallots are grand in themselves; spoon them over baked potatoes, poached eggs, steaks, barbecued chicken or fish or hot sandwiches. Add raw chopped shallots to salad dressings, chicken salad or sprinkle over cold roast beef. Glaze whole shallots with pears, apples or parsnip slices and brown sugar with butter for a special side dish. Add shallots to relishes, use in gravies and other savory sauces or mixed with fried potatoes.

Yield: 1 shallot = about 3 to 4 teaspoons, chopped.
1/4 lb. shallots = 1 serving.

Nutrition Facts: Shallots are low in calories, about 7 per tablespoon. They are an excellent source of iron.

SPROUTS

"Sprouts" is the culinary term for sprouting seeds, an ancient oriental art. In as little as five days, the seeds sprout tiny white and green shoots. When you buy sprouts, you're purchasing a miniature garden full of delicate, edible plants.

Sprout seeds or beans are planted in nothing but water; they do not need soil or sunlight to grow. That's why sprout enthusiasts can grow them on the kitchen counter, or almost anywhere, and still get a healthy harvest. Some sprouting beans, if harvested in 3 days, swell into tasty sprouting vegetables with a delicious bean flavor. New varieties of cress sprout into delicate stems with sweet to spicy green leaves. Look for sprouts year-round in markets; they are a refreshing change from lettuce.

Buying Tips: Fully sprouted seeds, like alfalfa sprouts, will be shipped in the containers in which they are grown. Look for fresh green sprouts or firm sprouted beans that are brightly colored and have a crisp-looking appearance.

Storage: Refrigerate sprouts or sprouted beans in the refrigerator crisper for up to 4 weeks for sprouts or sprouted beans for up to several weeks.

Basic Preparation: Neither sprouts nor sprouted beans require rinsing or washing. Simply snip off the sprouts or cress you need. Sprouts and cress are at their best served crisp and raw; sprouted mung or adzuki beans can be served raw or lightly stir-fried or sautéed for 1 to 2 minutes.

Serving Ideas: Use sprouts or cress as a substitute for lettuce in salads or to line a vegetable platter. Add sprouts to sandwiches or stuff in pita bread with meat or cheese for an easy filling. Add sprouted mung beans to stir-fried vegetables, scrambled eggs or fold into an omelet. Sprinkle a few sprouts over steamed vegetables or use small bouquets of gardencress to garnish a main dish platter or fruit salad.

Yield: 4 ounces sprouts = 2 to 4 servings.
1/4 lb. sprouted mung or adzuki beans = 1 serving.

Nutrition Facts: Sprouts are a concentrated source of nutrients such as A and C vitamins, calcium and iron. They are also high in protein. A 2-ounce serving of alfalfa sprouts has just 10 calories, a 4-oz. serving of sprouted beans about 40 calories.

Varieties:

Adzuki Bean Sprouts: Small, reddish beans sold just after sprouting. They have a nutty taste, crunchy texture; good for stir-fries as well as raw.

Alfalfa Sprouts: The most familiar sprouts, these delicate green shoots grow from alfalfa seed. Mildly nutty flavor.

Bean Sprouts: See Oriental Vegetables, page 128.

Clover Radish: Also called "spicy sprouts," these alfalfa-like shoots have a peppery, spicy flavor.

Danish Gardencress: An attractive, leafy version of alfalfa sprouts, gardencress has a uniquely spicy flavor.

Kaiware (kee-WAHR-ee): Also called "daikon radish" sprouts, these pretty sprouts have a leafy top and a refreshing, zingy taste.

Mung Bean Sprouts: Sprouted mung beans; they have a mild nutty flavor, crisp texture. Tiny green shoots grow from beans.

Sprouted Chicken Salad

Sprouts are a crunchy addition to lettuce-only salads. Look for sprout combinations often packaged in the produce section. It's an easy way to get acquainted with the different flavors and textures of various types of sprouts.

2 cups shredded lettuce
1-1/2 cups kaiware or alfalfa sprouts or azuki or mung bean sprouts
4 cooked chicken breasts, shredded
2 to 3 kiwi fruit, peeled, diced
1 large apple, cored, diced

Ginger-Lime Dressing:
1/3 cup salad oil
1/4 cup lime or lemon juice
2 tablespoons honey
1 tablespoon finely chopped fresh gingerroot or 1/4 teaspoon ground ginger

Prepare Ginger-Lime Dressing. Set aside. In a large bowl, toss together lettuce and sprouts. Add chicken, kiwifruit and apple pieces. Shake dressing; pour over salad. Toss well to coat. Makes 4 servings.

Ginger-Lime Dressing:
In a shaker jar, combine oil, lime or lemon juice, honey and gingerroot. Cover and shake well to mix. Makes about 3/4 cup.

Preparation time: 20 minutes

Sprouted Chicken Salad, above; Apricot Margarita, page 20.

SQUASH

(Summer & Winter) Along with corn, cranberries and bell peppers, squashes are another truly American crop. As new varieties have been cultivated here and throughout the world, squashes are becoming as diverse as our own culture. In shapes round and elongated, scalloped and pear-shaped; with meat that ranges from golden-yellow to brilliant orange, squashes add color and great taste to our tables.

Buying Tips: Soft-skinned squashes should be brightly colored, very firm and clean-looking. Look out for blemishes and mushy spots. Hard-shelled squashes should be heavy for their size with good color. Avoid cracked squashes or those with decayed areas.

Storage: Refrigerate soft-skinned squashes, tightly wrapped, in the crisper for up to 3 or 4 days. Store hard-shelled squashes in a cool, dry place for 3 to 6 months. (Exception: cut pieces of hard squash, such as banana, should be refrigerated tightly wrapped and used within a few days.) Cooked, mashed squash can be frozen up to 6 months.

Basic Preparation: For soft-shelled squashes, trim ends, do not peel. Bake, steam, boil, sauté or stir-fry briefly just until tender. Most squashes cook tender in less than 4 minutes, (cook chayote for 10 to 12 minutes) chopped or sliced. Micro-cook soft squashes, sliced or chopped, with 1/4 cup water in a shallow dish, loosely covered. Cook at High (100%) power for 2 to 4 minutes, turning once (5 to 6 minutes for chayote). Let stand 3 minutes.

For hard-shelled squashes, cook whole or cut into serving-size pieces or rings. To bake whole squash, bake in a 400F (205C) oven for 30 minutes to 1-1/4 hours, depending on size. Boil or steam quarters or rings for 25 to 35 minutes or until tender. To micro-cook squash, place halves or quarters cut side up with 1/4 cup water in a shallow dish; cover loosely. Microwave at High (100%) power for 5 to 13 minutes depending on size, turning once. Let stand 3 minutes.

Serving Ideas: Dress any cooked hard-shelled squash with butter and herbs, a cream sauce, cheese sauce, maple syrup and nuts, marinara sauce or stewed fruit. Serve raw summer squash with other fresh vegetables and a dip or add chunks or shreds to salads. Stuff summer or winter varieties with meats, cheeses, or cooked vegetables. Toss steamed summer squash with fresh pasta, such as tortellini or fettucine, and finish with a light cream sauce.

Yield: 1 lb. summer squash = 2 to 3 servings.
1 lb. summer squash = 3-1/2 cups sliced raw.
1 to 1-1/2 lbs. winter squash = 3 servings.
1 lb. winter squash = 1-2/3 to 2 cups cooked mashed squash.

Nutrition Facts: Squash is packed with nutrients; all are superb sources of vitamin A, especially orange-meat types. A serving of summer squash contains about 25 calories, winter squash, about 80.

Soft-Skinned or Summer Varieties:

Chayote (shy-OH-tay): With thin green or white skin, pear-shaped chayote has soft pale green melon-like meat and a narrow white edible seed in its center. It's flavor is bland and like cucumbers. Also called "merlitons," chayotes are southwestern in origin.

Golden Zucchini: A variety of zucchini with dazzling yellow skin and bright green stems. Pale yellow meat; mild zucchini flavor.

Pattypan: Smaller, 2- to 3-inch round squash shaped like small tops with scalloped edges. Pale green skin with creamy meat; mild squash flavor.

Scallopini: These look somewhat like pattypan with a plumper shape and very dark green skins. Mild, sweet flavor.

Sunburst: Like sunburst or pattypan with brilliant yellow skin. Mild, sweet squash flavor. A cross between summer squash and green zucchini.

Yellow Crookneck: With swan-shaped necks and bulbous bases, crook necks have bright green caps and pale yellow meat. Skin may be smooth or slightly bumpy; mild flavor.

Hard-Shelled or Winter Varieties:

Australian Blue: A squatty, square-shaped squash with a dull blue shell and brilliant orange meat. Flavor is hearty and rich.

Banana: Usually sold in pieces; banana squash has cream-colored to pale yellow skin and yellow meat. Shape is elongated with pointed ends. Flavor is hearty, mildly sweet.

Buttercup: This squatty round squash has a turban-like growth on top. Its dark green shell is streaked with gray; the orange meat has a drier texture, but is very sweet.

Butternut: Tan-colored, elongated shape with a bulbous end. Meat is bright orange and mildly sweet.

Calabaza: Bright orange squash, usually sold in pieces. May also be green, yellow or cream-colored on the outside; brilliant orange meat. Sweet and moist in flavor.

Delicata: Small, slender squash that's deep green with orange and white streaks along its length. Has less meat that is golden yellow with a mild squash flavor.

Golden Acorn: Also called "gold table queen," this small oval-shaped squash with its deep ridges looks like an orange acorn squash. Classic squash flavor. Golden meat; mildly sweet.

Golden Nugget: This small round orange squash is a one-serving size. Has a small amount of mildly sweet orange meat.

Hubbard: Has a misshapen, ugly duckling shell that may be pale gray to green-colored. The delicious orange meat is rich.

Jack-Be-Little: Mini pumpkins that look like individual-sized jack-o-lanterns. A small amount of orange meat, mildly sweet.

Kabocha: A Japanese variety; looks like a greenish gray globe that's flattened on top. Meat is golden, with a hearty squash flavor. "Sweet mama" is a sweet version of kabocha.

Mediterranean: Shape is like a giant butternut, but its sweet meat is stringy like spaghetti squash.

Spaghetti: Football-shaped squash with a bright yellow shell and intriguing yellow meat that becomes stringy like spaghetti when cooked. Can be served like spaghetti.

Sweet Dumpling: A small one-serving squash with a squatty shape. Its shell is cream-colored with dark green streaks. Orange meat; mildly sweet flavor.

Turban: An intriguing flattened round squash with three decorative knobs on top, turban is usually bright orange with green and white streaks. Meat is bright orange too, with a rich flavor.

Tip:

Squash blossoms are sometimes available, often attached to baby summer squash. These are entirely edible like lettuces. They can be lightly stir-fried, or served stuffed with chicken salad. Of course, they can also be used for a conversation-piece garnish.

Savory Squash Custards

Serve these individual souffle-like custards as an unusual side dish.

**2 cups cooked winter squash
(such as buttercup, butternut,
delicata, acorn, banana,
kabocha, turban, sweet mama or
Australian blue)
3 eggs
2 egg yolks
1 tablespoon chopped fresh basil
or 1 teaspoon dried basil
1/2 teaspoon salt
1/4 teaspoon ground nutmeg
1/8 teaspoon white pepper or
black pepper
3/4 cup milk
1/2 cup whipping cream
Fresh watercress sprigs or lemon
peel**

Preheat oven to 325F (165C). In blender or food processor fitted with a metal blade, process squash until puréed. In a medium bowl, beat eggs and egg yolks together until frothy; beat in squash purée, basil, salt, nutmeg and white or black pepper until blended. Whisk in milk and heavy cream. Lightly butter 6 individual 6-oz. custard cups or soufflé dishes. Pour mixture into cups, dividing evenly. Place cups in a shallow baking pan; pour boiling water into pan around cups to a depth of 1 inch. Cover pan loosely with foil. Bake 35 to 45 minutes or until a knife inserted near center of custards comes out clean. Carefully remove custards from water bath. Run a knife around edge of each custard; invert onto serving platter. Garnish custards with watercress and lemon peel. Makes 6 servings.

Preparation time: 15 minutes

Squash Soup with Cranberry Dollop

Winter squash puree is the basis for this rich soup. With the almost year-round availability of winter squash, you can enjoy this soup in any season.

3 lbs. winter squash, such as buttercup, butternut, acorn, turban, kabocha, Australian blue or banana, cooked
2 tablespoons butter or margarine
1 cup chopped onion
1 cup chopped carrots
1 cup chicken broth
1/2 teaspoon salt
1/8 teaspoon pepper
1/4 teaspoon ground nutmeg
1 pint half and half (2 cups)
1 cup whole-berry cranberry sauce

Remove cooked squash from shells; measure 4 cups pulp (reserve remainder for a side dish). In blender or food processor fitted with a metal blade, process squash until puréed. Set aside. In a large saucepan or Dutch oven, melt butter or margarine; sauté onion and carrots for 5 minutes or until tender but not brown. Stir in broth, salt, pepper and nutmeg; bring to boiling. Boil, uncovered, 5 minutes. Reduce heat to simmering; stir in squash purée and half and half. Simmer 5 minutes or until heated through. Taste for seasoning. To serve, ladle soup into bowls. Spoon 2 tablespoons of the cranberry sauce in the center of each bowl of soup. Makes 8 servings.

Preparation time: 30 minutes

Confetti Spaghetti Squash

Golden strands of spaghetti squash take the place of pasta. For another variation, top these vegetables with marinara sauce instead of the butter-herb mixture.

1 (1-lb.) spaghetti squash, quartered
1/2 cup julienne-cut carrots or bell pepper, cooked
1/2 cup fresh peas, shelled, cooked
1 cup julienne-cut zucchini, yellow crookneck or scallopine squash, cooked
2 tablespoons butter or margarine, room temperature
2 tablespoons chopped fresh parsley or chives
1 tablespoon chopped fresh dill or 1 teaspoon dillweed
1 tablespoon chopped fresh basil or 1 teaspoon dried basil

In a Dutch oven or large skillet, place squash pieces. Add water to a depth of 2 inches. Bring to boiling; simmer 20 minutes or until squash strands separate from rind. Meanwhile, in steamer basket over simmering water, cook carrots or bell pepper and peas 4 minutes. Add zucchini; cook 3 minutes more. Drain vegetables. In same pan, melt butter or margarine; stir in parsley or chives, dill and basil. With tongs, remove squash from pan; drain well. Using two forks, remove strands of squash from rind; pile into a large serving bowl. Add cooked vegetables and butter-herb mixture; toss well to mix. Makes 4 servings.

Preparation time: 20 minutes

1.Hubbard. 2.Spaghetti squash. 3.Kabocha. 4.Turban. 5.Sweet mama. 6.Butternut. 7.Sweet dumpling. 8.Pattypan. 9.Jack-be-little. 10.Scallopini. 11.Yellow crookneck. 12.Squash seeds. 13.Yellow sunburst. 14.Yellow crookneck. 15.Australian blue. 16.Delicata.

Summer Squash Skillet with Kielbasa

Accompany this easy dish with buttered noodles.

1 tablespoon vegetable oil
1 lb. Kielbasa or Polish sausage, cut into 1/2-inch slices
1/2 cup sliced onion
3 cups sliced summer squash (such as pattypan, sunburst, zucchini, scallopine, yellow crookneck or yellow zucchini)
1 medium tomato, chopped
1/2 cup marinara or spaghetti sauce
1 tablespoon chopped fresh basil or 1 teaspoon dried basil
1 tablespoon chopped fresh marjoram or oregano or 1 teaspoon dried leaf marjoram or oregano
Salt and pepper to taste

Heat oil in a large skillet. Brown sausage on all sides; remove from pan, reserving drippings in skillet. Sauté onion 3 minutes. Drain off excess fat. Add desired squash, tomatoes, cooked sausage and marinara or spaghetti sauce. Stir in basil, marjoram and salt and pepper to taste. Bring mixture to boiling; reduce heat and simmer, covered, 10 minutes. Makes 4 servings.

Preparation time: 15 minutes

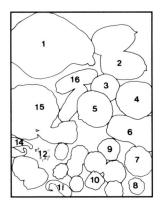

Squash. See diagram, opposite page.

SUNCHOKES/ JERUSALEM ARTICHOKES

A relative of the sunflower, sunchokes have long been called Jerusalem artichokes. The latter name is a misnomer, since this vegetable is native to America, not Jerusalem, and has no botanical relation to artichokes. Around 1605 in the Cape Cod area, the first American settlers discovered that the Indians were growing sunchokes and began trading for them. Ten years later, the plants were brought to Europe and the vegetable quickly became more popular there than in this country.

Sunchokes have a low calorie count and sweet, pleasant, nutty flavor. Though delicious, these ugly-duckling vegetables look like knobby brown potatoes. Sunchokes are crisp and sweet like water chestnuts when raw; baked in their skins, they become more like potatoes with a mild taste of artichoke hearts. Available all year, sunchokes are at their peak from October to March.

Buying Tips: Look for roots that are very firm, clean and free of moisture or soft spots. Some sunchokes will have dark brown skin, others will have lighter skin like that of gingerroot.

Storage: Refrigerate sunchokes in the crisper drawer in an airtight plastic bag. They can also be kept in a cool dark place as you would store potatoes. They will keep for several weeks.

Basic Preparation: Scrub sunchokes well; do not peel as the skin contributes both nutrients and flavor. Dip cut sunchokes into a lemon juice and water mixture to prevent discoloration; refrigerate sunchokes this way up to several days. Bake sunchokes as you would potatoes; sauté slices in butter or oil and sprinkle with herbs. Sauté or steam slices for 5 to 7 minutes. To microwave sunchokes, place slices in 1/4 cup water in a loosely covered shallow dish. Micro-cook on High (100%) power for 2-1/2 to 4 minutes. Let stand 3 minutes.

Serving Ideas: Sunchokes are a delicious substitute for recipes that call for water chestnuts or jicama. Use sliced sunchokes in marinated vegetable mixtures, on an appetizer vegetable platter with dips, deep-fried to serve with salsa or sautéed with bell peppers and onions. Sunchokes are also tasty fried like potatoes and served as a side dish with egg dishes and barbecued meats.

Yield: 1 lb. sunchokes = 4 to 5 servings.
1 lb. sunchokes = 2-2/3 to 3 cups chopped or sliced, uncooked.

Nutrition Facts: Sunchokes are an exceptional source of iron and also contribute B vitamins and phosphorous. Calorie content varies with age: a 3-1/2-ounce serving of fresh sunchokes is about 10 calories; after several months of storage, the count will be closer to 70.

Sunchokes with Yams

Here's a delicious Southern-style substitute for breakfast or dinner potatoes.

2 cups diced sunchokes
2 cups diced peeled yams or
  sweet potatoes
4 strips bacon, diced
1/2 cup chopped onion
1 clove garlic, minced
1 tablespoon minced fresh parsley
1/4 teaspoon salt
1/4 teaspoon pepper
1/8 teaspoon ground nutmeg

In a medium saucepan, place sunchokes and yams in water to cover. Bring to boiling; reduce heat. Simmer, uncovered, 5 to 6 minutes or until nearly tender. Drain well; set aside. In a large skillet, cook bacon until almost crisp. Drain bacon on paper towels; reserve 2 tablespoons of drippings. Add onion and garlic to drippings; sauté until onion is tender. Add bacon, cooked sunchokes and potatoes to skillet. Stir in parsley, salt, pepper and nutmeg, tossing gently to coat. Cook 1 to 2 minutes more until heated through. Makes 6 servings.

Preparation time: 20 minutes

Varieties:

Malanga (mul-AHNG-uh): A South American taro root with thin, somewhat shaggy skin that is brown with some yellow or red skin beneath. Its flavor is earthy with nutty overtones. Texture is soft.

Taro Root: May be round and turnip-shaped or slender and up to a foot long. They have brown shaggy skin and white to purple flesh with a mild, potato-like flavor. Highly digestible.

Yucca Root (YUKK-ah): From Brazil, yucca or yuca is a very large, elongated root with thick brown skin that is often waxed to hold in moisture. Flesh is white; very mild potato-like flavor.

Cuban-Style Malanga

Malanga tastes much like potatoes in this lightly spiced combination.

1 lb. malanga, scrubbed, peeled, cut into 1/2-inch pieces
2 cups chicken or beef broth
2 tablespoons butter or margarine
2 tablespoons lime juice
1 tablespoon chopped fresh cilantro
1/4 teaspoon chili powder
1/8 teaspoon cumin
Cilantro sprigs

In a medium saucepan, place malanga pieces with broth; bring to boiling. Reduce heat and simmer, partly covered, 20 to 25 minutes or until tender. Drain. Meanwhile, in a small saucepan, melt butter or margarine. Stir in lime juice, chopped cilantro, chili powder and cumin. Drizzle mixture over malanga. Garnish with cilantro sprigs. Makes 4 servings.

Preparation time: 10 minutes

TARO ROOT/ YUCCA ROOT/MALANGA

These tropical roots are grouped together because of their similarity in texture and cooking uses. All are staple foods of many people in the Pacific Rim, Central and South America, Asia and Hawaii. These roots are as important to Pacific cultures as potatoes are to us.

Taro root, often called "dasheen," is an important potato substitute. In Hawaii, poi, a thin paste, is made from taro. Yucca root, also called "cassava," and malanga, or "yautia," are other tropical varieties used in much the same way, though they are not botanically related. All can be found in Latin markets and larger produce markets during most of the year.

Buying Tips: All of these roots should be purchased in very firm condition with no shriveling or softness present. Roots should feel heavy for their size.

Storage: All of these roots should be refrigerated in the crisper drawer for up to 1 week.

Basic Preparation: Malanga, taro and yucca root must be cooked before eating. Cook taro in its skin; malanga and yucca should be peeled before cooking. Boil, steam, bake or microwave the roots until they are very tender. Boil chunks of the roots with water to cover for 15 to 25 minutes or until tender like potatoes. Bake the roots whole in a 375F (190C) oven for 40 to 60 minutes or until tender, depending on size of pieces. Micro-cook the roots, chopped or sliced, in 2 tablespoons water in a loosely covered shallow dish. Microwave on High (100%) power for 5 to 8 minutes or until tender, turning once. Let stand 3 minutes. Remove taro root skins after cooking.

Serving Ideas: All of these roots are as versatile as potatoes. Prepare them scalloped or au gratin style. They can be sliced and deep-fried as chips, cooked and added to soups or stews or mashed and seasoned like potatoes. Toss them in a cream or cheese sauce or add parboiled pieces to an oriental stir-fry. The mashed root can also be added to quick bread or pancake batter to substitute for a part of the flour. Shape the leftover cooked, mashed roots into cakes to fry in butter; season with salt and pepper.

Yield: 1 lb. root = 2 to 3 servings.

Nutrition Facts: All of these roots are high in carbohydrates; their calorie content is about 100 calories per 3-1/2-ounce serving. They are a good source of vitamin A and thiamin.

Vegetable-Topped Snapper

Of course, you can substitute any firm whitefish fillets for the red snapper.

1 cup peeled yucca root, finely chopped
1 onion, halved, thinly sliced
1 cup julienne-cut carrots
1 cup julienne-cut zucchini
2 large tomatoes, chopped
2 teaspoons chopped fresh thyme or 1/2 teaspoon dried leaf thyme
1 bay leaf
1/2 teaspoon salt
1/4 teaspoon cayenne pepper
1-1/2 lbs. red snapper fillets, thawed if frozen
2 tablespoons butter or margarine, melted

Preheat oven to 350F (175C). In steamer basket over simmering water, cook yucca root, onion and carrots 8 to 10 minutes or until nearly tender. Add zucchini; steam 2 minutes more. In a medium bowl, toss together steamed vegetables with tomatoes, thyme, bay leaf, salt and cayenne pepper. In a lightly oiled shallow baking dish, arrange fish fillets. Cover and bake 15 minutes. Spoon vegetable mixture over fillets; return to oven. Bake 10 to 15 minutes more or until fish flakes easily when tested with a fork. Drizzle with butter or margarine. Makes 4 to 6 servings.

Preparation time: 20 minutes

Vegetable-Topped Snapper, above.

TOMATOES

Unusual Varieties:

Dried Tomatoes: Sometimes called "sun dried," these tomatoes look like dried fruit with a reddish-orange color and wrinkled appearance. They must be simmered for 1 or 2 minutes to soften them for eating. Marvelous smoky tomato flavor.

Orange Tomatoes: A tomato variety that has a bright orange-yellow skin; orange flesh. Sweet and mild.

Roma: Also called "plum" or "Italian" tomatoes, these small, oval-shaped tomatoes are considered ideal for making sauces.

Tomatillos: A Mexican ground tomato. These are quite small, about 1 inch in diameter and covered with a papery greenish-gray husk. Inside the tomato is green, even when ripe. Used in Mexican salsa verde, tomato sauces and cooked dishes. Can also be served raw as a regular tomato. Mildly spicy flavor.

Yellow Cherry: Like cherry tomatoes except they have yellow skins and meat; very juicy.

Yellow and Red Teardrop: Tiny pear-shaped cherry tomatoes; as juicy and sweet as vine-ripened cherry tomatoes.

Yellow Tomatoes: Like the orange tomato only with a brilliant yellow-gold skin; sweet and juicy yellow flesh.

Aficionados can tell when a tomato is vine-ripened; it's sweet and juicy with a smooth, truly red skin. One of the succulent vegetables of summer, fresh tomatoes, whether sliced raw on a grilled burger or pulverized for marinara sauce, taste like everything they should be.

Aside from typical tomatoes and cherry tomatoes, some other attractive varieties appear seasonally in markets. Take advantage of these newcomers along with your old favorites; you'll discover why tomatoes were once dubbed "apples of paradise."

Buying Tips: Ripe tomatoes will have a healthy red or red-orange color; vine-ripened varieties often have the green stems attached. Press them gently between your palms; they should give slightly. Unripe tomatoes can be successfully ripened at home. Purchase them 3 to 4 days before you'll use them.

Storage: Refrigerate ripe tomatoes, never unripe ones. Store unripe tomatoes in a cool spot, out of direct sunlight (which promotes mushiness). Place unripe tomatoes in a closed paper bag or fruit ripening bowl. Use tomatoes within a few days after they are ripe.

Basic Preparation: Remove stems from tomatoes; quarter, slice or chop to enjoy as a raw vegetable or to use in recipes. Peel tomatoes by placing them in boiling water for 30 seconds, then in cold water. Skins should slip off easily. To seed tomatoes, halve them, then squeeze out seeds and watery pulp, scraping it out with a grapefruit knife or tip of a spoon. Tomato slices can be broiled, baked or microwaved for recipes. See individual recipes for timings.

Serving Ideas: Broil tomato slices, topped with seasoned bread crumbs or cheese, until hot. Hollow out large tomatoes and stuff with meats or cheeses, then bake. Sauté breaded sliced tomatoes for an unusual side dish. Use the smaller tomatoes as dippers on a fresh vegetable tray, or threaded on skewers and grilled with other tender vegetables. Season broiled, baked or grilled tomatoes with chopped fresh herbs and garlic, grated Parmesan cheese, or sour cream and onions. Fill fresh tomato cups with chicken or salmon salad or add chopped fresh tomatoes to tuna salad, relishes or guacamole. Use tomatoes to make homemade marinara or tomato sauce; both will freeze well.

Yield: 1 medium tomato or 6 cherry tomatoes = 1 serving.
1 lb. tomatoes = 3 to 4 medium.
1 lb. cherry tomatoes = about 24 tomatoes.
1 lb. tomatoes = 1-1/2 cups pulp.

Nutrition Facts: Low in sodium and free of cholesterol, tomatoes weigh in at a mere 30 calories per medium tomato. They are a good source of vitamins A and C, plus potassium and iron.

Greek-Style Tomato Salad

You can layer the same ingredients used in this salad on bread slices or in pita rounds to make pocket or open-faced sandwiches. Drizzle each sandwich with some of the Vinaigrette Dressing.

Lettuce leaves
2 large tomatoes, cored, thinly sliced
1/2 cup sliced red onion
1/2 cup pitted ripe olives, halved
2/3 cup crumbled feta or blue cheese

Vinaigrette Dressing:
1/3 cup olive oil or salad oil
1/4 cup red wine vinegar
1 tablespoon chopped fresh rosemary or thyme or 1 teaspoon crushed dried herb
1 tablespoon chopped fresh basil or 1 teaspoon dried basil
1 garlic clove, finely chopped
1/8 teaspoon salt
1/8 teaspoon pepper

On a salad platter, arrange lettuce leaves. Layer tomatoes over lettuce. Sprinkle with onions, olives and feta or blue cheese. Prepare Vinaigrette Dressing; drizzle over salad. Makes 4 servings.

Vinaigrette Dressing:
In a shaker jar, combine oil, vinegar, rosemary or thyme, basil, garlic, salt and pepper. Cover and shake well to mix. Makes 1/2 cup.

Preparation time: 10 minutes

Chicken with Sun Dried Tomatoes In Cream

Veal or thinly sliced turkey cutlets work well in this dish, too.

1 cup dried tomatoes
4 to 5 chicken breasts, boned, skinned
2 tablespoons butter or margarine
2 tablespoons vegetable oil
2 green onions, thinly sliced
1/2 cup dry white wine
1/2 pint half and half (1 cup)
1 tablespoon chopped fresh rosemary or 1 teaspoon crushed dried rosemary
1/4 teaspoon pepper
Hot cooked rice or noodles

In a small saucepan, place tomatoes with water to cover. Bring to boiling; reduce heat and simmer 2 minutes. Drain well. Cut tomatoes into thin strips; set aside. Place each chicken breast between 2 pieces of waxed paper. With a meat mallet, pound to 1/4-inch thickness. In a large skillet, melt butter or margarine and oil over medium-high heat. Brown chicken pieces on both sides for 4 to 5 minutes, turning once. Remove meat from skillet; cover and keep warm. Add onions and wine to drippings in skillet; bring to boiling. Reduce heat to low; whisk in half and half, rosemary and pepper. Simmer 2 minutes. Add chicken pieces and tomatoes to skillet; spoon sauce over. Cover and cook 1 minute more to heat through. Serve with hot cooked rice. Makes 4 or 5 servings.

Preparation time: 15 minutes

Quick Tomato Relish

Serve this spunky relish or salsa on burgers, hot dogs, barbecued meats and poultry or on fish fillets.

1 medium tomato or 6 cherry tomatoes, chopped
3/4 cup chopped tomatillos
1/2 cup finely chopped carrots
1/2 cup finely chopped red onion
1 garlic clove, finely chopped
2 tablespoons chopped fresh cilantro or parsley
1 jalapeño or serrano chili, seeded, finely chopped, or 2 tablespoons chopped mild green or Anaheim chilies
1/2 teaspoon salt

In a medium bowl, stir together tomato, tomatillos, carrot, onion, garlic, cilantro or parsley, desired chilies and salt until well mixed. Cover and chill at least 1 hour to blend flavors. If preparing ahead, cover and refrigerate up to 1 week. Serve chilled or at room temperature. Makes about 2-1/4 cups.

Preparation time: 10 minutes

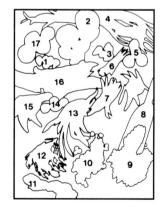

1.Roma plum tomatoes. 2.Yellow tomatoes. 3.Red pear tomatoes. 4.Chinese long beans. 5.Cherry tomatoes. 6.Haricots verts. 7.Yellow wax beans. 8.Purple wax beans. 9.Black-eyed peas. 10.Garbanzo beans. 11.Dried tomatoes. 12.Sea beans. 13.Cranberry beans. 14.Yellow cherry tomatoes. 15.Okra. 16.Fava beans. 17.Yellow pear tomatoes.

Beans & Tomatoes. See diagram, opposite page.

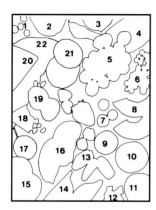

PAGE 15

1.Coquitos. 2.Passion fruit. 3.Kiwano. 4.Plantain. 5.Red seedless grapes. 6.Champagne grapes. 7.Coquitos. 8.Elberta peach slices. 9.Yellow tamarillo. 10.Red tamarillo. 11.Kiwi fruit. 12.Dried starfruit. 13.Deglet noor dates. 14.Perfumed quince. 15.Elberta peach. 16.Hosui Asian pear. 17.Lady apple. 18.Pomegranate seeds. 19.Calimyrna figs. 20.Red seedless watermelon. 21.Red and green prickly pears. 22.Yellow watermelon.

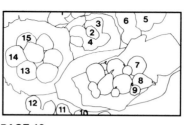

PAGE 18

1.Bosc pears. 2.Dried persimmons. 3.Hachiya persimmons. 4.Fuyu persimmons. 5.Granny Smith apples. 6.Snyrna quince. 7.Jona-gold apples. 8.Red Bartlett pears. 9.Lady apples. 10.Sapotas. 11.Comice pear. 12.Hosui Asian pear. 13.Comice pears. 14.Hosui Asian pears (russet). 15.Shinseiki Asian (yellow) pears.

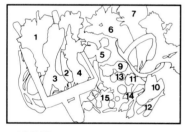

PAGE 47

1.Red tomarillo. 2.Kiwi fruit. 3.Kiwano. 4.Feijoas. 5.Kiwano. 6.Yellow tamarillo. 7.Passion fruit. 8.Yellow tamarillo. 9.Feijoa.

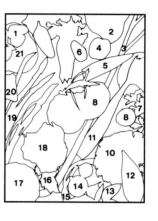

PAGE 79

1.Basil. 2.Yellowbell pepper. 3.Lemon grass. 4.Baby red potatoes. 5.Belgian endive. 6.Red pear tomatoes. 7.Italian parsley. 8.Baby planet carrots. 9.Shiitake mushrooms. 10.White salad savoy. 11.Baby corn. 12.Red Fresno chili. 13.Spearmint. 14.Red and gold pearl onions. 15.Chinese long beans. 16.Opal basil. 17.Sunburst squash. 18.Baby cauliflower. 19.Asparagus. 20.Woodear mushroom. 21.Red bell pepper. 22. Jalapeño pepper. 23.Kiware sprouts.

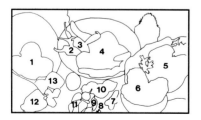

PAGE 85

1.Baby white turnips. 2.Green & red kohlrabi. 3.Baby beets. 4.Baby carrots. 5.Baby califlower. 6.Baby gold turnips. 7.Baby parsnips. 8.Planet carrots. 9.Baby artichokes. 10.Baby bok choy. 11.Baby broccoli. 12.Baby corn. 13.Baby eggplant. 14.Baby yellow zucchini with squash blossoms attached. 15.Baby summer squash: pale green-patty pan, dark green-scallopine, yellow round-sunburst, green zucchini.

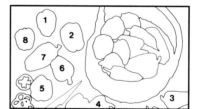

PAGE 89

1.Yellow. 2.Green Bell. 3.Purple Violetta. 4.Chocolate. 5.Yellow. 6.Red Bell. 7.Rouge Royale. 8.Chocolate.

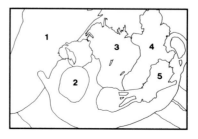

PAGE 97

1.Pomegranates. 2.Anaheim chiles. 3.Red jalapeños. 4.Hass avocados. 5.Jicama. 6.Cactus pads. 7.Cilantro. 8.Serrano chile. 9.Jalapeño chiles. 10.Tomatillos. 11.Cayenne pepper. 12.Pasilla chile. 13.Red prickly pear. 14.Green prickly pear.

PAGE 102

From left: 1.Cardoon; in basket. 2.Brown-skinned Celery Root. 3.White Fennel bulb with dill-like leaves. 4.Red Kohlrabi with leaves. 5.Green Kohlrabi with leaves.

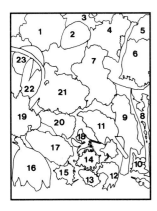

PAGE 119
1.Bibb Lettuce. 2.Radiccio.
3.Mustard Greens. 4.Kale.
5.Collards. 6.Chicory. 7.Escarole.
8.Dandelion greens. 9.White Swiss
chard. 10.Watercress. 11.Red
Swiss chard. 12.Kaiware sprouts.
13.Spicy sprouts. 14.Mung & azuki
bean sprouts. 15.Bean sprouts.
16.Sorrel. 17.Chinese (Napa)
cabbage. 18.Arrugula. 19.White
salad savoy. 20.Red leaf lettuce.
21.Purple salad Savoy. 22.Belgian
endive. 23.Red cabbage.

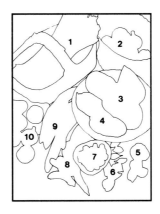

PAGE 133
1.Leeks. 2.Brown onions. 3.Italian
eggplant. 4.White eggplant.
5.Elephant garlic. 6.Shallots.
7.Red, gold and white pearl onions. 8.Japanese eggplant. 9.Hot-
house cucumber. 10.Maui onions.

METRIC CHART

Comparison to Metric Measure

When You Know	Symbol	Multiply By	To Find	Symbol
teaspoons	tsp	5.0	milliliters	ml
tablespoons	tbsp	15.0	milliliters	ml
fluid ounces	fl. oz.	30.0	milliliters	ml
cups	c	0.24	liters	l
pints	pt.	0.47	liters	l
quarts	qt.	0.95	liters	l
ounces	oz.	28.0	grams	g
pounds	lb.	0.45	kilograms	kg
Fahrenheit	F	5/9 (after subtracting 32)	Celsius	C

Fahrenheit to Celsius

F	C
200—205	95
220—225	105
245—250	120
275	135
300—305	150
325—330	165
345—350	175
370—375	190
400—405	205
425—430	220
445—450	230
470—475	245
500	260

Liquid Measure to Liters

1/4 cup	=	0.06 liters
1/2 cup	=	0.12 liters
3/4 cup	=	0.18 liters
1 cup	=	0.24 liters
1-1/4 cups	=	0.3 liters
1-1/2 cups	=	0.36 liters
2 cups	=	0.48 liters
2-1/2 cups	=	0.6 liters
3 cups	=	0.72 liters
3-1/2 cups	=	0.84 liters
4 cups	=	0.96 liters
4-1/2 cups	=	1.08 liters
5 cups	=	1.2 liters
5-1/2 cups	=	1.32 liters

Liquid Measure to Milliliters

1/4 teaspoon	=	1.25 milliliters
1/2 teaspoon	=	2.5 milliliters
3/4 teaspoon	=	3.75 milliliters
1 teaspoon	=	5.0 milliliters
1-1/4 teaspoons	=	6.25 milliliters
1-1/2 teaspoons	=	7.5 milliliters
1-3/4 teaspoons	=	8.75 milliliters
2 teaspoons	=	10.0 milliliters
1 tablespoon	=	15.0 milliliters
2 tablespoons	=	30.0 milliliters

INDEX